COUNTER THE COUNTERFEIT & BUILD A STRONG FOUNDATION FOR SUCCESS

Books are our best friends, is the adage we have grown up with. However, the pirates of piracy are continuously forging 'our best friends'. Our books and their supplementary online resources are copyrighted, and we don't lend any right-to-copy. Piracy is synonymous to stealing books.

Knowledge comes real, let's not encourage its counterfeit. Therefore, we appeal all our readers to discourage pirated books and **choose authentic ones.**

HOW TO IDENTIFY THE PIRATED BOOKS?

1 TRANSPARENCY CODE ON THE BOOK

Congratulations! The book you have purchased is protected by Transparency. Transparency by Amazon is a unit-level product serialization service that verifies a unit's authenticity and enables you to view rich information about the product you purchased. Please look for the Transparency logo and code on the book back cover (Transparency barcode is a square code that can be found next to the "T" symbol). You can scan the barcode with the Transparency app to verify the book's authenticity. Simply download the Transparency app from the App Store or Google Play. Scan the barcode with the app. The app will display a green checkmark when the book has been verified as authentic.

2 COVER AND SPINE

- Look and feel (new or used book)
- Blurred images on the cover
- Hologram pasted on front
- Defective spine (wrinkles) or air pocket at its bottom
- Unclear ISBN/bar codes
- Missing/non-operational access codes for supplemental online or e-learning materials

3 TEXT/PRINTING/BINDING

- Uneven inking of pages
- Poor quality or blurred photographs/images/ charts
- Substandard paper quality and opacity
- Misaligned pages
- Missing pages
- Inferior binding quality

You can further watch this video on How to identify a pirated book

For more information about identifying piracy, visit **https://www.mheducation.co.in/piracy**

To report a pirated book, send 'Hi' on WhatsApp code given on the back cover or write to us at **support.india@mheducation.com**.

Reported pirated books are examined to combat their piracy.

Let's fight the Pirates of Piracy and resolve to go for original!

2e

IMPORTANT JUDGMENTS THAT TRANSFORMED INDIA

FOR UPSC CIVIL SERVICES EXAMINATION

Alex Andrews George

Founder & Director, ClearIAS

Mc Graw Hill

McGraw Hill Education (India) Private Limited

Published by McGraw Hill Education (India) Private Limited
Registered Office: Anjana Complex No: 5/90 A, Butt Road, St. Thomas Mount, Chennai – 600016

Important Judgments that transformed India, 2e

First reprint

Print Edition
ISBN-13: 978-93-5532-129-9
ISBN-10: 93-5532-129-5

E-Book Edition
ISBN-13: 978-93-5532-137-4
ISBN-10: 93-5532-137-6

02 03 04 05 06 RAJ 26 25 24 23 22

Typeset at Transcend Content Solution, 163F Jaigirghat Road, Panchanantala, Kolkata – 700 063 and printed and bound in India at Rajkamal Electric Press, Plot No. 2, Phase-IV, Kundli, Haryana

Cover Designer: Neeraj Dayal
Cover Image Source: DAL

Visit us at: www.mheducation.co.in
Write to us at: info.india@mheducation.com
CIN: U80302TN2010PTC111532
Toll free Number: 1800 103 5875

About the Author

Alex Andrews George is a social entrepreneur, teacher and author. He is a problem-solver with diverse experience and interests.

Alex is the founder and director of *ClearIAS.com,* one of the most popular online learning platforms in India.

He is one of the expert Civil Service Exam trainers in India. A trusted mentor and pioneer in online training, Alex's classes, guidance, strategies, study materials, and mock exams have helped many aspirants become IAS, IPS and IFS officers.

He is the author of many bestselling books, like *Important Judgments that Transformed India* and *Important Acts that Transformed India.*

An engineer by graduation, Alex is passionate about creating content that makes learning an enjoyable experience. He strives hard to solve the problems associated with the affordability, accessibility and availability of quality education for all.

Alex aspires to create and mentor the leaders of tomorrow. His vision is to make the world a better place.

About ClearIAS: ClearIAS.com is one of the most popular websites in India, widely used by IAS/IPS/IFS aspirants for UPSC exam preparation. The platform is visited by more than 1 million learners every month.

Dedicated to

My Parents

Preface to the Second Edition

First of all, I would like to thank all the readers for the grand welcome given to the first edition of this book, '*Important Judgments that Transformed India*'.

This book got a wide reception from the IAS/IPS/IFS aspirant community, law students, and general readers-adding it to the best-sellers list on many online shopping websites like Amazon.

To be honest, the whopping initial response from the readers was a pleasant surprise to me. I thought books like this would take time to reach the intended users. However, the enthusiastic learners proved me wrong. I am always thankful to all who had faith in me and in this product.

In the last couple of years, the Supreme Court of India has come up with many new landmark judgments. It is against this background that I introduce you to the second edition of 'Important Judgments that transformed India'.

Salient Features

- A detailed overview of 40 landmark Supreme Court judgments
- An additional compilation of 100+ Supreme Court judgments with respect to the main area of conflict
- The complicated legal context behind various Supreme Court cases is made simple and easy to understand
- Each chapter is divided into introduction, background, legal issues involved, arguments, judgment, importance and impact

Special Attractions

- A lot of value-added content to make your answers stand out
- Each chapter starts with thought-provoking questions to understand the case's significance.
- Learn from easy-to-understand tables and mindmaps
- Master Judicial Doctrines and Judicial Terms
- Revise UPSC Civil Services Preliminary and Main Examination Previous Year Questions and Answers from the topic

What's new in the 2nd edition?

- The second edition of this book includes a detailed analysis of 40 important Supreme Court cases.
- A brief overview of more than 100 landmark judgments is also compiled in table format.
- A lot of additional information is added in boxes
- All chapters are revised and the latest updates are included

Before I conclude the Preface, I would like to acknowledge the contributions of many who were instrumental in the timely release of this edition.

We got hundreds of emails from the users of ClearIAS.com enquiring about the release date of the updated edition. To begin with, I would like to thank all the students of ClearIAS.com who were eagerly waiting for the new edition.

Next, I would like to express my gratitude towards my team, particularly Kirtika Goyal, Namratha M, Manu K Sabu, Jis Sebastian, Vivekanand, and Divakar Shenoy, who gave invaluable assistance and legal expertise while drafting the book. I owe the ClearIAS team a debt of gratitude for their constructive feedback regarding the design and layout as well.

My gratitude is also due to my family-my parents, wife, and sister for supporting me in all my aspirations.

Finally, I would like to express my sincere gratitude to my publisher, McGraw Hill India and their entire team-which has become an extended family of mine. My special thanks to McGraw Hill team for the unparallel support and encouragement given towards all new ideas of mine.

I welcome feedback from all the readers to further improve the book.

Alex Andrews George.

Preface to the First Edition

The study of **Indian Polity and Constitution** is incomplete without understanding the role played by the **Judiciary** in **transforming India** through various **landmark judgments**.

Indian Judiciary, particularly the Supreme Court of India, has been instrumental in shaping India, changing India, and transforming India.

This book, "Important Judgments that transformed India", presents an easy understanding of the landmark Court Cases that everyone needs to know about.

It is quite interesting to learn how the Supreme Court Judgments protected the essence of Indian Constitution, strengthened democracy, and transformed the lives of ordinary citizens of India. The way democracy now functions in India, owe a lot to many of these Supreme Court Judgments.

By going through these landmark Judgments, one can clearly understand not only the **evolution and transformation of the Indian Constitution** but also the emergence of Indian Judiciary as one of the most powerful among its tribe globally.

The constitutional court was bold enough to invent the 'Basic Structure Doctrine' in the case '*Kesavananda Bharati v. State of Kerala (1973)*' and to make a paradigm shift to 'due process of law' in '*Maneka Gandhi v. Union of India (1978)*' case.

Yes, as the **Custodian of the Indian Constitution**, the Supreme Court of India has been assertive on the constitutional values and creative in its interpretations **to resolve legal issues, and deliver justice**.

This book effectively caters to the requirements of many competitive examinations, particularly the UPSC Civil Services Examination (Prelims, Mains, and Interview). I hope, the book will be equally useful to all academics, legal students, and general readers who are interested in Indian Polity and Constitution.

Acknowledgements

The idea of collecting and consolidating important Supreme Court cases in an easy-to-understand fashion was there in my mind for quite some time. However, the book would not have been complete without the help I received from all quarters.

On this occasion, I would like to thank everyone who inspired me, one way or the other, to write this book.

To begin with, I would like to thank all readers of ClearIAS.com, who supported and encouraged me and my team, in all our initiatives of making learning simple and easy. I am also grateful to all my students, for making learning mutual - by asking so many thought-provoking questions in my classes and workshops.

I am indebted to every teacher of mine, specially Jijo Sir and Parampreet Sir, who nurtured interest in the subject. I am equally thankful for all renowned authors in Indian Polity and Constitution who produced exceptional books and thus opened the doors of constitutional wisdom to me.

I owe all my team members a debt of gratitude for their extensive research for this book. I am particularly thankful to Divakar Shenoy for the invaluable assistance provided in preparing the draft.

I am also thankful to all my friends, Lipu S Lawrence and Sreeraj S Menon in particular, for their inputs and timely feedback to improve the features. My gratitude is also due to my lawyer-friends, Balu G Nair and Sanal Cherian for providing crucial legal insights.

It is very odd for me to express my gratitude to my family. My parents are always my pillars of support in whatever I do. I am happy to dedicate this book to my father and mother, who taught me to dream big. Equally commendable is the role of my wife, Priyanka, in supporting my aspirations.

Finally, I would like to express my sincere gratitude to the publisher McGraw Hill, India, and their entire team. My special thanks to Lalit Singh, Tanmoy Roychowdhury, Tanweer Ahmed, Atul Gupta, Jyoti Nagpal, Aastha Khanna and Gunjan Rustagi for their constant backing and encouragement. Always receptive to new ideas, the team extended unparallel support to make this book possible.

The Usefulness of the Book for UPSC Civil Services Examination (Prelims, Mains, and Interview)

Indian Constitution and Polity is one subject that is directly connected to Civil Service and Public Administration; hence, a high-priority area for all aspiring civil servants.

From the broad area of Indian Polity, in recent years, many questions are asked about Indian judiciary and the landmark judgments. This trend is not surprising, thanks to the central role played by the Supreme Court as the custodian of the Indian Constitution.

A fair knowledge about the important judgments of the constitutional courts can help you fetch valuable marks in the UPSC Civil Services Prelims (objective), Mains (written), and Interview (personality-test).

UPSC CSE Prelims

Questions are asked about the basic concepts associated with Indian Constitution, Constitutional Amendments, Judicial Review, Landmark Judgments, etc.

To understand better, go through the question given below:

Consider the following statements: *(UPSC CSE - 2019)*

1. *The 44th Amendment to the Constitution of India introduced an Article placing the election of the Prime Minister beyond judicial review.*
2. *The Supreme Court of India struck down the 99th Amendment to the Constitution of India as being violative of the independence of the judiciary.*

Which of the statements given above is/are correct?

(a) *1 only*

(b) *2 only*

(c) *Both 1 and 2*

(d) *Neither 1 nor 2*

UPSC CSE Mains

In the UPSC Civil Services Main Exam (written), this book may turn really handy for you - directly and indirectly.

Almost every year, you can expect 1-2 direct questions - either about landmark cases or recent cases of the Supreme Court.

To get an idea, please go through the question given below:

Examine the scope of Fundamental Rights in the light of the latest Judgment of the Supreme Court on Right to Privacy. *(UPSC CSE 17)*

While the above question can be directly answered from this book, the indirect application of the book is also very significant to fetch valuable marks.

You can quote many of the landmark cases discussed in this book when you write answers of polity/constitution-related questions to provide a real-value addition to your answer.

UPSC CSE Interview

Awareness about important judgments will help you a lot in the UPSC CSE Interview.

Candidates are very often asked to express their opinion about recent judgments passed by the Supreme Court (*for example, your viewpoint on Sabarimala Verdict*).

Also, for other questions, when your viewpoint about a controversial topic is asked, it is always a good technique to supplement your answer with the Supreme Court judgments on the same topic. By bringing additional insights from the higher courts into your answer, you can impress the interview board.

Contents

Web Supplements

Important Judgments that Transformed India

S. No	Case Name and Year	Significance
1.	*Romesh Thappar v. State of Madras* (1950)	The *Romesh Thappar case* upheld the freedom of speech and expression of the citizens. It held that the liberty of the press is an essential part of the right to freedom of speech and expression. The judgment was quoted again and again by the Supreme Court, including in the *Shreya Singhal case,* in which it set aside Section 66A of the Information Technology Act.
2.	*State of Madras v. Smt. Champakam Dorairajan* (1951)	*Champakam Dorairajan case* is one of the first cases that dealt with the question of reservation in admission to educational institutions. The case decided the question of supremacy between the Fundamental Rights and the Directive Principles of State Policy.
3.	*K. M. Nanavati v. State of Maharashtra* (1959)	*K. M. Nanavati case* was the last case to be heard as a jury trial in India.
4.	*The Berubari Union v. Unknown* (1960)	*Berubari Union case* held that the Preamble is not a part of the Constitution. It held that a cession of a part of the territory of India can be made only by an amendment under Article 368.

S. No	Case Name and Year	Significance
5.	*Kedarnath Singh v. State of Bihar* (1962)	*Kedarnath Singh v. State of Bihar* deliberated upon the constitutional validity of Section 124A of IPC. The Supreme Court held that any form of expression by an individual would be deemed seditious only when such expression tends to cause public disorder or disturb public peace.
6.	*I. C. Golaknath and others v. State of Punjab and another* (1967)	*I. C. Golaknath case* held that the Parliament cannot amend Fundamental Rights. The judgment provided for the "Prospective Overruling of the law".
7.	*Keshavananda Bharati Sripadagalvaru v. State of Kerala* (1973)	The *Keshavananda Bharati case* deduced the 'Doctrine of Basic Structure'. It was held that the laws enacted to give effect to the Directive Principle of State Policy under Part IV are open to judicial review. The laws included in the ninth schedule can be challenged in a court of law on the ground that they abrogate the basic elements of the Constitutional structure. The judgment was quoted again and again by the Supreme Court in various judgments like in the *three judges' case.*
8.	*ADM Jabalpur v. Shivkant Shukla* (1976)	*ADM Jabalpur case* dealt with the power of the High Court to issue a writ of *habeas corpus.* Legal experts consider the *ADM Jabalpur judgment* as an unpopular judgment, but it is still continuing as a good law. There has been considerable judicial introspection and admission by former judges that ADM Jabalpur was wrongly decided. The Supreme Court in *Remdeo Chauhan* case *(2010)* officially admitted its mistake in the *ADM Jabalpur judgment.*

S. No	Case Name and Year	Significance
9.	*Maneka Gandhi v. Union of India* (1978)	*Maneka Gandhi case* established the interrelationship between Article 14 and Article 19. It expanded the scope of Article 21 of the Constitution.
10.	*Bachan Singh v. State of Punjab* (1980)	*Bachan Singh case* evolved the doctrine of 'rarest of rare case' for awarding the death penalty.
11.	*Minerva Mills Ltd v. Union of India* (1980)	*Minerva Mills case* held that the harmony and balance between fundamental rights and directive principles is an essential feature of the basic structure of the Constitution. It restored the power of the court to review any amendment to the Constitution.
12.	*Mohd Ahmad Khan v. Shah Bano Begum and others* (1985)	*Shah Bano judgment* upheld the right of divorced Muslim women to sufficient means to maintain themselves. It put an obligation on Muslim men to make provisions to provide maintenance to the divorced wife. The case also dwelt on the need to implement the **Uniform Civil Code**.
13.	*Dr. D. C. Wadhwa and others v. State of Bihar and others* (1986)	The *D. C. Wadhwa judgment* put a check on the process of re-promulgation of ordinances. By doing so, the court upheld the balance between executive and legislature.
14.	*M. C. Mehta v. Union of India and others* (1986)	*M. C. Mehta case* changed the scope of Environment Law in India. For the first time, an industry was held responsible for an accident and forced to pay compensation.

S. No	Case Name and Year	Significance
15.	*Mohini Jain v. State of Karnataka* (1989)	In the *Mohini Jain case* Supreme Court held that the 'right to education' is concomitant to the fundamental rights enshrined under Part III of the Constitution. The right to education flows directly from the right to life. The Parliament in 2002 passed the Constitution (86th Amendment) Act of 2002. It added Article 21A to the Constitution and expressly recognized 'right to education' as a fundamental right in the Constitution.
16.	*Indira Sawhney and others v. Union of India* (1992)	*Indira Sawhney case* upheld the constitutional validity of the Office Memorandum that provided 27% reservation to the Backward classes. It held that the reservations should not exceed 50%, and the reservation in promotion is constitutionally impermissible
17.	*S. R. Bommai v. Union of India* (1994)	*S. R. Bommai case* is related to the proclamation of emergency under Article 356 of the Constitution. The case also dealt with the power of the President to dissolve State Legislative Assemblies, and the issues relating to federalism and secularism as a part of the basic structure. It put an end to the arbitrary dismissal of State governments under Article 356. It was also held that the proclamation under Article 356(1) is not immune from judicial review.
18.	*L. Chandra Kumar v. Union of India* (1997)	In *L. Chandra Kumar v. Union of India* case, the Supreme Court held that Tribunals or other such courts can act as supplements to the High Courts but cannot take away their power of judicial review.

S. No	Case Name and Year	Significance
19.	*Vishakha and others v. State of Rajasthan* (1997)	*Vishakha case* is one of the first instances, where the judiciary tried to fill the vacuum left by the legislature and executive It dealt with the issue of Sexual Harassment in the workplace. The Supreme Court laid out Vishaka guidelines to curb Sexual Harassment of women in the workplace. Building on these guidelines, the Parliament passed the Sexual Harassment at Workplace (Prevention, Prohibition and Redressal) Act, 2013 which seeks to safeguard women from harassment at their place of work.
20.	*Vineet Narain and others v. Union of India* (1997)	*Vineet Narain case* laid out several steps to curb political influence in the functioning of the CBI. It also laid out similar guidance for the Enforcement Directorate. In issuing such guidelines, the Supreme Court referred to its precedent in the ***Vishaka case.***
21.	Three Judges Cases (1981, 1993, 1998)	The Collegium system was evolved by the Supreme Court through three different judgments. They are: • *S. P. Gupta v. President of India and others (1981)* • *Advocate on Record Association v. Union of India (1993)* • *Special Reference case of 1998* These are important judgments in preserving Judicial independence, which is one of the basic features of the Constitution as evolved in the *Keshavananda Bharati case.*
22.	*Prakash Singh and others v. Union of India and others* (2006)	*Prakash Singh judgment* issued seven binding directions on police reforms. The Supreme Court recalled its observation in the *Vineet Narain case* regarding the need for police reforms.

S. No	Case Name and Year	Significance
23.	*M. Nagaraj and Others v. Union of India* (2006)	*M. Nagaraj* case dealt with a challenge to constitutional amendments aimed at nullifying the impact of *Indira Sawhney* judgments of 1992. The judgment upheld the essence of the *Indira Sawhney* judgment. However, it provided flexibility to states to make a reservation for SC/ST in a matter of promotions. The Supreme Court reiterated the ceiling limit of 50%, the concept of creamy layer and the compelling reasons, namely, backwardness, the inadequacy of representation and overall administrative efficiency. Regarding the issue related to the 'extent of reservation', the Court said that the State will have to show in each case the existence of the compelling reasons.
24.	*Lily Thomas v. Union of India and others* (2013)	*Lily Thomas judgment* was aimed at freeing the political setup from the criminal elements. The Supreme Court held Subsection (4) of Section 8 of the Representation of Peoples Act is *ultra vires* the Constitution.
25.	*T. S. R. Subramanian and others v. Union of India and others* (2013)	*T. S. R. Subramanian* case aimed at professionalizing the bureaucracy, promote efficiency and good governance. Taking a cue from the *Vishaka* case, *Prakash Singh* case and *Vineet Narain* case, it issued directions to the government to make the bureaucracy free from unnecessary political interference, provide them with the security of tenure, increase the bureaucratic efficiency and thus to achieve good governance. It also sought to fix the accountability for any action taken, by requiring that the orders need to be in writing.

S. No	Case Name and Year	Significance
26.	*National Legal Services Authority v. Union of India* (2014)	*National Legal Services Authority (NALSA)* case recognized the Hijras/ Eunuchs as 'third gender'. It tried to address the grievances of the members of the Transgender Community in India and extended them all the benefits of socially and educationally backward classes.
27.	*Shreya Singhal v. Union of India* (2015)	*Shreya Singhal* case decided the questions related to the fundamental right of free speech and expression guaranteed by Article 19(1)(a) of the Constitution of India. Supreme Court in *Romesh Thappar* case stated that freedom of speech lay at the foundation of all democratic organizations. But, Section 66A of the IT Act 2000 authorized the imposition of restrictions on the 'freedom of speech and expression' in language wide enough to cover restrictions both within and without the limits of constitutionally permissible legislative action. Therefore, the Court held that Section 66A is unconstitutional.
28.	*Shayara Bano v. Union of India and others* (2016)	*Shayara Bano* judgment set aside the practice of *talaq-e-bidat,* which allowed Muslim men to divorce their wives instantaneously and irrevocably. Along with the *Shah Bano* case, it is one of the landmark judgments in protecting the rights of Muslim women in India.

S. No	Case Name and Year	Significance
29.	*Justice K. S. Puttaswamy (Retd) and another v. Union of India and others* (2017)	*Puttaswamy* case dealt with the question that whether privacy is a constitutionally protected value under the Indian Constitution. It held that 'right to privacy' emerges primarily from the guarantee of life and personal liberty in Article 21 of the Constitution. By holding that 'Right to Privacy' is a fundamental right, the court overruled its earlier judgments in *M. P. Sharma* case and *Kharak Singh* case. The Supreme Court relied on this ruling to declare Section 377 of IPC unconstitutional in *Navtej Singh Johar* case; decriminalize adultery in *Joseph Shine* case and in *Indian Young Lawyers Association* case which dealt with the entry of women into Sabarimala temple in Kerala.
30.	*Indian Young Lawyers Association v. the State of Kerala* (2018)	*Indian Young Lawyers Association* case allowed the entry of women aged between 10 and 50 to the Sabarimala temple in Kerala. It held that the devotees of Lord Ayyappa are just Hindus and do not constitute a separate religious denomination. The exclusionary practice followed at the Sabarimala temple cannot be treated as an essential practice. It upheld the women's right to profess practice and propagate a religion. The judgment reaffirms the Constitution's transformative character and derives strength from the centrality it accords to fundamental rights. While upholding the rights of women, the court also referred to *Puttaswamy* judgment.

S. No	Case Name and Year	Significance
31.	*Joseph Shine v. Union of India* (2018)	*Joseph Shine* case struck down Section 497 of the Indian Penal Code which criminalized adultery. It expanded the horizons of individual liberty and gender parity. The court referred to *Puttaswamy* judgment in decriminalizing adultery.
32.	*Navtej Singh Johar and others v. Union of India* (2018)	*Navtej Singh Johar* case partially struck down Section 377 of the Indian Penal Code (IPC). It upheld the right of LGBT community to have intimate relations with people of their choice, their inherent right to privacy and dignity and the freedom to live without fear. It corrected the judicial error committed by a two-member Bench in *Suresh Kumar Koushal* (2013). The court referred to the *Puttaswamy judgment* extensively in striking down Section 377.
33.	*Anuradha Bhasin v. Union of India and others* (2020)	In the *Anuradha Bhasin v. Union of India and others* case, Supreme Court declared the right to practice profession and that trade over the internet is a fundamental right under Article 19(1)(g).
34.	*Rambabu Singh Thakur v. Sunil Arora and others* (2020)	The Supreme Court in *Rambabu Singh Thakur v. Sunil Arora* case ensured that the general public will be properly aware of the criminal background of candidates contesting elections so that they can exercise their right to vote judiciously. However, the Supreme Court resisted banning candidates undergoing criminal trials to contest elections.

S. No	Case Name and Year	Significance
35.	*Internet and Mobile Association of India v. Reserve Bank of India* (2020)	In the *Internet and Mobile Association of India v. Reserve Bank of India* case, the Supreme Court decided in favour of cryptocurrency transactions in India after using the doctrine of proportionality. As a result, the RBI's circular to regulate cryptocurrencies was declared illegal and set aside. This paved the way for facilitating the exchanges of crypto traders not only in India but around the world.
36.	*Laxmibai Chandaragi and Another v. State of Karnataka and others* (2021)	Hon'ble Supreme Court in the *Laxmibai Chandaragi* case ruled that in India when two adult individuals agree to marry, consent of family, community or clan is not required. The Court has also stated that the choice of an individual to select a partner for marriage is an integral part of 'dignity'.
37.	*Mohammad Salimullah and Another v. Union of India and others* (2021)	The Supreme Court in the case of *Mohammad Salimullah v. Union of India* tried to answer the question of whether the detained refugees could be deported to their country of origin by the Government of India. The Apex Court considered the view that the fundamental right to reside and settle in India guaranteed under Article 19(1)(e) of the Indian Constitution is available only to the citizens. The Court ruled that the right not to be deported is ancillary (secondary) to the right to reside or settle in any part of the territory of India.

S. No	Case Name and Year	Significance
38.	*Farzana Batool v. Union of India and others* (2021)	In *Farzana Batool v. Union of India* case, Supreme Court pondered upon the fact whether higher education up to the professional level comes under the fundamental right to education or not. The Apex Court held that the right to pursue higher education is not explicitly mentioned as a fundamental right in Part III of the Constitution and thus access to professional education is not a governmental obligation.
39.	*Kerala Union of Working Journalists v. Union of India and others* (2021)	The Supreme Court of India in *Kerala Union of Working Journalists v. Union of India and others* case held that the fundamental right to life is available to undertrial prisoners. This case further established that undertrial prisoners are eligible to be provided with health and medical care.
40.	*Barun Chandra Thakur v. Master Bholu and Another* (2022)	In *Barun Chandra Thakur v. Master Bholu and Another* case, the Supreme Court ruled that the Juvenile Justice Board should consult with experts before making any preliminary decisions.

1

Romesh Thappar v. State of Madras (1950)

Freedom of Press is not explicitly mentioned in the Constitution of India.

However, is it part of the right to freedom of speech and expression?

Romesh Thappar case upheld the freedom of speech and expression of the citizens.

It held that liberty of the press is an essential part of the right to freedom of speech and expression.

The judgment was quoted again and again by the Supreme Court, including in ***Shreya Singhal case,*** in which it set aside Section 66A of the Information Technology Act.

INTRODUCTION

Romesh Thappar v. State of Madras is a landmark case delivered by the Supreme Court of India. The Supreme Court stated that freedom of speech lay at the foundation of all democratic organisations.[1]

Romesh Thappar was the petitioner in the case and the State of Madras was the respondent.

BACKGROUND

Romesh Thappar was the printer, publisher and editor of a weekly journal called *Cross Roads.* The journal was printed and published in the English language in Bombay.

The Government of Madras in an order dated 1 March 1950, issued under the Madras Maintenance of Public Order Act, 1949, imposed a ban on the entry and circulation of the *Cross Roads* journal in the State for reportedly publishing

1. https://indianexpress.com/article/india/india-others/for-free-speech-sc-cites-free-press/

views critical or defamatory of the Congress. The order cited 'public safety and the maintenance of public order' as the ground for imposing the ban.

The order read, 'In exercise of the powers conferred by Section 9 (I-A) of the Madras Maintenance of Public Order, Act, 1949 (Madras Act XXIII of 1949) His Excellency the Governor of Madras, being satisfied that for the purpose of securing the public safety and the maintenance of public order, it is necessary so to do, hereby prohibits, with effect on and from the date of publication of this order in the Fort St. George Gazette the entry into or the circulation, sale or distribution in the State of Madras or any part thereof of the newspaper entitled Cross Roads an English weekly published at Bombay'.[2]

The Madras Maintenance of Public Order Act was passed by the Provincial Legislature under Section 100 of the **Government of India Act 1935**, read with Entry 1 of List II of the Seventh Schedule to that Act, which comprised among other matters, 'public order'.

Romesh Thappar approached the Supreme Court under **Article 32** for a writ of **prohibition** and **certiorari**.

ARTICLE 32: RIGHT TO CONSTITUTIONAL REMEDIES

Article 32(1): The right to move the Supreme Court by appropriate proceedings for the enforcement of the rights conferred by the Part III is guaranteed.

Article 32(2): The Supreme Court shall have the power to issue directions or orders or writs, including writs in the nature of ***habeas corpus***, ***mandamus***, ***prohibition***, ***quo warranto***, and ***certiorari***, whichever may be appropriate, for the enforcement of any of the rights conferred by Part III.

ARGUMENTS

Romesh Thappar claimed that the order issued by the State of Madras under the Maintenance of Public Order Act, 1949, contravenes the fundamental right of speech and expression conferred on him by **Article 19(1)(a)** of the Constitution.

2. https://indiankanoon.org/doc/456839/

ARTICLE 19: PROTECTION OF CERTAIN RIGHTS REGARDING FREEDOM OF SPEECH, ETC.

Article 19(1): All citizens shall have the right–

(a) to freedom of speech and expression;
(b) to assemble peaceably and without arms;
(c) to form associations or unions or co-operative societies;
(d) to move freely throughout the territory of India;
(e) to reside and settle in any part of the territory of India;
(f) xx xx xx[3]; and
(g) To practice any profession, or to carry on any occupation, trade or business.

Thappar argued that Section 9 (1-A) of the Maintenance of Public Order Act, 1949, is inconsistent with the fundamental right of speech and expression, and hence void under **Article 13(1)** of the Constitution.

The State of Madras argued that the expression 'public safety' in the Act means the security of the Province, and therefore, 'the security of the State'. Therefore, it comes under the Article 19(2), as 'the State' has been defined in Article 12 as including, among other things, the Government and the Legislature of each of the erstwhile Provinces.

The State of Madras also objected to the petitioner approaching the Supreme Court directly for relief in the first instance. It said, as a matter of orderly procedure, the petitioner should first approach the High Court at Madras which has concurrent jurisdiction to deal with the matter under Article 226 of the Constitution.

UNDERSTANDING RIGHT TO FREEDOM OF SPEECH AND EXPRESSION

Article 19(1)(a) of the Constitution of India states that "*all the citizens have right to freedom of speech and expression*". But this provision of law has a very wide connotation which has been further expanded by Courts in India. Right to freedom of speech and expression includes:

1. Freedom of press – it includes no pre-censorship or stoppage of publication. The freedom of circulation also indicates that the press cannot be charged with excessive taxes.

3. Sub-Clause (f) was omitted by the Constitution (Forty-fourth Amendment) Act, 1978, with effect from 20 June 1979.

2. Right to Information - this is now exercised through the Right to Information Act.
3. Right to know the antecedents of candidates at an election.
4. Right to reply
5. Right to silence
6. Right to fly the national flag

THE JUDGMENT

The Supreme Court said that freedom of speech and expression includes freedom of propagation of ideas and that freedom is ensured by the freedom of circulation. It observed that the 'Liberty of circulation is as essential to that freedom as the liberty of publication. Indeed, without circulation, the publication would be of little value'.[4]

It further observed that the order of the Government of Madras would be a violation of the petitioner's fundamental right under Article 19(1)(a) unless Section 9(1-A) of the Madras Maintenance of Public Order Act is saved by the exceptions mentioned in Clause (2) of Article 19.

'Security of the State' is a reasonable restriction under Article 19(2) of the Constitution. However, the words used in Section 9 of the Act are 'public safety and public order'.[5]

In formulating the reasonable restrictions on the fundamental rights enumerated in Article 19(1), the Constitution has placed a distinct category of offences against public order which aim at undermining the security of the State or overthrowing it. Prevention of these offences is the sole justification for legislative abridgement of the freedom of speech and expression. In other words, nothing less than endangering the foundations of the State or threatening its overthrow could justify curtailment of the rights to freedom of speech and expression.

The Entry 3 of List III (Concurrent List) of the Seventh Schedule also differentiates between 'security of a State' and 'maintenance of public order' as distinct subjects of legislation.

Thus, the Supreme Court held that 'unless a law restricting freedom of speech and expression is directed solely against the undermining of the

---

4. https://indiankanoon.org/doc/456839/
5. https://globalfreedomofexpression.columbia.edu/cases/thappar-v-madras/

security of the State or the overthrow of it, such law cannot fall within the reservation under Clause (2) of Article 19. The Section 9 (1-A) which authorizes the imposition of restrictions for the wider purpose of securing public safety or the maintenance of public order falls outside the scope of authorized restrictions under Clause (2), and is therefore void and unconstitutional'.[6]

The Supreme Court quashed the order which prohibited the entry and circulation of the petitioner's journal in the State of Madras.

With regard to the petitioner approaching the Supreme Court for relief in the first instance, the Court said Article 32 provides a guaranteed remedy for the enforcement of the rights provided under Part III of the Constitution, and this remedial right is itself made a fundamental right by being included in Part III. Therefore, the **Supreme Court is the protector and guarantor of fundamental rights** and it cannot refuse to entertain applications seeking protection against infringements of such rights.

IMPORTANCE

The judgment in ***Romesh Thappar case*** is one of the finest in the history of the Supreme Court of India. It **upheld the freedom of speech and expression**, which lay at the foundation of all democratic organisations. The Court observed that **free political discussion is essential** for the proper functioning of a democratic government.

It held that the **liberty of the press is an essential part of the right to freedom of speech and expression** under Article 19(1)(a). It also said that the freedom of speech and expression is one of the most valuable rights guaranteed to a citizen by the Constitution and should be jealously guarded by the courts.

The judgment was quoted repeatedly by the Supreme Court, including in ***Shreya Singhal case***, in which it set aside Section 66A of the Information Technology Act.

IMPACT

'Romesh Thappar' case necessitated constitutional amendments. The first amendment to the Indian Constitution undid the effect of this judgment. In this regard, the first amendment to the Constitution amended Article 19.

6. https://indiankanoon.org/doc/456839/

In Article 19 of the Constitution, for Clause (2), the following Clause was substituted:

(2) Nothing in Sub-Clause (a) of Clause (1) shall affect the operation of any existing law, or prevent the State from making any law, in so far as such law imposes reasonable restrictions on the exercise of the right conferred by the said Sub-Clause in the interests of the security of the State, friendly relations with foreign states, public order, decency or morality, or in relation to contempt of court, defamation or incitement to an offence.

The amendment also inserted the following:

(2) No law in force in the territory of India immediately before the commencement of the Constitution which is consistent with the provisions of Article 19 of the Constitution as amended by Sub-Section (1) of this Section shall be deemed to be void, or over to have become void, on the ground only that, being a law which takes away or abridges the right conferred by Sub-Clause (a) of Clause (1) of the said Article, its operation was not saved by Clause (2) of that Article as originally enacted.

In other words, the amendment gave some protection to the pre-constitutional laws which are consistent with Article 19.

2

State of Madras v. Smt. Champakam Dorairajan (1951)

Can the government provide caste-based reservation in government jobs and college seats?

Between Fundamental Rights (FR) and Directive Principles of State Policy (DPSP), what is supreme?

Champakam Dorairajan case is one of the first cases that dealt with the question of reservation in admission to the educational institutions.

The case decided the question of supremacy between the Fundamental Rights and the Directive Principles of State Policy.

INTRODUCTION

State of Madras v. Smt. Champakam Dorairajan is a landmark case delivered by the Supreme Court of India that, along with ***Romesh Thappar v. State of Madras*** *(1950)*, led to the first amendment to the Indian Constitution in 1951.

The State of Madras was the petitioner in the case and Smt. Champakam Dorairajan was the respondent.

BACKGROUND

In 1927, the Province of Madras had issued a government order, known as the **Communal G.O.**, with regard to the admission of students to the Engineering and Medical Colleges of the state. The order stated that the seats in Engineering and Medical Colleges should be filled on the following basis:

'...out of every fourteen seats, six were to be allotted to Non-Brahmin (Hindus), two were to be allotted to Backward Hindus, two were to be allotted to Brahmins, two were to be allotted to Harijans, one to Anglo-Indians and Indian Christians and one to Muslims'.[1]

1. https://indiankanoon.org/doc/149321/

At that time, the State of Madras maintained only four Medical Colleges with a total of 330 seats. Out of these seats, 17 were reserved for students coming from outside the state and 12 for discretionary allotment by the state.

Similarly, the Madras state maintained four Engineering Colleges and only 395 seats were available in those colleges. Out of these, 21 seats were reserved for students coming from outside the state and 12 for discretionary allotment by the state.

Rest of the seats in the Medical and Engineering colleges were apportioned on the basis of Communal G.O. of 1927.

In 1950, Srimathi Champakam Dorairajan made an application to the High Court of Madras under Article 226 of the Constitution. She complained of a breach of her fundamental right to get admission into educational institutions maintained by the state. She stated that on inquiry, she came to know that she would not be admitted to the college as she belonged to the Brahmin community, and sought the protection of her fundamental rights under **Article 15(1) and Article 29(2)** of the Constitution.

Champakam Dorairajan prayed for the issue of a writ of mandamus 'restraining the State of Madras and all officers and subordinates thereof from enforcing, observing, maintaining or following or requiring the enforcement, observance, maintenance or following by the authorities concerned of the notification or order generally referred to as the Communal G.O. in and by which admissions into the Madras Medical Colleges were sought or purported to be regulated in such manner as to infringe and involve the violation of her fundamental rights'.[2]

The High Court of Madras delivered its judgment and ruled in favour of Champakam Dorairajan. The State of Madras appealed this ruling in the Supreme Court, and thus the case came before the Supreme Court of India.

ARTICLE 29: PROTECTION OF INTERESTS OF MINORITIES[3]

Article 29(1): Any section of the citizens residing in the territory of India or any part thereof having a distinct language, script or culture of its own shall have the right to conserve the same.

Article 29(2): No citizen shall be denied admission into any educational institution maintained by the State or receiving aid out of State funds on grounds only of religion, race, caste, language or any of them.

2. https://indiankanoon.org/doc/149321/
3. The Constitution of India, Ministry of Law and Justice (Legislative Department)

ARGUMENTS

Smt. Dorairajan argued that the denial of admission into the educational institution maintained by the state on the grounds of caste violated her fundamental rights under Article 15(1) and Article 29(2) of the Constitution.

Article 15(1) prohibits discrimination on grounds only of religion, race, caste, sex, place of birth or any of them.

The State of Madras contended that the provisions of these articles have to be read along with other articles in the Constitution. The state argued that '**Article 46** charges the state with promoting with special care the educational and economic interests of the weaker sections of the people, and, in particular, of the Scheduled Castes and the Scheduled Tribes, and with protecting them from social injustice and all forms of exploitation'.[4]

The State of Madras further argued that Article 46 under Part IV of the Constitution, though not enforceable by any court of law, is fundamental for the governance of the country. **Article 37** puts an obligation on the state to apply those principles in making laws. The state is entitled to maintain the Communal G.O. fixing proportionate seats for different communities, and the order is valid in law and not in violation of the Constitution.

Thus, if any person is unable to get admission into the educational institutions because of the Communal G.O., there is no infringement of their fundamental rights.

ARTICLE 15 v. ARTICLE 16

Articles 15 and 16 of the Indian Constitution deal with affirmative action by the State to protect backward communities and women in India. However, there is a slight difference between both provisions.

Article 15 is much wider in scope as it prohibits discrimination under general/all circumstances, whereas Article 16 is restricted to matters of public employment.

Also, Article 16 has two additional prohibited grounds of discrimination, i.e., descent and residence.

4. https://indiankanoon.org/doc/149321/

THE JUDGMENT

The Supreme Court held that the Communal G.O. constituted a violation of the fundamental right guaranteed to the citizens of India by Article 29(2) of the Constitution and was therefore void under Article 13.

Supreme Court held that the 'Clause (2) under Article 29 guarantees the fundamental right of an individual citizen. The right to get admission into any educational institution of the kind mentioned in clause (2) is a right which an individual citizen has as a citizen and not as a member of any community or class of citizens. This right is not to be denied to the citizen on grounds only of religion, race, caste, language or any of them'.[5]

In other words, if a citizen who seeks admission into any educational institution maintained by the state or receiving aid out of state funds, he/she **cannot be refused admission only on grounds of religion, race, caste, language** or any of them, provided he/she has the requisite academic qualifications. If the admission is denied only on such grounds, then that amounts to a breach of his/her fundamental right.

The Supreme Court further held that the **directive principles of State policy** laid down in Part IV of the Constitution **cannot in any way override or abridge the fundamental rights** guaranteed by Part III. On the other hand, they have to conform to and run as subsidiary to the fundamental rights laid down in Part III.

The Supreme Court said that 'the Directive Principles of State Policy, which by Article 37 are expressly made unenforceable by a Court, cannot override the provisions found in Part III which, notwithstanding other provisions, are expressly made enforceable by appropriate Writs, Orders or directions under Article 32'.

Thus, the Court held that the 'classification in the Communal G.O. proceeds on the basis of religion, race, and caste. The classification made in the Communal G.O. is opposed to the Constitution and constitutes a clear violation of the fundamental rights guaranteed to the citizen under Article 29(2). ...the Communal G.O. being inconsistent with the provisions of Article 29(2) in Part III of the Constitution is void under Article 13'.[6]

Thus, it upheld the judgment of the High Court of Madras.

---

5. https://indiankanoon.org/doc/149321/
6. https://indiankanoon.org/doc/149321/

IMPORTANCE

'Champakam Dorairajan' case decided the question of supremacy between the Fundamental Rights and the Directive Principles of State Policy.

It is one of the first cases that dealt with the question of reservation in admission to the educational institutions.

IMPACT

'Champakam Dorairajan' case along with ***'Romesh Thappar'*** case necessitated constitutional amendments. The first amendment to the Indian Constitution undid the effect of the two cases.

The first amendment, among other changes, inserted clause (4) to Article 15, which is:

'Nothing in this Article or in clause (2) of Article 29 shall prevent the State from making any special provision for the advancement of any socially and educationally backward classes of citizens or for the Scheduled Castes and the Scheduled Tribes'.

3

K. M. Nanavati v. State of Maharashtra (1959)

Almost immediately after the Indian Constitution came into effect, the abolition of the jury system began to be discussed in the corridors of power.

However, in many states, jury trials continued to exist.

The jury system became controversial after *K. M. Nanavati* case.

K. M. Nanavati case was one of the most famous jury trials in India. It changed the Indian justice system forever.

With the introduction of the new version of the Code of Criminal Procedure in 1974, the chapter of jury trials was closed.

INTRODUCTION

K. M. Nanavati v. State of Maharashtra is a landmark case which received unprecedented media coverage and inspired several books and movies. It was **one of the last cases to be heard as a jury trial** in India.

K. M. Nanavati was the petitioner in the case and the State of Maharashtra was the respondent.

BACKGROUND

K. M. Nanavati was a Naval Officer with the Indian Navy. He was second in command of the Indian Naval Ship "*Mysore*". He married Sylvia in 1949 and had three children.

He was put on trial under **Section 302 and Section 304** of the Indian Penal Code (IPC) for the alleged murder of his wife's paramour Prem Ahuja.

SECTIONS 302 AND 304 OF IPC

Section 302: Punishment for murder – Whoever commits murder shall be punished with death or imprisonment for life, and shall also be liable to fine.

Section 304: Punishment for culpable homicide not amounting to murder – Whoever commits culpable homicide not amounting to murder shall be punished with imprisonment for life, or imprisonment of either description for a term which may extend to ten years, and shall also be liable to fine, if the act by which the death is caused is done with the intention of causing death, or of causing such bodily injury as is likely to cause death, or with imprisonment of either description for a term which may extend to ten years, or with fine, or with both, if the act is done with the knowledge that it is likely to cause death, but without any intention to cause death, or to cause such bodily injury as is likely to cause death.

On the day of the alleged murder, his wife Sylvia confessed to him of her illicit intimacy with Ahuja.

There are different versions of the turn of events after the confession. But, the common thread is that K. M. Nanavati took a revolver and cartridges from the Naval stores on a false pretext, loaded the same and went to Ahuja's flat.

Nanavati asked whether Ahuja would marry Sylvia and look after the children. Ahuja retorted, 'Am I to marry every woman I sleep with?' Following the heated and abusive verbal exchange, Nanavati shot him dead. Thereafter, he surrendered himself to the police.

At that time, India had the 'Jury system'. Nanavati was initially declared not guilty by jury by a majority of 8:1. But the Sessions' Judge disagreed with that verdict and referred the matter to the Bombay High Court.

The verdict was dismissed by the Division Bench of the High Court and the case was re-tried as a bench trial. The Division Bench held that the appellant was guilty under Section 302 of the Indian Penal Code and sentenced him to undergo rigorous imprisonment for life.

K. M. Nanavati appealed to the Supreme Court by a **Special Leave Petition (SLP)**. Thus, the matter came before the Supreme Court of India.

At the same time, he made an application to the Governor under Article 161.

ARTICLE 161: POWER OF GOVERNOR TO GRANT PARDON[1]

The Governor of a State shall have the power to grant pardons, reprieves, respites or remissions of punishment or to suspend, remit or commute the sentence of any person convicted of any offence against any law relating to a matter to which the executive power of the State extends.

ARGUMENTS

Through the special leave petition, K. M. Nanavati contended that the High Court was not empowered by Section 307 (3) of the Indian Penal Code to set aside the verdict of the jury on the grounds that there were misdirections in the charge. It was also contended that there were no misdirections in the charge nor was the verdict perverse.

Further, since there was grave and sudden provocation, the offence committed, if any, was not murder, but **culpable homicide not amounting to murder**.

ARTICLE 136 – SPECIAL LEAVE PETITION

Generally, an appeal to the Supreme Court is made after an unsatisfactory judgment by the High Court, but under certain special circumstances, an appeal may lie directly to the Supreme Court from any Court in India under Article 136 of the Constitution.

According to Article 136, an appeal can be made to the Supreme Court directly from any order, decision, decree, judgment, etc. given by any court or tribunal in India.

This power of the Supreme Court under Article 136 is discretionary and Hon'ble Court may or may not allow special leave to appeal to any person.

1. The Constitution of India, Ministry of Law and Justice (Legislative Department)

LEGAL ISSUES INVOLVED

There were two issues in the case.

(1) Whether it was premeditated murder or 'the heat of the moment'?
(2) Whether the pardoning power of the Governor and the SLP can be moved together?

If it was 'the heat of the moment', Nanavati would be charged under Section 304 of the IPC for culpable homicide not amounting to murder. If it was a premeditated murder, Nanavati would be charged under Section 302 (murder), with the sentence being death or life imprisonment.

THE JUDGMENT

On the second issue, the Supreme Court held that **the SLP and pardoning power cannot operate together**. If SLP is filed, then the power of the Governor in such condition will cease to exist.

The Supreme Court reasoned that as per the **'rule of statutory coexistence'**, if two statutes are found in conflict as their objectives are different, then the language of each statute is restricted to its own object or subject. They run parallel and never meet.[2]

On the first issue, the Supreme Court upheld the judgment of the Bombay High Court, which held **K. M. Nanavati guilty under Section 302** of the Indian Penal Code and sentenced him to undergo rigorous imprisonment for life.

The Supreme Court's decision was based on the following grounds:

- There was a time lapse between Sylvia's confession and murder of Prem Ahuja. That was sufficient to regain the self-control.
- Nanavati asked Ahuja whether he would marry Sylvia and take care of the children. So, he was thinking of the future of his wife and children. This indicates that he had not only regained his senses, but also was planning for the future.
- Before shooting Ahuja, Nanavati abused him, which provoked an equally abusive reply. But, this cannot be a provocation for murder.

---

2. http://www.legalservicesindia.com/article/1347/K.M.Nanavati-V.-State-of-Maharashtra.html

IMPACT

- The case was **one of the last cases to be heard as a jury trial** in India, as the government abolished jury trials as a result of the case.[3]
- **Nanavati was pardoned by the then Governor** Vijay Lakshmi Pandit, after spending 3 years in jail.

3. http://www.legalservicesindia.com/article/1347/K.M.Nanavati-V.-State-of-Maharashtra.html

4

Berubari Union v. Unknown (1960)

Whether the Parliament of India has the power to cede Indian territory under the original Constitution?

Is the Preamble to the Constitution of India part of the Indian Constitution itself?

Berubari Union case held that the Preamble is not a part of the Constitution.

It held that a cession of a part of the territory of India can be made only by an amendment under Article 368.

INTRODUCTION

Berubari Union v. Unknown case is related to the exchange of territories between India and Pakistan as per the **Nehru-Noon Agreement of 1958**.

BACKGROUND

As per the Indian Independence Act, 1947, the boundaries of the new Provinces of India and Pakistan was to be determined by the 'award' of a **boundary commission** appointed by the Governor General. The expression 'award' means the decision of the chairman of the commission contained in his report to the Governor General at the conclusion of the commission's proceedings. Accordingly, the Governor General appointed a commission under the chairmanship of **Sir Cyril Radcliffe**.

However, soon the boundary dispute between India and Pakistan arose because of an erroneous depiction of the map by the Radcliffe award.

In order to resolve the boundary disputes between the two countries, the then Prime Ministers Shri. Jawaharlal Nehru and Shri. Feroze Khan Noon arrived at an **agreement in 1958**.

Among other things, the agreement provided for the **division of Berubari Union No. 12** and **exchange of enclaves** between the two countries. This exchange was on the basis of enclaves for enclaves without any consideration of territorial loss or gain.

Berubari Union No. 12 had an area of 8.75 square miles and a population of 10,000-12,000 residents. It is situated in the District of Jalpaiguri, West Bengal.

As per the agreement, 'Berubari Union No. 12' was to be divided horizontally, so as to give half the area to Pakistan and the other half adjacent to India to be retained by India.

The item 3 in paragraph 2 of the Agreement read:

'The division should be made in such a manner that the Cooch-Behar Enclaves between Pachagar Thana of East Pakistan and Berubari Union No. 12 of Jalpaiguri Thana of West Bengal will remain connected as at present with Indian Territory and will remain with India. The Cooch-Behar Enclaves lower down between Boda Thana of East Pakistan and Berubari Union No. 12 will be exchanged along with the general exchange of enclaves and will go to Pakistan'.[1]

Similarly, item 10 of the Agreement provided for 'Exchange of Old Cooch-Behar Enclaves in Pakistan and Pakistan Enclaves in India without claim to compensation for the extra area going to Pakistan...'.[2]

LEGAL ISSUES INVOLVED

While implementing the agreement, some legal issues came up. The issue was:

Whether the implementation of the Agreement in relation to the Berubari Union and the exchange of Enclaves require any legislative action either by way of the law of Parliament under **Article 3** of the Constitution or a suitable amendment of the Constitution under the provisions of **Article 368** or both?

1. https://www.sci.gov.in/jonew/judis/401.pdf
2. https://www.sci.gov.in/jonew/judis/401.pdf

ARTICLE 3

Article 3 deals with the formation of new States and alteration of areas, boundaries or names of existing States. It reads, 'Parliament may by law -

(a) Form a new State by separation of territory from any State or by uniting two or more States or parts of States or by uniting any territory to a part of any State;
(b) Increase the area of any State;
(c) Diminish the area of any State;
(d) Alter the boundaries of any State;
(e) Alter the name of any State'.

There was a chance of the constitutional validity of the exchange of enclaves and division of the Berubari Union being questioned in the courts. This involved avoidable and protracted litigation.

Therefore, the President of India thought that questions of law that have arisen are of such nature and importance that it is necessary that the opinion of the Supreme Court of India should be obtained. So, in the exercise of the powers conferred upon the President under **Article 143** of the Constitution, he referred the following three questions to the Supreme Court of India.[3]

Is any legislative action necessary for the implementation of the Agreement relating to Berubari Union?

If so, is a law of Parliament relatable to Article 3 of the Constitution sufficient for the purpose or is an amendment of the Constitution in accordance with Article 368 of the Constitution necessary, in addition, or in the alternative?

Is a law of Parliament relatable to Article 3 of the Constitution sufficient for implementation of the agreement relating to Exchange of Enclaves or is an amendment of the Constitution in accordance with Article 368 of the Constitution necessary for the purpose, in addition, or in the alternative?

3. https://www.sci.gov.in/jonew/judis/401.pdf

ARTICLE 143

Article 143 deals with the power of the President to consult the Supreme Court. It reads, 'If at any time it appears to the President that a question of law or fact has arisen, or is likely to arise, which is of such a nature and of such public importance that it is expedient to obtain the opinion of the Supreme Court upon it, he may refer the question to that Court for consideration and the Court may, after such hearing as it thinks fit, report to the President its opinion thereon'.[4]

ARGUMENTS

The Union of India contended that the agreement is merely a recognition of the boundary which had already been fixed and it is not a substitution of a new boundary or the alteration of the boundary. The ascertainment or the settlement of the boundary is not alienation or cession of the territory of India.

If any part of the territory has had to be yielded to Pakistan, as per the award of the boundary commission, it does not amount to the cession of territory. It is merely a mode of settling the boundary.

Hence, the government of India contended that no legislative action is required for the implementation of the Agreement in relation to Berubari Union as well as the exchange of enclaves.

A rival contention made by one Mr. Chatterjee said that the 'Parliament has no power to cede any part of the territory of India in favour of a foreign State either by ordinary legislation or even by the amendment of the Constitution'.[4]

So, according to him, the only opinion the Supreme Court can give on the Reference is that the Agreement is void and cannot be made effective even by any legislative process.

This argument was based on the following grounds:

- The preamble to the Constitution clearly postulates that like the democratic republic form of government, the entire territory of India is beyond the reach of the Parliament and cannot be affected either by ordinary legislation or even by constitutional amendment.

4. The Constitution of India, Ministry of Law and Justice (Legislative Department)

- **Article 1(3)(c)** of the Constitution has expressly given to the country the power to acquire other territories, but it has made no provision for ceding any part of its territory.

ARTICLE 1: NAME AND TERRITORY OF THE UNION[5]

Article 1(1): India, that is Bharat, shall be a Union of States.
Article 1(2): The States and the territories thereof shall be as specified in the First Schedule.
Article 1(3): The territory of India shall comprise -

(a) The territories of the States;
(b) The Union territories specified in the First Schedule; and
(c) Such other territories as may be acquired.

INDIA: AN INDESTRUCTIBLE UNION OF DESTRUCTIBLE STATES

Indian federalism is not part of an agreement between the Centre and States and hence States do not have a right to cede from the Union. India is famously referred to as an 'indestructible union of destructible states'.

In other words, the Centre is free to change the boundaries of States but States cannot under any circumstances cede from the Union.

This is in sharp contrast to American federalism which is referred to as an 'indestructible union of indestructible states'.

THE JUDGMENT

With regards to the contention of the Union government in implementing the agreement, the Supreme Court concluded that the parties have agreed upon the most expedient and reasonable way to resolve the dispute, which would be to divide the area in question half and a half. There was no attempt to interpret the award or to determine what the award really meant.

Therefore, the Supreme Court did not agree with the contention that the agreement is 'no more than ascertainment and delineation of the boundaries in the light of the award'.[6]

5. The Constitution of India, Ministry of Law and Justice (Legislative Department)
6. https://www.sci.gov.in/jonew/judis/401.pdf

With regards to the rival contention made by Mr. Chatterjee, the Supreme Court held that **the Preamble is not a part of the Constitution**, and hence found no merit in the rival contentions presented by Mr. Chatterjee.

Further, **Article 1(3)(c) does not confer power or authority on India to acquire territories**. It only makes a provision for absorption and integration of any foreign territories which may be acquired by India. This provision is not in pursuance of any expansionist political philosophy.

Article 368 of the Constitution provides for the procedure for the amendment of the Constitution and expressly confers power on the Parliament on that behalf. The **power to amend the Constitution includes the power to amend Article 1**. Thus, logically would include the power to cede national territory in favour of a foreign state.

Though not expressly conferred by the Constitution, the power to acquire foreign territory and the power to cede a part of the national territory are essential attributes of sovereignty. Cession of the national territory in law amounts to the transfer of sovereignty over the said territory by the owner state in favour of another state. So, some legislation is necessary to implement the Agreement.

Article 3 does not refer to the Union territories. So, if a part of the Union territories have to be ceded to a foreign state, no law relatable to Article 3 would be competent in respect of such cession. So, the cession of a part of the Union territories would inevitably have to be implemented by legislation relatable to Article 368.

In the light of these reasons, the **Supreme Court concluded** that it would not be competent to Parliament to make a law under Article 3 of the Constitution for the purpose of implementing the Agreement. This would mean that the law necessary to implement the Agreement has to be passed under Article 368.

The **Agreement amounts to a cession of a part of the territory of India** in favour of Pakistan. So, its implementation would involve the alteration of the content of Article 1 and the relevant part of the **First Schedule** to the Constitution, because such implementation would necessarily lead to the diminution of the territory of the Union of India. **Such an amendment can be made under Article 368**.

Thus, the Supreme Court **answered the three questions** referred to it:

1. A legislative action necessary for the implementation of the Agreement relating to the Berubari Union.
2. A law of Parliament under Article 3 of the Constitution would be incompetent and a law relatable to Article 368 of the Constitution is competent and necessary.

3. For exchange of the enclaves too, the same procedure is to be followed.

IMPORTANCE

The Supreme Court opinion in *Berubari Union* case concluded that:

- The Preamble is not a part of the Constitution.
- The Parliament has the power to amend the Constitution, including Article 1.
- A cession of a part of the territory of India would lead to the diminution of the territory of the Union of India. Such an amendment can be made only under Article 368.

IMPACT

The Parliament of India enacted the Constitution (Ninth Amendment) Act, 1960, to give effect to the Nehru-Noor agreement of 1958.

The Berubari Union was divided and enclaves were exchanged on the basis of enclaves for enclaves without any consideration of territorial loss or gain.

5

Kedarnath Singh v. State of Bihar (1962)

Freedom of speech and expression is a fundamental right under Article 19 of the Indian Constitution.

However, does this right include the right to criticise the government of India?

If somebody criticises the government of India, can he/she be booked under the law of sedition in India–Section 124A of the Indian Penal Code (IPC)?

Are Section 124A and Section 505 of IPC constitutionally valid as per Article 19(1)(a)?

Kedarnath Singh v. State of Bihar deliberated upon the constitutional validity of Section 124A of IPC.

The Supreme Court held that any form of expression by an individual would be deemed seditious only when such expression tends to cause public disorder or disturb public peace.

The Court held Section 124A and Section 505 of IPC to be constitutionally valid but within the bounds of this interpretation.

INTRODUCTION

Section 124A of the Indian Penal Code provides for the law of sedition in India.

The law states that *whoever, by words, either spoken or written, or by signs, or by visible representation, or otherwise, brings or attempts to bring into hatred or contempt, or excites or attempts to excite disaffection towards the Government established by law shall be punished with imprisonment for life, to which fine may be added.*

The law defines 'disaffection' as a feeling of enmity or disloyalty towards the government.

Section 124A also states that any 'disapprobation' against any government measure or administrative action is not an offence under Section 124A.

BACKGROUND

Kedarnath Singh was convicted for sedition (Section 124A, IPC) and inciting public mischief (Section 505, IPC) because of his speech, wherein he criticised members of the ruling party, then Congress. He appealed his conviction before the Supreme Court and challenged the constitutional validity of Section 124A as unreasonably violating Article 19(1)(a) of the Constitution of India.

LEGAL ISSUES INVOLVED

1. Whether Sections 124A and 505 of IPC are constitutionally invalid as per Article 19(1)(a)?
2. Does Section 124A enact a law which is in the interest of public order and impose reasonable restrictions in the interest of public order?

WHY 'FREEDOM OF SPEECH AND EXPRESSION' IS CONSIDERED AS A HIGHLY IMPORTANT FUNDAMENTAL RIGHT IN A DEMOCRATIC COUNTRY?

Right to freedom of speech and expression is considered as a very important fundamental right because it allows citizens to freely express their ideas and participate in political discourse. This political discourse plays an important role in elections as it allows them to choose their representatives wisely. Thus, freedom of speech and expression is an important pillar of democracy.

ARGUMENTS

Appellants argued that in a democratic setup, citizens should be entitled to criticise the government. In this regard, Section 124A of IPC affects this right of citizens. Section 124A is *ultra vires* of the Constitution because it affects both kinds of speech, one which may disturb public order and the other which does not. Section 124A of IPC should be interpreted in light of the law of sedition in England and hence only the speech which tends to disturb public order should be held liable under Section 124A.

However, respondents were of the view that Section 124A is valid as the tendency of a speech to disturb public order is inherent in its interpretation and the mere fact that some speech which does not disturb public order may be held liable under it, cannot make the entire provision of law invalid. Also, if the disturbance of public order was a necessary condition under Section 124A, the explanations added to it would become redundant.

CONSTITUTIONALITY OF A LAW

Whenever the Court deliberates upon constitutionality of any law, it always presumes the law to be constitutional and declares it unconstitutional only when the law in its entirety is in violation of the Constitution. The Court may also save the law/legal provision by declaring a part as unconstitutional or changing the interpretation of law to bring it within the bounds of the Constitution.

THE JUDGMENT

The Hon'ble Court in this case quashed the sedition charges against Kedarnath Singh and stated that the remarks made by him were criticism of the government and cannot be termed seditious. Regarding the constitutional validity of Section 124A and Section 505 of IPC, the following observations were made:

1. 'Government established by law' as stated under Section 124A is not synonymous with criticism of a specific party or person.
2. Any form of expression by an individual would be deemed seditious only when such expression tends to cause public disorder or disturb public peace.
3. Section 124A and its interpretation were limited to include only such form of expression that incites or tends to incite public disorder.
4. The Court held Section 124A to be constitutionally valid but within the bounds of this interpretation.
5. Section 505 of IPC was also held constitutionally valid by the Court based upon the same reasoning.

IMPORTANCE AND IMPACT

The Law of sedition in a democratic country needs to be drafted very carefully as it can have an overarching effect on the free speech of citizens.

The Law of sedition is one of the most controversial provisions in Indian legislation. Many great freedom fighters were subjected to this law in British India. There was a strong demand to remove the law completely from independent India. However, it still exists in the statutes. The irony lies in the fact that the colonial masters, Britain, have removed the law of sedition from their books.

Kedarnath Singh judgment is a landmark case which prevented the misuse of the provision of sedition in IPC to a great extent. However, the Supreme Court, in this case, did not consider Section 124A unconstitutional. Many claims challenging its validity are pending currently in the Supreme Court and therefore it is very important to look forward to any developments made under it.

SECTION 124A OF IPC

On May 11, 2022, the Supreme Court of India observed that Section 124A of IPC was meant to maintain colonial control and that it should not be employed until further orders were issued. The Supreme Court's order has kept sedition under abeyance until it rules on the constitutionality of the law.

6

I. C. Golaknath v. State of Punjab (1967)

Can the Parliament of India amend the Fundamental Rights of Indian Citizens?

Is a constitutional amendment under Article 368 of the Constitution an ordinary 'law'?

I. C. Golaknath case held that the Parliament cannot amend the Fundamental Rights.

The judgment provided for the 'Prospective Overruling of the law'.

INTRODUCTION

I. C. Golaknath v. State of Punjab is an important judgment of the Supreme Court, which dealt with the amending power of the Parliament with respect to the Fundamental Rights conferred under Part III of the Constitution.

I. C. Golaknath was the petitioner and the State of Punjab was the respondent.

BACKGROUND

In 1953, the then Punjab State Government enacted Punjab Security of Land Tenures Act, 1953. This Act was placed under the **ninth schedule** of the Constitution of India by the **17th Constitutional Amendment Act, 1964.**

The Golaknath family in Punjab had over 500 acres of land. Exercising its authority under the Punjab Security of Land Tenures Act, 1953, the state government informed Golaknath that he can possess only 30 acres of land and rest will be treated as surplus.

At that time, the 'right to hold and acquire property' was a fundamental right under Article 19(1)(f).[1]

Golaknath filled a writ petition under Article 32 of the Constitution and challenged the validity of the Punjab Security of Land Tenures Act. He contended that the said Act violated his fundamental right to hold and acquire the property.

LEGAL ISSUES INVOLVED

The case involved two important legal issues:

- Whether the Parliament by law can amend the Fundamental Rights or not?
- Whether such an amendment is a law under Article 13(2) of the Constitution?

ARGUMENTS

The main contention of the petitioner was that the **fundamental rights** provided under Part III of the Constitution of India **are the essential and integral part of the Constitution**. They **cannot be taken away** by an act of Parliament. The Constitution without the fundamental rights is like a body without a soul.

He contended that the Constitution drafted by the constituent assembly is of permanent nature. Any Act which changes or tries to bring about a change is constitutional. The amendment cannot bring in new ideas into the Constitution. Any changes, if made, should be in accordance with the **'basic idea'** of the Constitution.

He further contended that Article 368 merely prescribes the procedure for amending the constitution. It does not confer any power or authority on the Parliament to amend the Constitution.

Golaknath argued that any 'law' under Article 13(3)(a) includes both statutory and constitutional. Therefore, **any law which violates the fundamental right conferred under Part III is unconstitutional**.

The State of Punjab responded by saying that the **power to amend the Constitution is an exercise of sovereign power**. It is different from the legislative power of the Parliament.

1. The 44th amendment eliminated the right to acquire, hold and dispose of property as a fundamental right and made it a legal right under Article 300A.

The argument of the State of Punjab was based on the reason that the **changing needs of society require changes in the Constitution**; otherwise, the Constitution would become too rigid.

The state further argued that all provisions of the Constitution are of equal status and equal importance. There is **no special status to the fundamental rights** under Part III.

NINTH SCHEDULE OF THE CONSTITUTION

The Ninth Schedule was added to the Indian Constitution by the Constitution (First Amendment) Act, 1951. This schedule provides for a list of central and state legislations which cannot be challenged in a court of law even if they violate fundamental rights.

The major objective behind the Ninth Schedule was to abolish the Zamindari system in India and ensure that land was re-distributed in the country. Most of the laws in the Ninth Schedule relate to land reforms.

But after the judgment of the Supreme Court in *I. R. Coelho v. State of Tamil Nadu* (2007) case, any law added into the Ninth Schedule after April 24, 1973 (Keshavananda Bharati judgment) can be challenged in Courts.

THE JUDGMENT

Prior to ***Golaknath case,*** the Supreme Court in ***Shankari Prasad v. Union of India (1951)*** and ***Sajjan Singh v. State of Rajasthan (1965)*** held that 'no part of our Constitution was unamendable'. The Parliament by passing a Constitution Amendment Act under Article 368 can amend any provision of the Constitution, including Fundamental Rights and Article 368 itself.

It was held that the 'law' under Article 13 referred to ordinary legislation made by the Parliament as a legislative body and would not include an amendment of the Constitution which was passed by the Parliament in its constituent capacity.

In ***Golaknath case,*** the Supreme Court overruled this position and held that the **Fundamental Rights** provided under Part III of the Constitution **cannot be subjected to the process of amendment** provided in Article 368. If any of such rights provided under Part III is to be amended,

a new Constituent Assembly must be convened for making a new constitution or radically changing it.[2]

The ruling of the Supreme Court was based on the view that the power to amend the Constitution was also a legislative power conferred by Article 245 by the constitution so that a Constitution Amendment Act was also a 'law' within the purview of Article 13(2).

IMPORTANCE

Since 1950, the Parliament by invoking the power under Article 368 passed numerous legislations which violated the Fundamental Rights. Therefore, to check the **'colourable exercise'** of power and save the Constitution from autocratic actions of the Parliament, the Supreme Court held that the Parliament cannot amend Fundamental Rights.

The Supreme Court held that the Fundamental Rights are the *'primordial rights necessary for the development of human personality'*.

The judgment provided for the **'Prospective Overruling of the law'**. It implies that the effects of the law to be laid down will be applicable on future dates only, that is past decisions will not be affected by this decision.

IMPACT

The Parliament tried to supersede the ***Golaknath case*** ruling by amending Article 368 itself. The Parliament passed the Constitution (24th Amendment) Act, 1971.

As per the **24th amendment**, an **amendment of the Constitution** passed under Article 368 **will not be considered as 'law' under the meaning of Article 13**. It further stated that the validity of an amendment to the Constitution shall not be challenged on the ground that it takes away or affects the Fundamental Rights.

2. Introduction to the Constitution of India, DD Basu, *Introduction the Constitution of India,* 24th Edition, Lexis Nexis.

7

Keshavananda Bharati Sripadagalvaru v. State of Kerala (1973)

Whether the Indian Parliament has the power to amend the fundamental rights.

While the Parliament has 'wide' powers, does it have the power to destroy or emasculate the basic elements or fundamental features of the Constitution?

What is the limit of judicial review?

Keshavananda Bharati case deduced the 'Doctrine of Basic Structure'.

It was held that the laws enacted to give effect to the Directive Principle of State Policy under Part IV are open to judicial review.

The laws included in the ninth schedule can be challenged in the court of law on the grounds that they abrogate the basic elements of the Constitutional structure.

The judgment was quoted again and again by the Supreme Court in various judgments like in the ***three judges' case***.

INTRODUCTION

Kesavananda Bharati Sripadagalvaru v. State of Kerala is a landmark verdict given by the 13-judge bench of the Supreme Court. The verdict set the principle that the **Supreme Court is the guardian of the 'basic structure'** of the Constitution.

Kesavananda Bharati Sripadagalvaru was the petitioner and the State of Kerala was the respondent.

BACKGROUND

The Kerala Land Reforms Act, 1963 (amended again in 1969), was enacted to fullfil the socio-economic obligation of the state government of Kerala.

Under this Act, the state government acquired land belonging to the Edneer Mutt in the Kasaragod district of Kerala.

Challenging this land acquisition, his holiness Kesavananda Bharati - the head of Edneer Mutt - filed a writ petition under Article 32 for the enforcement of rights under Article 25 (Right to practice and propagate religion), Article 26 (Right to manage religious affairs), Article 14 (Right to Equality), Article 19(1)(f) (Freedom to acquire property) and Article 31 (Compulsory Acquisition of Property).

Meanwhile, the ***Golaknath case*** judgment put severe restrictions on the power of the Parliament to amend the Constitution.

In the years that followed *Golaknath case,* the Supreme Court struck down the Bank Nationalization Act, 1969, in *R. C. Cooper v. Union of India.* In *Madhav Rao Scindia v. Union of India,* the Supreme Court again struck down the Presidential order that aimed at the abolition of Privy Purses.

Following these setbacks, the Government of India passed **24th and 25th Constitutional Amendment Acts** to nullify the effects to these judgments.

The **Constitution (29th Amendment) Act**, 1972, placed the Kerala Land Reforms Act, 1963, in the ninth schedule of the Constitution.

So, the petitioners in the case challenged the constitutional validity of the 24th, 25th and 29th Amendment Acts.

ARGUMENTS

The petitioners in the argument contended that the power of the Parliament to amend the Constitution is limited and restrictive. They said, '*the Constitution gave the Indian citizen freedoms which were to subsist forever and the Constitution was drafted to free the nation from any future tyranny of the representatives of the people.*' According to the petitioners, this freedom has been taken away by the Article 31C which has been inserted by the 25th Amendment.

Their argument for restricted power to the Parliament was also based on the 'Basic Features principle' propounded by Justice Mudholkar in his dissenting judgment in ***Sajjan Singh case (1964)***.

They pleaded for the protection of their **'fundamental right to property'**[1] under Article 19(1)(f) that was violated by the enactment of the 24th and 25th Constitutional Amendments.

1. The 44th amendment eliminated the right to acquire, hold and dispose of property as a fundamental right and made it a legal right under Article 300A.

On the other hand, the State of Kerala argued that the power of the Parliament to amend the Constitution is absolute and unlimited. In order to fulfil the socio-economic obligations guaranteed to the citizens in Preamble, there should be no restriction on the power of the Parliament to amend the Constitution.

The structure of the Constitution has been erected on the concept of an egalitarian society. If the power to amend is restricted and arguments of the petitioners are accepted, then the laws made by the state to fulfil its socio-economic obligations will come into direct conflict with the Fundamental Rights given under Part III. Article 31C essentially lifts the ban placed on the State Legislatures and Parliament under Articles 14, 19 and 31.

The respondents went on to claim that '*Parliament can abrogate fundamental rights such as freedom of speech and expression, freedom to form associations or unions, and freedom of religion. The democracy can even be replaced and one-party rule established.*'[2]

ARTICLE 13

Article 13 incorporates the power of judicial review of the Courts. It states that any law, regulation, order, etc. inconsistent with Part III will be declared unconstitutional.

It protects the fundamental rights provided in the Constitution and acts as a check on the powers of the legislature and executive.

It is interesting to note that, initially Article 13 was one of the major causes of the rift between the legislature and judiciary but finally after the judgment, in this case, the law is more or less settled now.

THE JUDGMENT

The Supreme Court by a 7:6 majority held that the Parliament in the exercise of constituent power **can amend any provision of the Constitution**. The Court gave the following reasons:

- First, the power to amend the Constitution is located in Article 368.
- Second, **neither the Constitution nor an amendment of the Constitution can be or is law within the meaning of Article 13**. Law in Article 13 means laws enacted by the legislature subject to the provision of the Constitution. Law in Article 13(2) does not mean the Constitution. The **Constitution is the supreme law**.

2. Para 11, *Kesavananda Bharati v. State of Kerala* (1973)

- Third, an amendment of the Constitution is an exercise of the constituent power. The majority view in ***Golaknath case*** is, with respect, wrong.
- Fourth, there are **no express limitations to the power of amendment**.
- Fifth, there are **no implied and inherent limitations on the power of amendment**. Neither the Preamble nor Article 13(2) is at all a limitation on the power of amendment.
- Sixth, **the power to amend is wide and unlimited**. The power to amend means the **power to add, alter or repeal any provision** of the Constitution.

The Supreme Court also observed that '*The Indian Constitution is first and foremost a social document. The majority of its provisions are either directly aimed at furthering the goals of social revolution by establishing the conditions necessary for its achievement yet despite the permeation of the entire Constitution by the aim of national renaissance, the core of the commitment to the social revolution lies in Parts III and IV, in the Fundamental Rights and the Directive Principles of State Policy. These are the conscience of the Constitution. Therefore to implement the duties imposed on the States under Part IV, it may be necessary to abridge in certain respects the rights conferred on the citizens or individuals under Part III...*'

So, the Court held the 24th Amendment to the Constitution as valid.

On the question **to which extent the Constitution can be amended,** the Court deduced the **'Doctrine of Basic Structure'**. It implies that though Parliament has the power to amend any provision of the Constitution, it cannot in any manner interfere with the features so fundamental to the Constitution without which the Constitution would be spiritless.

With regard to the 25th Amendment, the Court held the first part of the amendment valid. However, the Court declared the part which read '*and no law containing a declaration that it is for giving effect to such policy shall be called in question in any court on the ground that it does not give effect to such policy*' as unconstitutional.

In other words, **the laws enacted to give effect to the Directive Principle of State Policy under Part IV are open to judicial review**.

The court also held the 29th Amendment valid. However, it said that '*the question whether the Acts included in the Ninth Schedule by that amendment or any provision of those Acts abrogates any of the basic elements of the Constitutional structure or denudes them of their identity will have to be examined when the validity of those Acts comes up for consideration.*'

In other words, **the laws included in the ninth schedule can be challenged in the court of law on the grounds that they abrogate the basic elements of the Constitutional structure**.

IMPORTANCE

Kesavananda Bharati case overruled ***Golaknath case*** with regard to the power to amend the Constitution.

All the amendments to the Constitution were subjected to the test of **'Basic Structure' doctrine**. It reflected the judicial creativity of a very high order.

The Supreme Court gave an **illustrative list of basic elements** of the Constitution. The list included:

1. The supremacy of the Constitution.
2. The sovereignty of India.
3. Republican and Democratic forms of Government.
4. The secular character of the Constitution.
5. A free and independent judiciary.
6. Separation of powers between the Legislature, the executive and the judiciary.
7. Federal character of the Constitution.
8. The dignity of the individual secured by the various freedoms and basic rights in Part III and the mandate to build a welfare State contained in Part IV.
9. The unity and integrity of the nation.

Note: At least 20 features have been described as "basic" or "essential" by the Courts in numerous cases. Those have been incorporated in the basic structure in subsequent years. Any claim of any particular feature of the Constitution to be a "basic" feature would be determined by the Court on a case by case basis. Only the Judiciary can decide what is to be considered as the basic feature of the Constitution. The above list is for illustrative purpose only and should not be catalogued.

IMPACT

There were political controversies surrounding the judgment. As a reaction to the judgment, the Government elevated Justice A. N. Ray to the office of Chief Justice despite there being three other judges who were senior to him on the bench at the time.

In 1975, the then Chief Justice A. N. Ray set up a bench of 13 Judges to review the ***Kesavananda Bharati case***. But the bench was unilaterally dissolved after two days of argument, on the ground that '*no review petition had been filed and the review had been initiated over an oral request, making the review process improper.*'

The government headed by Indira Gandhi sought to undo the implications of ***Kesavananda Bharati case.*** The government enacted the **42nd Amendment Act, 1976**, giving 'unlimited power to the Parliament to amend the Constitution.' It also provided that 'validity of no constitutional amendment shall be called in question in any court on any ground'.

8

ADM, Jabalpur v. Shivkant Shukla (1976)

Is Article 32 – the right to approach the court to defend the fundamental rights – suspended under National Emergency?

ADM Jabalpur case dealt with the power of the High Court to issue a writ of *habeas corpus*.

Legal experts consider the *ADM Jabalpur judgment* as an unpopular judgment, but it still continues as a good law. There has been considerable judicial introspection and admission by former judges that the *ADM Jabalpur case* was wrongly decided.

The Supreme Court in ***Remdeo Chauhan case (2010)*** officially admitted its mistake in the *ADM Jabalpur* judgment.

INTRODUCTION

Additional District Magistrate (ADM), Jabalpur v. Shivakant Shukla case is popularly known as **Habeas Corpus case**. It was decided by the Supreme Court on 28 April 1976.

Additional District Magistrate, Jabalpur, was the petitioner and Shivkant Shukla was the respondent in the case.

BACKGROUND

In the general election of 1971, Smt. Indira Gandhi contested and won from the Rae Bareilly constituency. The election of Indira Gandhi was challenged by Raj Narain, a defeated candidate who contested against Mrs. Gandhi, in the Allahabad High Court.

On 12 June 1975, Justice Jagmohan Lal Sinha delivered the verdict in ***State of Uttar Pradesh v. Raj Narain***. The Allahabad High Court convicted Indira Gandhi of having indulged in electoral wrong practices and declared her election void. She was barred from contesting any election or holding office for the period of the next six years.

On her appeal to the Supreme Court, it granted her only a conditional stay. Her powers in the matter of vote and speech in the Lok Sabha was restrained.

In desperation to hold on to the power, Smt. Indira Gandhi requested the then President Fakruddin Ali Ahmad to declare an emergency under the **Article 352** Clause (1) of the Indian Constitution. The ground for imposing the emergency was that '*a grave emergency existed whereby the security of India was threatened by internal disturbances.*' The government also cited the 1971 war with Pakistan and the drought of 1972 as the reasons for imposing emergency.

Thus, an emergency was imposed on 26 June 1975. In exercise of powers conferred by Clause (1) of Article 359, the President declared that '*the right of any person including a foreigner to move any Court for the enforcement of the rights conferred by **Article 14**, **Article 21** and **Article 22** of the Constitution and all proceedings pending in any Court for the enforcement of the above mentioned rights shall remain suspended for the period during which the Proclamations of Emergency made under Clause (1) of Article 352 of the Constitution on 3 December 1971 and on 25 June 1975 are both in force*'.[1]

On 8 January 1976, the President declares that '*the right of any person to move to any Court for the enforcement of the rights conferred by **Article 19** of the Constitution and all proceedings pending in any Court for the enforcement the above-mentioned rights shall remain suspended for the period during which the Proclamation of Emergency is in force*'.[2]

During the emergency, the government started arresting people who could raise his/her political opinion freely and who were considered as 'political threat' under the **Maintenance of Internal Security Act** (MISA).

The arrested people filed a petition in various High Courts for the issue of a writ of ***habeas corpus*** and challenged their detention. Most of the High Courts ruled in favour of the arrested people. High courts broadly took the view that despite the Presidential order, it is open to the detenus to challenge their detention on the grounds that it is *ultra vires*.

Additional District Magistrate (ADM) of Jabalpur Kiran Vijay Singh appealed against the **Madhya Pradesh High Court's verdict** that was in favour of the detenu, Shivakant Shukla.

It was the lead case. Hence, it is known as ADM, *Jabalpur v. Shivkant Shukla.*

---

1. https://indiankanoon.org/doc/1735815/
2. https://indiankanoon.org/doc/1735815/

THE LEGAL ISSUE INVOLVED

- Despite the Presidential proclamation, can the High Court entertain a writ of ***habeas corpus*** filed by a person challenging his detention?

ARGUMENTS

The government contended that the object and purpose of emergency provisions are that the Constitution provides special powers to the executive because at times of emergency the considerations of the State assume importance.

National emergency demands grant of special power to the Executive. The emergency provisions contained in Part XVIII, including Articles 358, 359(1) and 359(1A), are constitutional imperatives.

It further said that the validity of any law cannot be challenged on the grounds of infringing a fundamental right mentioned in the Presidential Order under Article 359(1).

If the executive takes any action depriving a person of a fundamental right mentioned in the Presidential Order, such executive action cannot be challenged.

The reason given by the State for the aforementioned arguments is that 'in times of emergency the executive safeguards the life of the nation.'

On the other hand, respondents contended that the object of Article 359(1) is to prevent moving to the Supreme Court under Article 32 for the enforcement of certain rights. It does not affect the enforcement of common law and statutory rights to personal liberty under **Article 226** before the High Court.

Article 359(1) removes the restriction put on the Executive under Part III, but does not remove the restrictions arising from the principles of '**limited power of the executive**' under the system of checks and balances based on '**separation of powers**'.

The Presidential Order operates only in respect of fundamental rights mentioned in the Presidential Order. The Order would not affect the rights of personal liberty under the common law or under statute law or under natural law.

Respondents also contended that the purpose of Article 359(1) is not to protect illegal orders of the Executive. Executive cannot show disregard to the command of Parliament relying on a Presidential order under Article 359(1).

They argued that there is no reason to equate the State with the Executive. The suspension of the fundamental right only enables the Legislature to make laws violative of the suspended fundamental rights and the Executive to implement such laws. The suspension of the fundamental right does not enable the Executive to flout legislative mandates and judicial decisions.

The right to arrest is conferred by the Maintenance of Internal Security Act on the State and their officers only if the conditions laid down under Section 3 of the Act is fulfilled. If the conditions are not fulfilled, then the order of detention would be *ultra vires* of the Act.

EMERGENCY

The Constitution under Part XVIII provides for three types of emergency:

1. Article 352 (National Emergency) - It can be proclaimed in an exigency caused due to war, external aggression or armed rebellion.
2. Article 356 (President's rule) - This type of emergency is declared in a State or part of the country when there is a failure of constitutional machinery.
3. Article 360 (Financial Emergency) - It can be imposed when there is a threat to the financial stability or credit of the country.

THE JUDGMENT

Considering the arguments by the petitioners and the respondents, the Supreme Court by majority held that '*In view of the Presidential order dated 27 June 1975* ***no person has any locus standi to move any writ petition under Article 226 before a High Court for habeas corpus or any other writ*** *or order or direction to challenge the legality of an, order of detention on the ground that the order is not under or in compliance with the Act or is illegal or is vitiated by malafides factual or legal or is based on extraneous consideration*'.[3]

3. https://indiankanoon.org/doc/1735815/

In other words, the Supreme Court dismissed the contentions of the respondents. It **accepted the appeal filed by the ADM Jabalpur** and the judgments of various High Courts (*which were in favour of detenus*) were set aside.

The Supreme Court also upheld the constitutional validity of Section 16A(9) of the Maintenance of Internal Security Act.

IMPORTANCE

Legal experts consider the ***ADM Jabalpur judgment*** as an unpopular judgment, but it is still continuing as a good law. There has been considerable judicial introspection and admission by former judges that the ADM Jabalpur was wrongly decided.[4]

The Supreme Court and the High Courts have continued to cite *ADM Jabalpur case* for different points of law.

The Supreme Court in ***Remdeo Chauhan v. Bani Kant Das (2010)*** officially admitted its mistake in the *ADM Jabalpur* judgment.

IMPACT

The *ADM Jabalpur* judgment **read Article 21 in a restrictive manner**. The judgment reversed the several courageous high court judgments and denied thousands of Emergency detenues the right of *habeas corpus*. The government singled out political opponents and activists for arrest and imprisonment.

4. https://thewire.in/law/supreme-court-emergency-era-judgment

9

Maneka Gandhi v. Union of India (1978)

What is the scope of Article 21 (right to life and personal liberty)?

Should not any procedure established by law under Article 21 be 'fair, just and reasonable' and not 'fanciful, oppressive or arbitrary'?

Maneka Gandhi case established the interrelationship between Article 14 and Article 19.

It expanded the scope of Article 21 of the Constitution.

INTRODUCTION

Maneka Gandhi v. Union of India is a landmark case decided by the Supreme Court of India, in which the Court departed from its earlier straitjacketed interpretation of Fundamental rights.

Maneka Gandhi was the petitioner and the Union of India was the respondent in the case.

BACKGROUND

Maneka Gandhi, the daughter-in-law of the former Prime Minister Indira Gandhi, started a political magazine *Surya*. She used it as a political platform to restore the image of the Congress Party, which was dented by the imposition of Emergency. The magazine also published some controversial images of the son of the then Defence Minister Jagjivan Ram.

She was issued a passport on 1 June 1976. On 4th July 1977, the time around which she wanted to travel out of India for a speech, she received a letter from the Regional Passport Officer, Delhi, informing her that under **Section 10(3)(c) of the Passport Act, 1967**, the Government of India has decided to impound her passport 'in public interest'. She was asked to surrender her passport within seven days from the receipt of the letter.

She wrote a letter to the Regional Passport Officer requesting him to furnish a copy of the statement of reasons for making the order as provided in **Section 10(5).** But in its reply, the Ministry of External Affairs, Government of India, stated that 'in the interest of the general public' it has decided not to furnish her copy of the statement of reasons for the making of the order.

Maneka Gandhi filed a Writ Petition challenging the action of the Government in impounding her passport and declining to give reasons for doing so.

LEGAL ISSUES INVOLVED

- Whether the right to go abroad is part of personal liberty?
- Whether the right under Article 19(1)(a) has any geographical limitation?
- Whether the Section 10(3)(c) of the Passport Act, 1967, is violative of Article 14, Article 19(1)(a) and Article 21?

SOME SECTIONS OF THE PASSPORT ACT RELEVANT TO THE CASE[1]

Sub-section (1) of Section 10 of the Passport Act, 1967, empowers the Passport Authority to cancel the endorsement on a passport or travel document or to vary or cancel it on the conditions subject to which a passport or travel document has been issued.
Sub-section (3) provides that the Passport Authority may impound or cause to be impounded or revoke a passport or travel document on the grounds set out in Clauses (a) to (h).

1. https://main.sci.gov.in/judgments

Clause (c) reads as follows: '*If the passport authority deems it necessary so to do in the interest of the sovereignty and integrity of India, the security of India, friendly relations of India with the foreign country, or in the interests of the general public*'.

Sub-section (5) requires the Passport Authority impounding or revoking a passport to record in writing a brief statement of the reasons for making such order and furnish to the holder of the passport or travel document on demand a copy of the same; in any case, the Passport Authority is of the opinion that it will not be in the interest of the sovereignty and integrity of India, the security of India, friendly relations of India with any foreign country or in the interest of the general public to furnish such a copy.

ARGUMENTS

The petitioner contended that:

1. The **right to go abroad is part of 'personal liberty'** within the meaning of that expression as used in Article 21 and no one can be deprived of this right except according to the procedure prescribed by law. There is no procedure prescribed by the Passport Act for impounding or revoking a passport.
2. The Act does not provide for giving an opportunity to the holder of the passport to be heard against the making of the order.
3. Section 10(3)(c) is violative of fundamental rights guaranteed under Articles 14, 19(1)(a) and (g) and 21.
4. The order impounding the passport is made in contravention of the rules of natural justice and is therefore null and void.
5. A passport may be impounded under Section 10(3)(c), public interest must actually exist in the present and the mere likelihood of public interest arising in future would be no ground for impounding the passport. It was not correct to say that the presence of the petitioner was likely to be required for giving evidence before the **Shah Commission**.

SHAH COMMISSION

Shah Commission was appointed by the Janata Government in 1977 to inquire into the excess committed during the Emergency.

On the other hand, the Union government submitted that the petitioner's passport was impounded because her presence was likely to be required in connection with the proceedings before a Commission of Inquiry.

Under Article 21 of the Constitution, a person can be deprived of his right to 'Protection of life and personal liberty' as per the procedure established by law. Such a procedure need not pass the test of reasonability.

The respondents also contended that the Constitution makers chose the **British concept of 'procedure established by law'** over the **American concept of 'due process of law'**. It is the reflection of the mind of the framers of the Constitution which should be protected and respected.

THE GOLDEN TRIANGLE

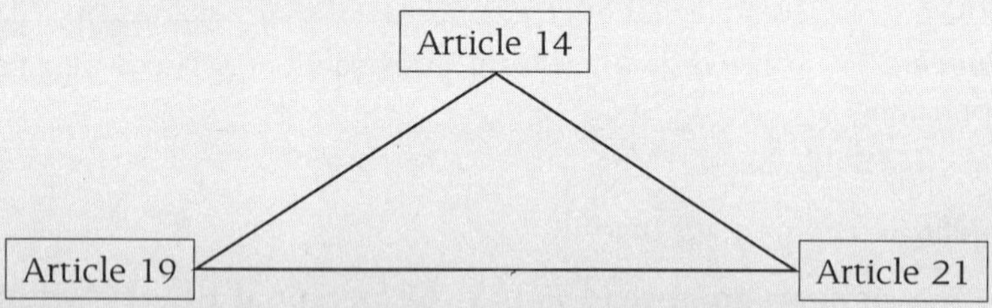

These three provisions-Article 14, Article 19 and Article 21-are interconnected and fundamental for all citizens. Any law to be just, fair and reasonable should not violate any of these three provisions.

THE JUDGMENT

The Supreme Court held that, though Article 21 mentions the 'procedure established by law', it has to be fair, just and reasonable, not oppressive or arbitrary. The mere prescription of some kind of procedure cannot even meet the mandate of Article 21.

The court gave Article 21 an expansive interpretation. The Court held that '*the expression "personal liberty" in Article 21 is of the widest amplitude and covers a variety of rights which go to constitute the personal liberty of man and some of them have been raised to the status of distinct fundamental, rights and given additional protection under Article 19(1).*'

Earlier in ***Satwant Singh Sawhney case,*** the Court held that the '*right of travel and to go outside the country is included in the right to personal liberty.*'

The court overruled the A. K. Gopalan judgment, which held that '*certain Articles in the Constitution exclusively deal with specific matters and where the requirements of an Article dealing with the particular matter in question are satisfied and there is no infringement of the fundamental right guaranteed by that Article, no recourse can be had to a fundamental right conferred by another Article.'*[2]

The Court held that there is a unique relationship between the provisions of Article 14, Article 19 and Article 21. Therefore, a law depriving a person of 'personal liberty' has not only to stand the test of Article 21, but it must also stand the test of Article 19 and Article 14 of the Constitution.

IMPORTANCE

By establishing the interrelations, the Court extended the protection of Article 14 to the personal liberty of every person and additional protection of Article 19 to the personal liberty of every citizen.

Maneka Gandhi case gave the term 'personal liberty' the widest possible interpretation.

IMPACT

Based on this ruling, the Supreme Court expanded the scope of Article 21, which now includes, among other rights, right to Clean Air, right to Food, right to Clean Environment and more.

The judgment made India a true welfare state, as enshrined in the Preamble to the Constitution.

2. https://indiankanoon.org/doc/1766147/

10

Bachan Singh v. State of Punjab (1980)

Is the death penalty for murder provided in Section 302 constitutionally valid?

When should Capital Punishment be awarded?

Bachan Singh case evolved the doctrine of 'rarest of rare case' for awarding the death penalty.

INTRODUCTION

Bachan Singh v. State of Punjab is a landmark judgment in which the Supreme Court evolved the doctrine of 'rarest of rare case' for awarding the death penalty.

Bachan Singh was the petitioner and the State of Punjab was the respondent.

BACKGROUND

Bachan Singh was tried and convicted and sentenced to death under Section 302 of the Indian Penal Code for the murders of Desa Singh, Durga Bai and Veeran Bai by the Sessions Judge.

When he appealed in the High Court against the conviction, the court upheld the judgment of the Sessions Court. It confirmed the death sentence and dismissed his appeal.

Bachan Singh then filed a special leave petition in the Supreme Court. Thus, the case came before the Supreme Court.

ARGUMENTS

The only question for consideration in the appeal was whether the facts found by the Sessions and High Courts would be 'special reasons' for awarding the death sentence as required under Section 354(3) of the Code of Criminal Procedure, 1973.

It was submitted that neither the fact that the appellant was previously convicted for murder and committed these murders after he had served the life sentence in the earlier case nor the fact that three murders were extremely heinous and inhuman constitutes a 'special reason' for imposing the death sentence.

In his appeal, Bachan Singh also submitted that the Courts below (i.e. Sessions Court and High Court) were not competent to impose the extreme penalty of death on the appellant.

The petitioner also contended that the provision of Section 302 of the IPC offends Article 19, Article 21 and the basic structure of the Constitution.

The Court provided guidelines that are to be followed when applying 'rarest of rare doctrine' in the case of *Macchi Singh v. the State of Punjab*. They are:

a. Modus Operandi: Committed crime is extremely brutal and can shock the collective consciousness of society.
b. Motive: deliberate plan to torture the victim, hiring assassins, compromising the security of State, etc. are some of the conditions wherein 'rarest of the rare doctrine' can be made applicable.
c. The severity of the Crime .
d. Profile of Victim: Killing an innocent or a vulnerable person will fall under the purview of rarest of rare circumstances.
e. The tilt of balance between aggravating and mitigating factors will also be considered while applying the doctrine.

LEGAL ISSUES INVOLVED

- Whether the death penalty for murder provided in Section 302 of the IPC constitutionally valid?
- Whether the sentencing procedure embodied in Sub-section (3) of Section 354 of the CrPC, 1973, constitutionally valid?

- Whether the provision of Section 302 of the IPC offends Article 19, Article 21, the basic structure of the Constitution and Article 6(1) of the International Covenant on Civil and Political Rights adopted by the UN General Assembly?
- Powers of the Supreme Court to lay down norms restricting the area of the imposition of the death penalty to a narrow category of murders.

THE JUDGMENT

The Supreme Court held that the **right to life is not one of the rights mentioned in Article 19(1)** of the Constitution and the six fundamental freedoms guaranteed under Article 19(1) are not absolute rights.

The court made a **distinction between 'law and order' and 'public order'**. It said violent crimes similar in nature but committed in different contexts and circumstances might cause different reactions. The real distinction between the areas of 'law and order' and 'public order' lies not merely in the nature or quality of the act but in the degree and extent.

If a law prohibits and penalises any activity that is within the purview of and protection of Article 19(1), then only the protection under Article 19 can be sought and the Article 19 is applied.

The mere fact that certain Sections of the IPC and CrPC incidentally, remotely or collaterally have the effect of abridging rights under Article 19 will not satisfy the test.

It cannot be contended that any of the rights mentioned in Article 19(1) of the Constitution confers the freedom to commit murder or for the matter of that the freedom to commit any offence whatsoever.

Therefore, **penal laws**, which define offences and prescribe punishment for the commission of offences, **do not attract the application of Article 19(1)**.

Placing its reason on the ***Maneka Gandhi judgment***, the court read **Article 21** in a positive form as '*A person may be deprived of his life or personal liberty in accordance with fair, just and reasonable procedure established by valid law*'.[1]

By implication, the Founding Fathers recognized the right of the state to deprive a person of his life or personal liberty in accordance with fair,

1. https://indiankanoon.org/doc/1766147/

just and reasonable procedure established by valid law. Thus, it cannot be said that the death sentence for murder or the mode prescribed for its execution is a degrading punishment which would defile 'the dignity of the individual'.

The procedure provided in the Criminal Procedure Code for imposing capital punishment for murder and some other capital crimes is not unfair, unreasonable or unjust.

Thus, **it cannot be said that the death penalty for the offence of murder violates the basic structure of the Constitution**.

The Court also observed that statistical attempts to assess the true **penological value** of capital punishment remain inconclusive. On the one hand, the statistics of capital punishment deterring the potential murderers are hard to obtain, and on the other, those who support the abolition of capital punishment have adopted an oversimplified approach.

International Covenant on Civil and Political Rights does not abolish or prohibit the imposition of the death penalty in all circumstances. All that they require is that, first, the death penalty shall not be arbitrarily inflicted, and second that it shall be imposed only for most serious crimes in accordance with the law.

The Court held that India's penal laws are entirely in accord with its international commitment.

The Court held that **capital punishment can be given in the 'rarest of rare cases'** where the alternative option is unquestionably foreclosed. It laid down the broad criteria to guide the Courts in the matter of sentencing a person convicted of murder under Section 302 of the Penal Code. They are:

1. The extreme penalty can be inflicted only in gravest cases of extreme culpability.
2. In making the choice of sentence, due regard must be paid to the circumstances of the offender also.

IMPORTANCE

- ***Bachan Singh case*** evolved **the doctrine of 'rarest of rare case'** for awarding the death penalty.
- The Supreme Court laid down **broad guidelines** for awarding the death penalty.

IMPACT

Though the Supreme Court was of the view that **minimal use of capital punishment** to penalise the criminals, this view is **contradicted by the legislation** by increasing the number of crimes for which capital punishment is awarded.

In 2018, the Supreme Court judge Justice Kurian Joseph, in ***Chhannu Lal Verma v. the State of Chattisgarh*** observed that the time had come to **review the need for the death penalty** as a punishment, especially its purpose and practice. However, the other judges on the bench observed: '*since the constitution bench in Bachan Singh v. State of Punjab had upheld capital punishment, there was no need to re-examine it at this stage.*'[2]

2. https://thewire.in/law/justice-kurian-joseph-retirement-death-penalty

Minerva Mills Ltd. v. Union of India (1980)

Is the power of the Parliament to amend the Constitution limited by the Constitution?

Should there be a balance between Fundamental Rights and Directive Principles of State Policy?

Minerva Mills case held that the harmony and balance between fundamental rights and directive principles is an essential feature of the basic structure of the Constitution.

It restored the power of the court to review any amendment to the Constitution.

INTRODUCTION

Minerva Mills Ltd. v. Union of India is a landmark decision of the Supreme Court which dealt with the 'Basic structure doctrine' that was deduced in ***Kesavananda Bharati case***.

Minerva Mills Ltd. and Others were the petitioners in the case and Union of India was the respondent.

BACKGROUND

Minerva Mills Ltd. was a textiles production company. In 1970, the Central Government appointed a committee under Section 15 of the Industries (Development Regulation) Act, 1951, to investigate the affairs of the Minerva Mills. The government was of the opinion that there had been a substantial fall in the volume of production of the mill.

The committee submitted its report to the Central Government in January 1971. On the basis of this report, the government passed an order under Section 18A of the Industries (Development Regulation) Act, 1951, authorising the National Textile Corporation Ltd. to take over the management of the Minerva Mills. The order was based on the grounds that the affairs of the Mill are being managed in a manner highly detrimental to the public interest.

Minerva Mill was nationalised and taken over by the Central Government under the provisions of the Sick Textile Undertakings (Nationalization) Act, 1974.

Minerva Mill and other petitioners challenged the following in the Supreme Court:

1. The constitutional validity of certain provisions of the Sick Textile Undertakings (Nationalization) Act, 1974
2. The government order that authorized the National Textile Corporation Ltd. to take over the management of the Minerva Mills
3. The constitutionality of the Constitution (Thirty-Ninth Amendment) Act which inserted the Nationalization Act as Entry 105 in the Ninth Schedule to the Constitution
4. The validity of Article 31B of the Constitution
5. Constitutionality of Sections 4 and 55 of the Constitution (Forty-Second Amendment) Act, 1976

SECTIONS 4 AND 55 OF THE CONSTITUTION (42nd AMENDMENT) ACT, 1976

Section 4: Section 4 made an Amendment of Article 31C. It states, '*Notwithstanding anything contained in Article 13, no law giving effect to the policy of the State towards securing* ***all or any of the principles laid down in Part IV*** *shall be deemed to be void on the ground that it is inconsistent with, or takes away or abridges any of the rights conferred by Article 14 or Article 19...*'.

Section 55: Section 55 made an amendment to Article 368. It inserted Clause 4 and Clause 5 under Article 368.[1]

1. Clauses (4) and (5) have been declared invalid by the Supreme Court in *Minerva Mills v. Union of India* (1980)

Clause 4 reads, '*No amendment of this Constitution (including the provisions of Part III) made or purporting to have been made under this Article [whether before or after the commencement of Section 55 of the Constitution (Forty-second Amendment) Act, 1976] shall be called in question in any court on any ground.*'

Clause 5 reads, '*For the removal of doubts, it is hereby declared that there shall be no limitation whatever on the constituent power of Parliament to amend by way of addition, variation or repeal the provisions of this Constitution under this Article.*'

ARGUMENTS

Petitioners challenged the constitutionality of Sections 4 and 55 of the Constitution (42nd Amendment) Act, 1976, on the grounds that '*though by Article 368 of the Constitution Parliament is given the power to amend the Constitution, that power cannot be exercised so as to damage the basic features of the Constitution or so as to destroy its basic structure.*'

The petitioners also challenged the constitutionality of the Constitution (39th Amendment) Act, which inserted the Sick Textile Undertakings (Nationalization) Act, 1974, as Entry 105 is the 9th Schedule to the Constitution.

They also challenged the primacy given to the Directive Principles of State Policy contained in Part IV over the fundamental rights conferred by Part III of the Constitution.

They argued that Section 55 of the Constitution (42nd Amendment) Act deprived them of their right to seek legal remedies, as the concerned section bars the 'judicial review.'

On the other hand, the respondents argued that the issue formulated for consideration of the court that is, 'whether the provisions of the 42nd Amendment of the Constitution which deprived the Fundamental Rights of their Supremacy and made them subordinate to the Directive Principles of State Policy are *ultra vires* the amending power of Parliament?' is too wide and academic.

The union of India argued that securing the implementation of directive principles by the elimination of obstructive legal procedures cannot ever be said to destroy or damage the basic features of the Constitution. Further, laws made for securing the objectives of Part IV would necessarily be in the public interest.

The directive principles being themselves fundamental in the governance of the country, no amendment to achieve the goals specified in the directive principles can ever alter the basic structure of the Constitution.

It further argued that a law which fulfils the directive of **Article 38** is incapable of abrogating fundamental freedoms or of damaging the basic structure of the Constitution in as much as that structure itself is founded on the principles of justice, social, economic and political.

The deprivation of some of the fundamental rights for the purpose of bringing about a social order to achieve social, economic and political justice cannot possibly amount to a destruction of the basic structure of the Constitution.

42ND AMENDMENT ACT, 1976

This amendment made very significant changes to the Indian Constitution and is popularly known as a mini-constitution. Some important changes include:

a. Added words 'socialist', 'secular' and 'integrity' to the Preamble
b. Article 51A (Fundamental duties) was added to the Constitution
c. Part XIV-A was added, i.e., provisions in relation to administrative tribunals and tribunals for other matters
d. New directive principles were added to the Constitution

LEGAL ISSUES INVOLVED

1. Whether the Sections 4 and 55 of the 42nd Amendment Act are beyond the amending power of the Parliament under Article 368 of the Constitution and therefore void?
2. Whether the Directive Principles of State Policy contained in Part IV of the Constitution can have primacy over the fundamental rights conferred in Part III of the Constitution?

THE JUDGMENT

The Supreme Court held that the introduced **Clause (5) of Article 368** transgresses the limitations on the amending power of Parliament and hence **unconstitutional**. Since Clause (4) and Clause (5) of Article 368 are interrelated, the court declared **Clause (4), too, as unconstitutional**.

Clause (5) of Article 368 removed all limitations on the amending power of the Parliament and Clause (4) deprived the courts of their power to review any amendment to the Constitution.

Court opinioned that '*if courts are totally deprived of the power to review, the fundamental rights conferred upon the people will become a mere adornment because rights without remedies are as writ in water.*'[2] Clause (4) of Article 368 totally deprives the citizens of a right guaranteed by Article 32.

Directive Principles of State Policy are fundamental in the governance of the country and Fundamental rights occupy a unique place in the lives of civilised societies. Parts III and IV together constitute the core of the commitment to social revolution and they together are the conscience of the Constitution. The Indian Constitution is founded on the bedrock of the balance between Parts III and IV. **Giving absolute primacy to one over the other will disturb the harmony** of the Constitution. The Supreme Court held that the **harmony and balance between fundamental rights and directive principles is an essential feature of the basic structure of the Constitution**.

IMPORTANCE AND IMPACT

The 42nd Amendment Act made the challenge of Constitutional Amendments in the courts of law unjustifiable. Further, it gave unlimited power to the Parliament to amend the Constitution. This amendment even gave the power to the Parliament to rewrite the entire Constitution and turn this Democratic nation into a Totalitarian regime.

However, the apex court in ***Minerva Mill case*** held some of the provisions of the 42nd Amendment Act as unconstitutional, and thus saved the democracy from turning into a Totalitarian state.

The ***Minerva Mill case*** substantiated the 'basic structure' doctrine by holding that the balance between fundamental rights and directive principles as being a part of the basic structure of the Constitution.

2. https://indiankanoon.org/doc/1939993/

Mohd. Ahmad Khan v. Shah Bano Begum (1985)

Are not muslim women discriminated by denying the right to basic maintenance available to non-muslim women under secular law?

Whether Section 125 of the Code of Criminal Procedure applies to muslims also?

Should not India need a Uniform Civil Code?

The *Shah Bano judgment* upheld the right of divorced Muslim women to sufficient means to maintain themselves. It put an obligation on Muslim men to make provision for or to provide maintenance to the divorced wife.

The case also dwelt on the need to implement the **Uniform Civil Code.**

INTRODUCTION

Mohd. Ahmad Khan v. Shah Bano Begum, famously known as ***Shah Bano case,*** is one of the landmark judgment in Muslim women's fight for rights in India and against the set Muslim personal law.

Mohd. Ahmed Khan was the petitioner and Shah Bano Begum and others were the respondents in the case.

BACKGROUND

Mohd. Ahmad Khan, a renowned lawyer from Madhya Pradesh, was married to Shah Bano. The two were married in 1932 and had five children. In 1975, Ahmad Khan asked Shah Bano to move out of his residence where she was living with Khan and his second wife.

In April 1978, Shah Bano filed a petition in the court of the Judicial Magistrate, Indore, seeking maintenance from her divorced husband Mohd. Ahmad Khan under **Section 125** of the Code of Criminal Procedure, 1973.

SECTIONS 4 AND 55 OF THE CONSTITUTION (42nd AMENDMENT) ACT, 1976

Section 125 of the Code of Criminal Procedure, 1973, puts a legal obligation on a man to provide maintenance for his wife during the marriage and after divorce, too.

Shah Bano sought maintenance at the rate of ₹500 per month, in view of the professional income of Ahmad Khan which was about ₹60,000 per annum.

In August 1979, the Magistrate court directed Khan to pay a sum of ₹25 per month to Shah Bano. On appeal, the High Court of Madhya Pradesh enhanced the amount to ₹179.20 per month.

In November 1978, Ahmad Khan had granted Shah Bano irrevocable talaq. He said Shah Bano had ceased to be his wife by reason of the divorce and therefore, he was under no obligation to provide maintenance for her.

He also claimed he had already paid maintenance for her at the rate of ₹200 per month for about two years, and had deposited a sum of ₹3,000 in the court by way of dower or **'Mahr'** during the period of **'iddat'**.

SECTIONS 4 AND 55 OF THE CONSTITUTION (42nd AMENDMENT) ACT, 1976

Iddat is the waiting period a woman must observe after the death of her husband or divorce before she can marry another man.

Mohd. Ahmad Khan appealed against the judgment of the High Court of Madhya Pradesh in the Supreme Court by the way of **Special Leave Petition**.

ARGUMENTS

Mohd. Ahmad Khan maintained that after the irrevocable talaq, Shah Bano had ceased to be his wife and he is under no obligation to provide maintenance to her.

The **All India Muslim Personal Law Board** supported the petitioner and went on to assert that it is irrelevant to inquire as to how a Muslim divorced woman should maintain herself. The board maintained that interfering in these matters would violate **The Muslim Personal Law (Shariat) Application Act, 1937**.

LEGAL ISSUES INVOLVED

1. Whether on the pronouncements of 'talaq' and on the expiry of the period of 'iddat' a divorced wife ceases to be a wife?
2. Whether there is any conflict between the provisions of Section 125 of Code of Criminal Procedure and that of the Muslim Personal Law on the liability of the Muslim husband to provide for the maintenance of his divorced wife?
3. Whether the liability of the husband to maintain a divorced wife is limited to the period of 'iddat'?

UNIFORM CIVIL CODE

Article 44 of the Constitution states that the State shall endeavour to secure for the citizens a uniform civil code throughout the territory of India.

Since Article 44 falls under Part IV (DPSPs), it is not mandatory for the government to implement it. A uniform civil code would provide a generic set of regulations for all citizens of the country irrespective of their religion.

THE JUDGMENT

On the question of applicability of **Section 125 of the Code of Criminal Procedure** applies to Muslims, the court held that '*the* ***religion professed by a spouse or by the spouses has no place in the scheme of these provisions****. The reason for this was that Section 125 is a part of the Code of Criminal Procedure, not of the Civil Laws which define and govern the rights and obligations of the parties belonging to particular religions... Section 125 was enacted in order to provide a quick and summary remedy to a class of persons who are unable to maintain themselves.*'[1]

The court said neglect by a person of sufficient means to maintain these and the inability of these persons to maintain themselves are the objective criteria which determine the applicability of Section 125. Clause (b) of the Explanation to Section 125(1) defines **'wife' as including a divorced wife**. It **does not exclude Muslim women** from its scope.

The court also held that **Section 125 would prevail over the personal law** of the parties, in cases where they are in conflict.

1. https://indiankanoon.org/doc/823221/

Based on its interpretation of the Holy Quran, the court held that there is an obligation on the Muslim husband to make provision for or to provide maintenance to the divorced wife. The court held the liability cannot be limited to the period of *iddat*.

The Supreme Court upheld the decision of the High Court that gave orders for maintenance to Shah Bano under CrPC. For its part, the apex court **also increased the maintenance sum**.

In its judgment, the court also observed that '***a common Civil Code will help the cause of national integration*** *by removing disparate loyalties to laws which have conflicting ideologies*.'[2]

IMPORTANCE

- The ***Shah Bano case*** was a step ahead of the general practice of deciding cases on the basis of interpretation of personal law.
- The case also dwelt on the need to implement the **Uniform Civil Code**.
- The case took note of different personal laws and the need to recognise and address the issue of gender equality and perseverance in matters of religious principles.

The judgment, in general, was a step towards creating an equal society of men and women.

IMPACT

The then central government headed by Rajiv Gandhi passed the **Muslim Women (Protection on Divorce Act), 1986**. It was passed to overturn *Shah Bano case* judgment.

Highlights of the Act are:

- The maintenance can only be made liable for the iddat period.
- If a woman is not able to provide for herself, the magistrate had the power to direct the Wakf Board for providing the means of sustenance to the aggrieved woman as well as her dependent children.

The Act's Constitutional validity was challenged by Danial Latifi, lawyer of Shah Bano. However, the **Supreme Court upheld the validity of the Act** but said that the liability cannot be restricted to the period of iddat.

2. https://indiankanoon.org/doc/823221/

13

Dr. D. C. Wadhwa v. State of Bihar (1986)

Ordinances are not permanent. They lapse unless they are converted into Acts within a specified duration.

Article 123 of the Constitution authorises the President to promulgate Ordinances if a law is 'immediately necessary' and at any time, except when both Houses of Parliament are in session.

Then, is it unconstitutional to repromulgate Ordinances?

The *D. C. Wadhwa judgment* put a check on the process of repromulgation of Ordinances. By doing so, the court upheld the balance between executive and legislature.

INTRODUCTION

Article 123 of the Constitution authorises the President to promulgate Ordinances, if he is satisfied that circumstances exist which render it necessary for him to take immediate action when both Houses of Parliament are not in session.

Under **Article 213**, similar power was granted to the Governor of a state.

But how many times an Ordinance can be repromulgated? This issue was addressed by the Supreme Court in *Dr. D. C. Wadhwa v. State of Bihar* case.

Dr. D. C. Wadhwa and others were the petitioners and the State of Bihar was the respondent in the case.

BACKGROUND

The State of Bihar adopted a practice of repromulgating the Ordinances on a massive scale from time to time without any attempt to replace them with the acts of the legislature.

Between 1967 and 1981, the Governor of Bihar promulgated 256 Ordinances, and all these Ordinances were kept alive for periods ranging from 1-14 years by repromulgation from time to time.

After the session of the State Legislature was prorogued, the same Ordinances which had ceased to operate were repromulgated without any substantial changes in the provisions.

Dr. D. C. Wadhwa, a professor of economics in Gokhale Institute of Politics and Economics, Pune, challenged the validity of this practice. He was interested in the preservation and promotion of constitutional functioning of the administration in the country.

Dr. Wadhwa carried out a thorough and detailed research in the matter of repromulgation of Ordinances by the Governor of Bihar from time to time. He filed a Writ petition in the Supreme Court challenging in general the process of repeated repromulgation of Ordinances.

Other petitioners who were affected by some of the Ordinances challenged the following Ordinances in particular:

1. Bihar Forest Produce (Regulation of Trade), Third Ordinance, 1983
2. The Bihar Bricks Supply (Control), Third Ordinance, 1983
3. The Bihar Intermediate Education Council, Third Ordinance, 1983

These Ordinances also suffered the same process of repromulgation from time to time.

During the pendency of the Writ Petition, the first two Ordinances were enacted into acts of the legislature. A bill to replace the third Ordinance was pending in the state legislature.

ARGUMENTS

The petitioners challenged the repeated repromulgation of Ordinances by the Governor on the grounds that it **violates the constitutional functioning of the administration** in the country.

On the other hand, the respondent opposed the Writ petition on the following grounds:

1. Two of the three Ordinances already lapsed and a bill to replace the third Ordinance is introduced in the state legislature. So, the petitioners have no locus standi to maintain the writ petitions.
2. Petitioners are outsiders and have no legal interest to challenge the validity of the process of the promulgation of Ordinances.

3. The question raised before the Court is academic in nature and should not be adjudicated upon by the Court.
4. The Court is not entitled to examine whether the conditions precedent for the exercise of the power of the Governor under Article 213 existed or not for the purpose of determining the validity of an Ordinance.

WHAT IS AN ORDINANCE?

An Ordinance is a law which is promulgated by the President at the Centre when either Lok Sabha or Rajya Sabha or both the houses of Parliament are not in session.

Governor can also promulgate an Ordinance at the State level when the legislative assembly is not in session.

Originally, the provision for Ordinance making was provided as an emergency provision but over the years it has become like an Ordinary course of law-making.

LEGAL ISSUES INVOLVED

- The scope of Article 213, which authorizes the Governor to promulgate an Ordinance.
- Power of the Governor to repromulgate Ordinances from time to time without getting them replaced by Acts of Legislature.
- Whether a **colourable exercise of power** is violative of the constitutional scheme?

THE JUDGMENT

The primary law making authority under the Constitution is the Legislature and not the Executive. The power conferred on the Governor to issue Ordinances is in the nature of an emergency power which is vested in the Governor for taking immediate action at a time when the Legislature is not in session.

The Supreme Court held that the **Governor cannot assume legislative function by crossing the limits laid out in the Constitution**. Any excess would amount to usurpation of a function which does not belong to him.

Repeated repromulgation of Ordinances is clearly contrary to the constitutional scheme and it must be held to be **improper and invalid**.

The court also observed that the power to promulgate an Ordinance is essentially a power to be used to meet an extraordinary situation and it cannot be allowed to be 'perverted to serve political ends'. A constitutional authority cannot do indirectly what it is not permitted to do directly.

The court held that the **exercise of the power by the state,** whether it be the Legislature or the Executive or any other authority, **should be within the constitutional limitations**. If such limitations are violated, a member of the public can challenge such practice by filing a writ petition.

The court also observed that **it cannot examine the question of satisfaction of the Governor in issuing an Ordinance**.

The court struck down The Bihar Intermediate Education Council Ordinance 1983 (which is still in operation) as unconstitutional and void.

IMPORTANCE

The primary authority to enact legislation is the legislature. Repromulgation of Ordinances circumvents the legislature's primacy. The judgment put a check on the process of repromulgation of Ordinances. By doing so, the court upheld the balance between executive and legislature.

IMPACT

Wadhwa case came before the Supreme Court in 1986. Interestingly, before 1986, the Central government had never repromulgated Ordinances. The practice began only in 1992.[1]

Even after the ***Wadhwa judgment,*** the governments are resorting to promulgation and repromulgation of Ordinances. This is because the judgment provided some exceptions. It said the government may occasionally repromulgate when in situations like 'the Legislature has a too much legislative business' or the time at its disposal is short.

It is opinioned that, in the era of coalition politics, the ***Wadhwa judgment*** has encouraged rather than prohibited repromulgations and incentivised shorter parliamentary sessions.

1. https://www.thehindu.com/opinion/columns/legal-eye-column-repromulgation/article7275518.ece

14

M. C. Mehta v. Union of India (1986)

Whether hazardous industries be allowed to operate in densely populated areas?

If they are allowed to work in such areas, should not there be regulating mechanisms?

How is the liability and amount of compensation determined?

What is the scope of Article 32 of the Constitution?

M. C. Mehta case changed the scope of Environment Law in India.

For the first time, an industry was held responsible for an accident and forced to pay compensation.

INTRODUCTION

M. C. Mehta v. Union of India case, also known as ***Oleum Gas Leak case***, is a landmark judgment that changed the scope of Environment Law in India.

M. C. Mehta was the petitioner and the Union of India and others were respondents in the case.

BACKGROUND

Shriram Food and Fertilizers, a subsidiary of Delhi Cloth Mills Limited, was manufacturing caustic chlorine and oleum. The company was based in Delhi. The manufacturing units of the company were surrounded by densely populated areas.

Mahesh Chandra Mehta, an attorney, filed a writ petition under **Article 32** seeking a direction for the closure of the various units of Shriram Food and Fertilizers, on the grounds that they were hazardous to the community.

During the pendency of the petition, there was leakage of oleum gas from one of the units of Shriram Food and Fertilizers. The **Delhi Legal Aid and**

Advice Board and the **Delhi Bar Association filed applications for the award of compensation** to the persons who had suffered harm on account of the escape of oleum gas.

A three Judges Bench of the Supreme Court permitted Shriram Food and Fertilizers to restart its plants subject to certain conditions. However, it referred to the applications for compensation to a larger Bench of five Judges as it involved the following issues of constitutional importance.

LEGAL ISSUES INVOLVED

1. Whether letters addressed even to an individual judge entertainable?
2. What is the scope and ambit of the jurisdiction of the Supreme Court under Article 32, since the applications for compensation are sought to be maintained under that Article?
3. Whether Article 21 is available against Shriram Food and Fertilizers which is owned by Delhi Cloth Mills Limited, a public company limited, and is engaged in an industry vital to the public interest and with the potential to affect the life and health of the people?
4. What is the measure of liability of an enterprise, which is engaged in a hazardous industry, if accidents occur, persons die or are injured?

ARGUMENTS

Shriram Food and Fertilizers objected by saying that the Court should not proceed to decide these constitutional issues since the original writ petition did not make any claim for compensation.

They also submitted that the escape of oleum gas took place subsequent to the filing of the writ petition. The petitioner could have applied for amendment of the writ petition so as to include a claim for compensation for the victims of oleum gas, but no such application for amendment was made. Therefore, these constitutional issues did not arise for consideration.

Shriram Food and Fertilizers cautioned against expanding **Article 12** so as to bring within its ambit private corporations. It contended that control or regulation of a private corporation functions by the state under statutory law is only the power of regulation by the state. Such regulation does not convert the activity of the private corporation into that of the state.

ARTICLE 12: DEFINITION OF STATE

Article 12 states that '...*the State includes the Government and Parliament of India and the Government and the Legislature of each of the States and all local or other authorities within the territory of India or under the control of the Government of India.*'[1]

On the other hand, the petitioners argued that a sizable aid in loans, land and other facilities were granted by the Government to Shriram Food and Fertilizers in carrying on the industry. Any private activity, if supported, controlled or regulated by the state, would be subject to the same constitutional restraints on the exercise of power as the state.

THE DOCTRINE OF ABSOLUTE LIABILITY

In this case, Hon'ble Supreme Court propounded the doctrine of absolute liability which states that if any person undertakes any activity which can be dangerous to the life and property of others, then such person is bound to pay compensation for any unfortunate accident.

This doctrine is also called no-fault liability because such a person is required to pay compensation even without fault. It acted as a game-changer because now industries cannot escape any liability by citing reasons like all the safety procedures were followed.

THE JUDGMENT

On the issue of letter addressed to the court, the Supreme Court held that *'if a person who by reason of poverty or disability or socially or economically disadvantaged position cannot approach a Court for justice, it would be* ***open to any public-spirited individual to bring an action for vindication of the fundamental or other legal right of such individual*** *and this can be done not only by filing regular writ petition under Article 226 in the High Court and under Article 32 in this Court, but also by addressing a letter to the Court.*'[2]

The Supreme Court also said that even if a letter is addressed to an individual Judge of the Court, it should be entertained, provided if it is by or on behalf of a person in custody or on behalf of a woman or a child or a class or deprived or disadvantaged persons.

1. The Constitution of India, Ministry of Law and Justice (Legislative Department)
2. https://main.sci.gov.in/judgments

Accordingly, the Delhi Legal Aid and Advice Board was directed to take up the cases of all those who claimed to have suffered on account of oleum gas leak and to file actions on their behalf in the appropriate Court for claiming compensation.

On the issue of scope and ambit of the jurisdiction of the Supreme Court under Article 32, it held that *'Article 32 lays a constitutional obligation on this Court to protect the fundamental rights. For this purpose, the* ***Court has all incidental and ancillary powers including the power to forge new remedies and design new strategies to enforce the fundamental rights****, in addition to issue order, give directions and issue writ for enforcement of the fundamental rights.'*[3]

In other words, the Supreme Court held that its **power under Article 32** includes **not only preventing the infringement of fundamental right,** but also **providing relief against a breach of the fundamental right** already committed. The power to grant such remedial relief may include the power to award compensation in appropriate cases.

The applications for compensation in the writ petition were for enforcement of the fundamental right to life enshrined in Article 21. Therefore, the Court held that the applications for compensation are maintainable under Article 32.

The Supreme Court observed that in the past, it had expanded the horizon of Article 12 primarily to inject respect for human rights and social conscience in the corporate structure. Thus, it included those **'private corporations whose activities have the potential of affecting the life and health of the people' within the ambit of Article 12** and thus subject to the discipline of Article 21.

IMPORTANCE AND IMPACT

- It is a landmark judgment that changed the scope of **Environment Law** in India.
- Coming just one year after the Bhopal Disaster, ***M. C. Mehta case*** sought to address and rectify the miscarriage of justice of that time and reinstate faith in the judiciary.
- For the **first time, an industry was held responsible for an accident** and forced to pay compensation.
- The Supreme Court performed an **extra-judiciary role**. The verdict was decided on taking into account the need for industrialisation and the fact that accidents are an unavoidable consequence of it.

3. https://main.sci.gov.in/judgments

15

Mohini Jain v. State of Karnataka (1989)

Whether Right to Education is guaranteed to the Indian citizens under the Constitution of India?

In *Mohini Jain case*, the Supreme Court held that the 'Right to Education' is concomitant to the fundamental rights enshrined under Part III of the Constitution. The Right to Education flows directly from right to life.

The Parliament in 2002 passed the Constitution (Eighty-Sixth Amendment) Act of 2002. It added Article 21A to the Constitution and expressly recognized 'Right to Education' as a fundamental right in the Constitution.

INTRODUCTION

Mohini Jain v. the State of Karnataka is a landmark judgment related to **'Right to Education'**.

Mohini Jain was the petitioner and State of Karnataka and others were respondent in the case.

BACKGROUND

The State Government of Karnataka issued a **notification** dated 5 June 1989, under Section 5(1) of the **Karnataka Educational Institutions (Prohibition of Capitation Fee) Act, 1984,** fixing the tuition fee, other fees and deposits to be charged from the students by the private Medical Colleges in the state.

As per this order, **three different fee slabs** were fixed:

- For the candidates admitted against **'Government seats'**, the tuition fee per year was ₹2,000.

- For the **Karnataka students** (other than those admitted against 'Government seats'), the maximum tuition fee was ₹25,000.
- The students belonging to the category of **'Indian students from outside Karnataka'** were to pay the tuition fee not exceeding ₹60,000 per annum.

Mohini Jain was a resident of Uttar Pradesh and she came under the category of Indian students from outside Karnataka.

Mohini Jain was informed by Sri Siddhartha Medical College (a private medical college in Karnataka), that she could be admitted to the MBBS Course in the session commencing February/March 1991, provided she would deposit ₹60,000 as the tuition fee for the first year and furnish a bank guarantee in respect of the fees for the remaining years of the MBBS Course.

When she could not pay the exorbitant annual tuition fee, she was denied admission.

Mohini Jain, under **Article 32** of the Constitution, challenged the notification dated 5 June 1989, issued by the Government of Karnataka, which permitted private medical colleges to charge exorbitant tuition fees from the students other than those admitted to the 'Government seats'.

ARGUMENTS

Sri Siddhartha Medical College, which denied admission to Ms. Jain, contended that the students from whom higher tuition fee was charged belong to a different class. It said that those who were admitted to the Government seats were meritorious and the remaining non-meritorious. The classification of candidates into those who possessed merit and those who did not was a valid classification and the college management was within its right to charge more fee from those who did not possess merit. The object was to collect money to meet the expenses incurred by the college in providing medical education to the students.

The Karnataka Private Medical Colleges Association argued that private medical colleges in the State of Karnataka did not receive any financial aid from either the Central or the State Governments.

They submitted that the private medical colleges would incur about ₹500,000 per student as expenditure for a 5-year MBBS course and 40 per cent of the seats in the colleges were set apart as Government seats to be filled by the Government. The students selected and admitted against Government seats would pay only ₹2,000 per annum and the rest of the burden was on those who were admitted against management quota. The tuition fee was not excessive and as such there was no question of making any profit by the private medical colleges in the State of Karnataka.

Sri Siddhartha Medical College and the Karnataka Private Medical Colleges Association submitted that in order to run the medical colleges, the managements were justified in charging the capitation fee.

They also submitted that there was no provision under the Constitution or under any other law, except the law passed by the State of Karnataka, which prohibited the charging of capitation fee.

LEGAL ISSUES INVOLVED

1. **Was there a 'Right to Education' guaranteed** to the people of India under the Constitution? If so, did the concept of 'capitation fee' violate this right?
2. Whether the charging of capitation was arbitrary, unfair, unjust and as such violated Article 14 of the Constitution?
3. Whether the notification issued by the Government of Karnataka permitted the private medical colleges to charge capitation fee in the guise of regulating fees under the Act?
4. Whether the notification was violative of the provisions of the Karnataka Educational Institutions (Prohibition of Capitation Fee) Act, 1984?

THE JUDGMENT

The dignity of man is inviolable. It is education which brings forth the dignity of a man. It is the duty of the state to respect and protect the same. For this, the framers of the Constitutions brought Articles 41 and 45 in Chapter IV of the Constitution.

The Supreme Court observed that '*without making "Right to Education" under Article 41 of the Constitution a reality, the fundamental rights under Chapter III shall remain beyond the reach of the large majority which is illiterate.*'[1]

Based on this reasoning, the Supreme Court held that the **'Right to Education' is concomitant to the fundamental rights enshrined under Part III** of the Constitution.

The court observed that the 'Right to Life' is the expression for all those rights which the Court must enforce because they are basic to the dignified enjoyment of life. **The Right to Education flows directly from right**

1. https://indiankanoon.org/doc/40715/

to life. Charging capitation fee in consideration of admission to educational institutions amounts to a denial of a citizen's Right to Education. So, the State Government is under an obligation to make an endeavour to provide educational facilities at all levels to its citizens.

Capitation fee makes the availability of education beyond the reach of the poor. It brings out a clear class bias. So, the court held that '*the capitation fee to be charged by State recognized educational institutions is wholly arbitrary and as such violative of Article 14...*'[2]

The court observed that the Karnataka Educational Institutions (Prohibition of Capitation Fee) Act, 1984, was brought with the objective of curbing the evil practice of collecting capitation fee for admitting students into the educational institutions in Karnataka.

The Court observed that 'If the State Government fixes ₹2,000 per annum as the tuition fee in government colleges and for "Government seats" in private medical colleges then it is the responsibility of the State to see that any private college recognized by the Government is prohibited from charging more than ₹2,000 from any student who may be resident of any part of India.'

The Court held that '***charging capitation fee by the private educational institutions as a consideration for admission is wholly illegal*** *and cannot be permitted.*'

The **court set aside the notification** dated 5 June 1989 on the grounds that it goes beyond the scope of the Act and contrary to Section 3 of the Act. It held that '*It is not permissible in law for any educational institution to charge capitation fee as a consideration for admission.*'

IMPORTANCE

- The **'Right to Education' was declared as a fundamental right**.
- The judgment reminded the state of its constitutional obligation to provide educational institutions at all levels for the benefit of the citizens.
- The judgment brought equality in access to education.
- Capitation fee is nothing but a price for selling education. By holding that charging of capitation fee as unconstitutional, the court prevented, at least theoretically, the educational institutions from becoming 'teaching shops'.

2. https://indiankanoon.org/doc/40715/

IMPACT

Prior to the judgment, the Right to Education was not a fundamental right.

The Parliament in 2002 passed the **Constitution (Eighty-sixth Amendment) Act** of 2002. It added **Article 21A** to the Constitution and expressly recognized the 'Right to Education' as a fundamental right in the Constitution.

16

Indira Sawhney v. Union of India (1992)

Can there be reservation for Other Backward Classes (OBCs)? Is the OBC reservation constitutionally valid?

Indira Sawhney case upheld the constitutional validity of the Office Memorandum that provided 27 per cent reservation to the BCs.

It held that the reservations should not exceed 50 per cent, and the reservation in promotion is constitutionally impermissible.

INTRODUCTION

Indira Sawhney v. Union of India case is one of the landmark cases that dealt with the issue of reservation in Government jobs for Backward Classes (BCs).

BACKGROUND

In 1979, the Union Government under **Article 340** of the Constitution appointed the **second BCs commission** (famously known as **Mandal Commission**) to investigate the status of Socially and Educationally Backward Classes (SEBCs) and recommend steps to be taken for their advancements.

ARTICLE 340

Article 340 empowers the President to appoint a Commission to investigate the conditions of socially and educationally backward classes within the territory of India.

FIRST BACKWARD CLASS COMMISSION

The first Backward Class Commission is known as **Kaka Kallelkar Commission**. It was set up on 29 January 1953, and submitted its report on 30 March 1955. The commission listed out 2,399 castes as socially and educationally backward on the basis of criteria evolved by it, but the Central Government did not accept that report.

The **terms of reference** of the Commission were:

- To determine the criteria for defining the SEBCs;
- To recommend steps to be taken for the advancement of the SEBCs of citizens so identified;
- To examine the desirability or otherwise of making provision for the reservation of appointments or posts in favour of such BCs of citizens which are not adequately represented in public services and posts in connection with the affairs of the Union or of any State; and
- Present to the President a report setting out the facts as found by them and making such recommendations as they think proper.

The commission in its report, submitted in December 1980, identified 3,743 castes as SEBC and recommended 27 per cent reservation in Government jobs for them.

Till 1989, the successive governments did not take any action on this report. In 1989, the newly elected Janata government issued an **Office Memorandum (O.M.)** to implement the recommendations in the report. Issuance of Office Memoranda was followed by the violent 'anti-reservation' movement that rocked the country for three months.

In 1990, a **writ petition** was filed on behalf of the **Supreme Court Bar Association** challenging the validity of the O.M. and for staying its operation. A five Judges bench of the Supreme Court issued a stay order till the final disposal of the case.

In the meantime, the Janata Government collapsed and the newly elected government headed by Shri. P. V. Narasimha Rao issued **another O.M.** on 25 September 1991.

It **introduced the economic criterion** in granting reservation by giving preference to the poorer Sections of SEBCs in the 27 per cent quota. It **also reserved another 10 per cent of vacancies** for economically backward sections who are not covered by any of the existing schemes of reservation.

The five judges' bench referred the case to the **nine judges' bench**. The bench issued a notice to the Government to show the criteria upon which the Government has proposed to make the 27 per cent reservation.

ARGUMENTS

Petitioners argued that the Mandal Report **perpetuates the evils of the caste system** and accentuates caste consciousness besides obstructing the doctrine of secularism. According to them, the O.M. issued on the basis of the Mandal Report, which is solely based on the caste criterion, is violative of Article 16(2).

They demanded a fresh Commission under Article 340(1) to make a fresh survey throughout the length and breadth of the country, as the Mandal Report was based on the 1931 census and therefore, it can never serve a correct basis for identifying the 'backward class'.

Caste can never be the basis for identification. Survey to identify BCs should be from individual to individual; it cannot be caste-wise. A secular socialist society can never approve of identification of BCs on the basis of caste.

Yet another argument of the petitioners was that if the recommendations of the Commission are implemented, **it would result in the substandard replacing the standard** and the reins of power passing from meritocracy to mediocrity. They said it **would result in demoralisation and discontent** and **revitalisation of the caste system**, and divide the nation into two - forward and backward.

The petitioner submitted that the 'provision' considered by Clause (4) of Article 16 can and should necessarily be made only by the legislative wing of the state and not by the Executive or any other authority.

They contended that the **'equal protection' Clause** prohibits the State from making unreasonable discrimination in providing preferences and facilities for any Section of its people.

On the other hand, respondents refuted each and every contention of the petitioners'. According to them, the criteria evolved, the methodology adopted, the identification made and lists prepared were valid and legal.

The respondents contend that the Constitution guarantees liberty, equality and fraternity for all classes of people irrespective of their religion, community, caste, occupation, residence or the like. To elevate BCs to the positions of equality with the more fortunate, affluent and enlightened Sections of our country, it is necessary to provide reservations.

The respondents argued that though 'equal protection' Clause prohibits the State from making unreasonable discrimination in providing preferences for any Section of its people, it requires the State to provide equal opportunities to those placed unequally. The basic policy of reservation is to off-set the inequality.

They supported the identification of backward classes solely and exclusively on the basis of caste.

LEGAL ISSUES INVOLVED

The following constitutional questions were considered by the nine judges' bench:

1. Whether Article 16(4) is an exception to Article 16(1) and would be inclusive of the right to the reservation to posts in services under the State?
2. What would be the content of the phrase Backward Class in Article 16(4) of the Constitution and whether caste by itself could constitute a class and whether economic criterion by itself could identify a class for Article 16(4)?
3. Whether reservation of posts in services under the State based exclusively on economic criteria would be covered by Article 16(1) of the Constitution?
4. Can the extent of the reservation to posts in the services under the State under Article 16(4) exceed 50 per cent of the posts in a cadre or Service under the State?
5. Does Article 16(4) permit the classification of 'Backward Classes' into BCs and MBCs or permit classification among them based on economic or other considerations?
6. Will making 'any provision' under Article 16(4) for reservation 'by the State' necessarily have to be by law made by the Legislatures of the State or by law made by Parliament? Or could such provisions be made by Executive order?
7. Will the extent of judicial review be limited to the identification of BCs and the percentage of reservations made for such classes?
8. Would reservation of appointments or posts 'in favour of any Backward Class' be restricted to the initial appointment to the post or would it extend to promotions as well?

ARTICLE 16(4)

Article 16(4) empowers the state to make any provision for reservation of appointments or posts in favour of any backward class of citizen which in the opinion of the state is not adequately represented in the services under the state.

THE JUDGMENT

After hearing the arguments of the petitioners and the respondents, the court held that:[1]

1. **Clause (4) of Article 16 is not an exception to Clause (1) of Article 16**. It is an instance of classification implicit in and permitted by Clause (1). Even without Clause (4), it would have been permissible for the State to make a provision for reservation of appointments/posts in their favour. Clause (4) merely puts the matter beyond any doubt in specific terms.
2. The 'provision' contemplated by Article 16(4) can also be made by the executive wing of the Union or of the State.
3. **Backward class** of citizen in Article 16(4) **can be identified on the basis of the caste and not only on an economic basis**.
4. The wards of those BCs of persons who have achieved a particular status in society, either political or social or economic, or if their parents are in higher services, then such individuals should be excluded to avoid monopolisation of the services reserved for BCs by a few. **Exclusion of 'creamy layer' is a social purpose**.
5. Article 16(4) **permits the classification of backward classes** into BCs and MBCs. Such a classification would be necessary to help the MBCs, otherwise, those of the BCs who might be a little more advanced than the MBCs might walk away with all the seats.
6. The **reservations** contemplated in Clause (4) of Article 16 **should not exceed 50 per cent**.
7. **Reservation in promotion is constitutionally impermissible** as once the advantaged and disadvantaged are made equal and are brought in one class, then any further benefit extended for promotion

1. https://indiankanoon.org/doc/1363234/

based on the inequality existing prior to the initial benefits would be like treating equals unequally.

IMPORTANCE

The judgment laid down a reasonable solution to the problem of reservation.

The court made an attempt to balance between the interests of society and educationally BCs and a person belonging to the general category in matters of government employment.

However, some opinioned that the Court should have taken into consideration the interest of the poor Section that is not covered by any of the existing schemes of reservation.

IMPACT

From time to time, various governments have made an attempt to change the effect of the decision of this case with the intention of political gain.

- The **Constitution 77th Amendment** in 1995 inserted a new Article 16(4)(A) that empowers the State to make a provision for reservation in the matter of promotion to any class or classes of posts in the service of the State in favour of the SC and ST.
- The **Constitution 81st Amendment in 2000** inserted Article 16(4)(B). By this amendment, it was fixed that reservation can exceed above 50 per cent reservation for SC, ST and BCs if backlog vacancies could not be filled up in the previous years due to the non-availability of eligible candidates.
- By the **Constitution 85th Amendment in 2001**, the word 'in the matter of promotion to any classes' was substituted by the words 'in the matter of promotion with consequential seniority, to any classes'. It provided for 'consequential seniority' in the case of promotion by the virtue of the rule of reservation for the government servants belonging to the SCs and STs.

S. R. Bommai v. Union of India (1994)

Is the power of the Center (President of India) to dismiss a state government absolute?

Whether the Presidential Proclamation under Article 356 justiciable, and if so, to what extent?

S. R. Bommai case is related to the proclamation of emergency under Article 356 of the Constitution. The case also dealt with the power of the President to dissolve State Legislative Assemblies and the issues relating to federalism and secularism as a part of the basic structure.

It put an end to the arbitrary dismissal of State governments under Article 356.

It was also held that the proclamation under Article 356(1) is not immune from judicial review.

INTRODUCTION

S. R. Bommai v. Union of India case is a landmark case related to the **proclamation of emergency under Article 356** of the Constitution. The case also dealt with the power of the President to dissolve State Legislative Assemblies and the issues relating to **federalism and secularism** as a part of the basic structure.

S. R. Bommai was the petitioner and Union of India was the respondent in the case.

BACKGROUND

S. R. Bommai was the chief minister of Karnataka between 13 August 1988 and 21 April 1989. The President of India on 21st April 1989 dismissed S. R. Bommai government on the grounds that the government had lost the majority following large-scale defections and imposed President's Rule in the State of **Karnataka**.

S. R. Bommai sought an opportunity to test his majority in the Assembly, but the then Governor of Karnataka P. Venkatasubbaiah refused.

Bommai filed a writ petition in the High Court of Karnataka against the Governor's decision to recommend President's Rule. The High Court dismissed his writ petition. He, then, moved to the Supreme Court.

There were **other cases** of dismissal of governments and dissolution of Legislative Assemblies:

- On 7th August 1988, the President issued a Proclamation dismissing the Government of **Nagaland** and dissolving the State Legislative Assembly.
- On 11th October 1991, the President issued a Proclamation dismissing the Government of **Meghalaya** and dissolving the Legislative Assembly.
- On 6 December 1992, the disputed Ram Janmabhoomi Babri Masjid structure was demolished. This was followed by large-scale violence which resulted in the loss of lives and damage to property. The Uttar Pradesh government resigned. On this ground, on 15th December 1992, the President issued a Proclamation under Article 356 dismissing the State Governments and dissolving the Legislative Assemblies of **Rajasthan**, **Madhya Pradesh** and **Himachal Pradesh**.

The validity of these Proclamations was challenged by Writ Petitions in the appropriate High Courts and later withdrawn to the Supreme Court.

S. R. Bommai case took almost five years to see a logical conclusion. On 11 March 1994, a nine-judge Constitution Bench of the Supreme Court issued the historic order.

ARGUMENTS

The main argument against the order was that the power to issue a **proclamation under Article 356 is not on subjective discretion or opinion,** but on objective facts. The circumstances must exist to conclude that the relevant situation had arisen in which the Government of the State cannot be carried on in accordance with the provisions of the Constitution.

The petitioners also argued that the **Proclamation must provide the grounds and reasons for reaching the satisfaction**, supported with the materials or the gist of the events in support of it.

It is contended that the imposition of the President's rule in the States of Madhya Pradesh, Rajasthan and Himachal Pradesh was mala fide, based on no satisfaction and was purely a political act. The counsels on behalf of these states argued that **mere fact that communal disturbances and/or instances of arson and looting took place is no ground for imposing the President's rule**.

The counsel for petitioners strongly refuted the idea of 'secularism'. According to them, it is a vague concept not defined in the Constitution and hence, cannot be a ground for taking action under Article 356.

On the other hand, the Union of India argued that the ground to issue the **Presidential Order is the subjective satisfaction of the President** and it is in his discretion and opinion to dissolve the National Assembly.

It was contended on behalf of the Union of India that since the Proclamation under **Article 356(1)** would be issued by the President on the advice of the Council of Ministers given under **Article 74(1)** of the Constitution and since Clause (2) of Article 74 bars inquiry into the question whether any and what advice was tendered by Ministers to the President, **judicial review of the reasons which led to the issuance of tile Proclamation also stands barred**.

The respondents' contended that **secularism being a basic feature** of the Constitution, a State Government can be dismissed if it is guilty of unsecular acts. They considered the events that led to the **demolition of the disputed Ram Janmabhoomi Babri Masjid** structure as unsecular act.

ARTICLE 356

When Article 356 was being discussed in the constituent assembly, Dr. B.R. Ambedkar thought that this provision would remain a 'dead letter' to the Constitution. However, it has become one of the most misused provisions in the Constitution.

Sarkaria Commission on Centre-State Relations recommended that Article 356 should be used very sparingly. The Punchhi Commission on Centre-State Relations recommended that principles laid down by the Supreme Court should be followed when applying the President's rule.

THE JUDGMENT

The Supreme Court held that Articles 352 to 360 in Part XVIII of the Constitution relating to emergency provisions can be invoked only when there is an emergency and the emergency is of nature described therein and not of any other kind.

It was held that the **President's satisfaction has to be based on objective material**. That material may be available in the report sent to him by the Governor or otherwise or both from the report and other sources. Therefore, the **conditions** for the issuance of the Proclamation are[1]:

(a) The President should be satisfied either on the basis of a report from the Governor of the State or otherwise.
(b) A situation has arisen in which the Government of the State cannot be carried on in accordance with the provisions of the Constitution.

The **Proclamation under Article 356(1) is not immune from judicial review**. The Court held that the exercise of power by the President under Article 356(1) to issue Proclamation is subject to the judicial review, at least to the extent of examining whether the conditions precedent to the issuance of the Proclamation have been satisfied or not.

Even though **Article 74(2)** bars judicial review of the advice given by the Ministers concerned, it **does not bar scrutiny of the material on the basis of which the advice is given**.

The power of dissolving the Legislative Assembly shall be exercised only after the Proclamation is approved by both Houses of Parliament under Clause (3) of Article 356 and not before. Until such approval, the President can only suspend the Legislative Assembly.

In case both Houses of Parliament disapprove or do not approve the Proclamation, the Proclamation lapses. In such a case, the Government which was dismissed revives. The Legislative Assembly, which may have been kept in suspended animation, gets reactivated.

If the **court** strikes down the Proclamation, it **has the power to restore the dismissed Government and revive the Legislative Assembly** wherever it may have been dissolved or kept under suspension.

With regard to the **issue of 'federalism'**, the Court held that the Constitution of India has created a federation but with a bias in favour of the Centre. **Within the sphere allotted to the States, they are supreme**.

The Court observed that while freedom of religion is guaranteed to all persons in India, from the point of view of the State, the religion, faith or belief of a person is immaterial. To the State, all are equal and are entitled to be treated equally. The Court held that **'Secularism is one of the basic features of the Constitution'**.

Based on the relevant facts and available materials, the Supreme Court held that the Proclamation in respect of Karnataka, Meghalaya and Nagaland

1. https://main.sci.gov.in/judgments

are unconstitutional. The Proclamations in respect of Madhya Pradesh, Rajasthan and Himachal Pradesh are **not unconstitutional**.

IMPORTANCE

- The judgment has become **one of the most cited** whenever hung Assemblies were returned, and parties scrambled to form a government.
- By imposing some restrictions, the Court **put an end to the arbitrary dismissal of State governments** under Article 356.
- It categorically said that **the floor of the Assembly is the only forum to test the majority** and not the subjective opinion of the Governor.

IMPACT

In one of the first instances of the impact of the case was seen in 1999. The Central Government headed by Shri. A. B. Vajpayee had sacked the Bihar Government headed by Smt. Rabri Devi on 12 February 1999. But the Central Government was forced to reinstate the Bihar Government on 8 March 1999.

In 2016, the Supreme Court based on ***Bommai case*** asked the Centre to revoke the proclamation of President's Rule in Uttarakhand and allowed Mr. Harish Rawat to assume the chief minister's office once again.

18

L. Chandra Kumar v. Union of India (1997)

As per the original Indian Constitution, both the Supreme Court and the High Courts have the power of judicial review.

This power conferred under Articles 32 and 226 is a part of the basic structure of the Indian Constitution.

However, the power of judicial review of High Courts became questionable, when Parliament tried to give that role to Tribunals.

Can the power of judicial review under Articles 32 and 226 of the Indian Constitution be curtailed by an Act of legislature?

This question became prominent when Parliament enacted the Administrative Tribunals Act to give effect to the law under Articles 323A and 323B.

In *L. Chandra Kumar v. Union of India*, the Supreme Court held that Tribunals or other such courts can act as supplements to the High Courts but cannot take away their power of judicial review.

INTRODUCTION

L. Chandra Kumar v. Union of India is a landmark case which clarified the disputes and ambiguity of the constitutional amendment which inserted Articles 323A and 323B and declared the power of Administrative Tribunals in relation to Articles 32 and 226.

BACKGROUND

Part XIVA of the Constitution was inserted through Section 46 of the Constitution (42nd Amendment) Act, 1976 with effect from March 1, 1977. The amendment inserted two articles dealing with Tribunals in India, that is, Article 323A and Article 323B. These provisions curtailed the power of all courts in India, except the power under Article 136 of the Supreme Court.

The legislature also enacted the Administrative Tribunals Act to give effect to the law under Articles 323A and 323B. Hence, this case challenged the constitutional validity of the Administrative Tribunals Act and dealt with the question, whether Articles 323A and 323B can curtail the power of the Supreme Court and High Courts under Articles 32 and 226.

LEGAL ISSUES INVOLVED

1. Whether the Sub-clause (d) of Clause (2) of Article 323A or Sub-clause (d) of Clause (3) of Article 323B of the Constitution, totally excludes the jurisdiction of 'all courts', except that of the Supreme Court under Article 136, in respect of disputes referred section itself?
2. Whether the Tribunals, constituted either under Article 323A or under Article 323B of the Constitution, possess the competence to test the constitutional validity of a statutory provision/rule?
3. Whether these Tribunals, as they are functioning at present, can be said to be effective substitutes for the High Courts in discharging the power of judicial review? If not, what are the changes required to make them conform to their founding objectives?

ARGUMENTS

The state argued by quoting the decision in *Sampath Kumar v. Union of India,* where the Court held that though the judicial review is a basic feature of the Constitution, the vesting of the power of judicial review in an alternative institutional mechanism, after taking it away from the High Courts, would not violate the basic structure of Indian Constitution so long as it is ensured that the alternative mechanism is an effective and real substitute for the High Court. Even though the Administrative Tribunal cannot be seen as a substitute for the High Court it can deal with service matters that of the High Court.

It was also argued that in *M. B. Majumdar v. Union of India,* the court held that Tribunals under the Administrative Tribunal Act had been equated with High Courts only to the extent that the former was to act as substitutes for the latter in adjudicating service matters.

The petitioner on the other hand argued that the Supreme Court and the High Courts are the sole repositories of the power of judicial review. Such power, being inclusive of the power to pronounce upon the validity of statutes, actions taken and orders passed by individuals and bodies falling within the ambit of the impression 'State' under Article 12 of the

Constitution, has only been entrusted to the constitutional courts, i.e., the High Courts and this Court. Constitutional Courts alone are competent to exercise the power of judicial review to pronounce upon the constitutional validity of statutory provisions and rules.

While the Tribunals constituted under Articles 323A and 323B can be vested with the power of judicial review over administrative action, the power of judicial review of legislative action cannot be conferred upon them. This proposition has been asserted by the court in *Keshavanada Bharathi v. Union of India.*

Further, the petitioner argued that the High Courts can never be equated with the Tribunals for the following reasons:

- High Courts enjoy vast powers as a consequence of they being Courts of Record under Article 215 of the Constitution and also possess the power to issue Certificates of Appeal under Articles 132 and 133 of the Constitution in cases where they feel that a decision of the Supreme Court is required. This is not so for Tribunals.
- The qualifications for being High Court Judges and the constitutional safeguards provided to High Court Judges are not at all comparable with that of Tribunal composition.
- The jurisdiction of the High Court is constitutionally protected whereas the jurisdiction of the Tribunal can be simply taken away by the repeal of the parent Act.
- The expenditure of the High Court is charged upon the Consolidated Fund of India whereas the Tribunal is dependent on the appropriate government for grants and aids.
- Under our constitutional scheme, every High Court has, under Articles 226 and 227 of the Constitution, the power to issue prerogative writs or orders to all authorities and instrumentalities of the State which function within its territorial jurisdiction. In such a situation, no authority or Tribunal located within the territorial jurisdiction of a High Court can disregard the law declared by it. The impugned constitutional provisions, insofar as they seek to divest the High Courts of their power of superintendence over all Tribunals and Courts situated within their territorial jurisdiction, violate the basic structure of the Indian Constitution.

THE JUDGMENT

The Hon'ble Supreme Court held that Clause 2(d) of Article 323A and Clause 3(d) of Article 323B, to the extent they exclude the jurisdiction of the High Courts and the Supreme Court under Articles 226/227 and 32 of the Constitution, are unconstitutional.

The jurisdiction conferred upon the High Courts under Articles 226/227 and upon the Supreme Court under Article 32 of the Constitution is a part of the inviolable basic structure of our Constitution.

The court further held that Tribunals may perform a supplemental role in discharging the powers conferred by Articles 226/227 and 32 of the Constitution.

The Tribunals created under Article 323A and Article 323B of the Constitution have the competence to test the constitutional validity of statutory provisions and rules. All decisions of these Tribunals will, however, be subject to scrutiny before a Division Bench of the High Court within whose jurisdiction the concerned Tribunal falls.

IMPORTANCE AND IMPACT

The importance of this judgment is that it addressed the question that whether the Parliament by way of an alternative mechanism can take away the right of the judicial review which is a basic structure of the Constitution.

The Tribunals established (through statutes) from the authority conferred by Article 323A and Article 323B have got the competence to test the constitutional validity of statutory provisions and rules in India.

However, the judgment demanded the review of the appropriate High Court to verify the decisions the tribunals have taken in respect of the constitutional matters relating to the service for which they are authorised to do so.

This reaffirmed the authority of the constitutional court in the matters of judicial review.

19

Vishakha v. State of Rajasthan (1997)

How an incident involving sexual harassment at the workplace should be dealt with by an employer?

Vishakha case is one of the first instances where the judiciary tried to fill the vacuum left by the Legislature and Executive

It dealt with the issue of sexual harassment in the workplace.

The Supreme Court laid out the Vishakha guidelines to curb sexual harassment of women at the workplace. Building on these guidelines, the Parliament passed the sexual harassment at workplace (Prevention, Prohibition and Redressal) Act, 2013, which seeks to safeguard women from harassment at their place of work.

INTRODUCTION

Gender equality includes protection from sexual harassment and the right to work with dignity, which is a universally recognized basic human right.

Vishakha v. the State of Rajasthan is a landmark judgment which dealt with the issue of **sexual harassment at the workplace**. The Supreme Court laid out the Vishaka Guidelines to curb sexual harassment of women at the workplace.

Vishaka and others were the petitioners and State of Rajasthan and others were the respondents in the case.

BACKGROUND

Bhanwari Devi was employed as a village-level social worker under the Women's Development Project (WDP) run by the Government of Rajasthan. One of the objectives of the WDP was to curb child marriages.

As a part of her work, Bhanwari Devi tried to stop a child marriage in the family of one Ramakant Gujjar. Even though there was widespread protest, the marriage was successful.

In 1992, to seek vengeance upon her, Ramakant Gujjar along with his five men gangraped Bhanwari Devi in front of her husband. Initially, the police dissuaded her from filing any complaint, but Bhanwari Devi was determined and lodged a complaint against the accused.

The trial court acquitted the accused. But Bhanwari Devi, supported by fellow social workers, filed a **writ petition** in the Supreme Court under the name 'Vishaka'.

This particular petition was concerned only with the realisation of 'gender equality' and prevention of sexual harassment of working women in all workplaces through the judicial process.

The incident of the brutal gang rape of the social worker was considered as the subject matter of a separate criminal action.

ARGUMENTS

The petitioners asked for the enforcement of the fundamental rights of working women under **Articles 14, 19 and 21** of the Constitution of India.

It mainly dealt with the responsibility of the employers for sexual harassment ***by*** and ***to*** its employees.

THE JUDGMENT

The Supreme Court held that incidents **like Sexual Harassment result in a violation of the fundamental rights of 'Gender Equality' and the 'Right of Life and Liberty'**. It is a clear violation of the rights under Articles 14, 15 and 21 of the Constitution. One of the logical consequences of such an incident is also the **violation of the victim's fundamental right under Article 19(1)(g)** 'to practice any profession or to carry out any occupation, trade or business'.

Therefore, such violations attract the remedy under Article 32 for the enforcement of these fundamental rights of women.

The Court observed that the **fundamental right to carry on any occupation, trade or profession depends on the availability of a safe working environment**. Right to life means life with dignity. Therefore, it is the primary responsibility of the Legislature and the Executive to ensure such safety and dignity through suitable legislation and to create a mechanism for its enforcement.

In the **absence of domestic law** relating to the Sexual Harassment at workplaces, the Court depended on International Conventions and norms for the interpretation of the guarantee of gender equality, right to work with human dignity in Articles 14, 15, 19(1)(g) and 21 of the Constitution and the safeguards against sexual harassment.

The court also observed that the meaning and content of the fundamental rights guaranteed in the Constitution of India sufficiently cover all the facets of gender equality, including prevention of sexual harassment or abuse.

In view of the above, and the absence of enacted law to prevent sexual harassment at workplaces, the Supreme Court **laid down the following guidelines and norms**[1].

1. It shall be the duty of the employer or other responsible persons in workplaces or other institutions to prevent or deter the commission of acts of sexual harassment and to provide the procedures for the resolution, settlement or prosecution of acts of sexual harassment by taking all steps required.
2. For this purpose, **sexual harassment includes** such unwelcome sexually determined behaviour (whether directly or by implication) as:
   (a) Physical contact and advances;
   (b) A demand or request for sexual favours;
   (c) Sexually coloured remarks;
   (d) Showing pornography;
   (e) Any other unwelcome physical verbal or non-verbal conduct of sexual nature.
3. All employers or persons in charge of work place whether in the **public or private sector** should take appropriate steps to prevent sexual harassment.
4. If any conduct amounts to a specific offence under the Indian Penal Code or under any other law, the employer shall initiate appropriate action in accordance with law by making a complaint with the appropriate authority. It should be ensured that victims or witnesses are not victimised or discriminated against while dealing with complaints of sexual harassment.
5. If the conduct amounts to misconduct in employment as defined by the relevant service rules, appropriate disciplinary action should be initiated by the employer in accordance with those rules.
6. An **appropriate complaint mechanism** should be created in the employer's organisation for redress of the complaint made by the victim. A complaints committee - headed by a woman and at least half of its member are women - should be set up.

1. https://main.sci.gov.in/jonew/judis/13856.pdf

7. Employees should be allowed to raise issues of sexual harassment at workers meeting and in other appropriate forum and it should be affirmatively discussed in Employer-Employee Meetings.
8. Awareness of the rights of female employees in this regard should be created in particular by prominently notifying the guidelines.

The Supreme Court directed that these guidelines and norms would be strictly observed in all workplaces for the preservation and enforcement of the right to gender equality of the working women.

JUDICIAL ACTIVISM

Judicial refers to a proactive role played by the judiciary while deciding matters in the Court of law.

Generally, Judicial Activism involves the Courts taking over the functions of the executive and legislature by entering into the domain of law-making. The Vishakha case is one of the most cited examples of judicial activism in India.

Sometimes, judicial activism involves an overarching role of judges wherein their personal views regarding a public policy matter play a greater role while deciding a case rather than the letter of the law.

IMPORTANCE

This incident of brutal gang rape revealed the safety concerns employed women face and the pressing need for their protection.

The judgment is a step towards the realisation of the true concept of 'gender equality'.

It tried to fill the vacuum in existing legislation and prevent sexual harassment of working women in all work places through the judicial process.

IMPACT

Building on the ***Vishaka Guidelines***, the Parliament passed the **sexual harassment at workplace (Prevention, Prohibition and Redressal) Act, 2013,** which seeks to safeguard women from harassment at their place of work.

20

Vineet Narain v. Union of India (1997)

Should not the CBI be insulated from executive interference?

Vineet Narain case laid out several steps to curb political influence in the functioning of the CBI.

It also laid out similar guidance for the Enforcement Directorate.

In issuing such guidelines, the Supreme Court referred to its precedent in the ***Vishaka case.***

INTRODUCTION

The landmark judgment in *Vineet Narain v. Union of India,* in 1997, laid out several steps to curb political influence in the functioning of the CBI.

Vineet Narain and others were the petitioners and Union of India and another were the respondents.

BACKGROUND

On 25th March 1991, Ashfak Hussain Lone, alleged member of the terrorist organization Hizbul Mujahideen, was arrested in Delhi. Upon his interrogation, the **Central Bureau of Investigation** (CBI) conducted raids on the premises of Surrender Kumar Jain and his businesses.

During the raid, the CBI seized **two diaries** from the premises. They contained details of huge payments made to various persons who were identified only by initials. The initials corresponded to the initials of various high-ranking politicians of different political parties and of high-ranking bureaucrats. The source of funding was linked to suspected terrorists.

The scandal, popularly known as **'Hawala Scandal'**, attracted widespread media coverage and public attention. The CBI was criticised for its failure to initiate investigations of the politicians and officials with the apparent intent to protect certain implicated individuals who were extremely influential in government and politics.

Nothing having been done in the matter of investigating the Jains or the contents of their diaries, **Vineet Narain**, a journalist, filed a writ petitions on 4th October 1993 in the public interest under Article 32 of the Constitution of India.

Though the primary purpose of the case was to compel a proper investigation into the scam, the focus of the judgment was on the future and autonomy of the CBI.

Following the Court orders, investigations were conducted and charge sheets were filed against certain accused. However, all the cases collapsed at the stage of prosecution in court.

ARGUMENTS

The petitioners alleged that the Government agencies, like the CBI and the revenue authorities, have failed to perform their duties and legal obligations. They have failed to conduct proper investigations in the matters arising out of the seizure of the **'Jain Diaries'** in certain raids conducted by the CBI.

They also alleged that arrest of a certain terrorist led to the discovery of financial support to them by illegal means and a nexus between several important politicians, bureaucrats and the illegal source of such funding.

The CBI failed to investigate the matter. This is being done with a view to protecting the persons involved, who are very influential and powerful in the political setup.

The petitioners argued that the scandal discloses the nexus between crime and corruption in public life in high places, which poses a serious threat to the integrity, security and economy of the nation.

They demanded that the **Government agencies be compelled to duly perform their legal obligations**, to prevent erosion of the rule of law and the preservation of democracy in the country.

In particular, the **petitioners pleaded for**[1],

1. The direction of the Court to investigate the scandal in accordance with the law.

1. https://main.sci.gov.in/judgments

2. Appointment of police officers, in whose integrity, independence and competence the Court has confidence, for conducting and/or supervising the said investigation.
3. Suitable directions to ensure that the culprits are dealt with according to law.
4. Directions by the Supreme Court, so that such evil actions on the part of the investigating agencies and their political superiors are not repeated in the future.

CBI

CBI is an investigating police agency which derives its powers from the Delhi Special Police Establishment Act, 1946.

It is one of the best investigating agencies in the world with a conviction rate as high as 70%.

CBI coordinates on behalf of India with Interpol member countries.

THE JUDGMENT

Referring to the ***Vishaka case*** judgment, the Supreme Court said, '*it is the duty of the executive to fill the vacuum by executive orders because its field is coterminous with that of the legislature, and where there is inaction even by the executive, the judiciary must step in*'.

In exercise of its constitutional obligations to provide a solution till such time as the Legislature acts to perform its role by enacting proper legislation, the Supreme Court laid down the following important guidelines:

1. The Central Vigilance Commission (CVC) shall be given **statutory status**.
2. **Selection for the post of Central Vigilance Commissioner** shall be made by a Committee comprising the Prime Minister, Home Minister and the Leader of the Opposition from a panel of outstanding civil servants and others with impeccable integrity to be furnished by the Cabinet Secretary.
3. The **CVC shall be responsible for the efficient functioning of the CBI**. While Government shall remain answerable for the CBI's functioning, the CVC shall be entrusted with the responsibility of superintendence over the CBI's functioning.
4. The Central Government shall take all measures necessary to ensure that the CBI functions effectively and efficiently and is viewed as a non-partisan agency.

5. **Recommendations for appointment of the Director, CBI shall be made by a Committee** headed by the Central Vigilance Commissioner with the Home Secretary and Secretary (Personnel) as members. The final selection shall be made by the Appointments Committee of the Cabinet (ACC) from the panel recommended by the Selection Committee.
6. The **Director, CBI shall have a minimum tenure of two years**, regardless of the date of his superannuation.
7. The transfer of an incumbent Director, CBI in an extraordinary situation, including the need for him to take up a more important assignment, should have the approval of the Selection Committee.
8. The Director, CBI shall have full freedom for allocation of work within the agency as also for constituting teams for investigations.

The Supreme Court also laid out **similar guidance for the Enforcement Directorate**.

The Supreme Court also struck down **the 'Single Directive'**. As per this directive, '*prior sanction of the designated authority is required to initiate the investigation against officers of the Government and the Public Sector Undertakings (PSUs), nationalized banks above a certain level*'.

> The **Central Vigilance Commissioner Act, 2003**, reinstated the 'Single directive' requiring the prior sanction of the government for pursuing an investigation against bureaucrats of the level of Joint Secretary and above.
>
> This directive was **again struck down** by the Supreme Court in the course of another judgment **in 2014**, on the basis that it **violated the right to equality guaranteed by the Constitution**.

IMPORTANCE

Vineet Narain case was a step in the direction to ensure **accountability in public life**.

The Supreme Court liberally interpreted its powers under the Constitution to devise various innovative procedural techniques. It gave detailed directions to the executive and formulated guidelines to fill a legislative vacuum on the issue of public corruption.

It created public awareness about the issue of public corruption and inspired people to engage with the judicial system through the process of public interest litigation.

IMPACT

Though in ***Vineet Narain case*** the Supreme Court laid out guidelines to secure the functional autonomy of the CBI, the guidelines are rarely followed in letter and spirit. The guidelines were heavily diluted by the successive governments during implementation.

For example, one of the guidelines gave fixed two-year tenure to the Director of CBI. But recently, the Central Government sent the CBI director Alok Kumar Verma on compulsory leave. Though the government has not removed the Director from the post, in forcibly sending him on leave and appointing joint director M. Nageswara Rao as interim director, it has effectively done the same. It runs contrary to a Supreme Court directive.

THE SEVEN PRINCIPLES OF PUBLIC LIFE

While dealing with the issue of accountability in Public life in *Vineet Narain case*, the Supreme Court of India referred to **'the Seven Principles of Public Life'** stated in the Report by **Lord Nolan**.

Selflessness

Holders of public office should take decisions solely in terms of the public interest. They should not do so in order to gain financial or other material benefits for themselves, their families or their friends.

Integrity

Holders of public office should not place themselves under any financial or other obligation to outside individuals or organisations that might influence them in the performance of their official duties.

Objectivity

In carrying out public business, including making public appointments, awarding contracts or recommending individuals for rewards and benefits, holders of public office should make choices on merit.

Accountability

Holders of public office are accountable for their decisions and actions to the public and must submit themselves to whatever scrutiny is appropriate to their office.

Openness

Holders of public office should be as open as possible about all the decisions and actions that they take. They should give reasons for their decisions and restrict information only when the wider public interest clearly demands.

Honesty

Holders of public office have a duty to declare any private interests relating to their public duties and to take steps to resolve any conflicts arising in a way that protects the public interest.

Leadership

Holders of public office should promote and support these principles by leadership and example.

21

Three Judges Cases (1981, 1993, 1998)

How should the Judges of the Supreme Court be selected?

Should the court themselves appoint judges?

Or, should there be another body for Judicial Appointments?

The Collegium system was evolved by the Supreme Court through three different judgments. They are:

- *S. P. Gupta v. President of India and others* (1981)
- *Advocate on Record Association v. Union of India* (1993)
- Special Reference case (1998)

These are important judgments in preserving Judicial independence, which is one of the basic features of the Constitution as evolved in ***Keshavananda Bharati case.***

INTRODUCTION

In India, the judges of the Supreme Court and High Courts are appointed and transferred on the recommendation of the 'Collegium system'. However, this collegium has no place in the Indian Constitution.

The present form of the Collegium system was evolved by the Supreme Court through three different judgments. They are:

- *S. P. Gupta v. President of India and others* (1981)
- *Advocate on Record Association v. Union of India* (1993)
- Special Reference case (1998)

These three are collectively known as 'Three Judges cases'.

BACKGROUND

On 18th March 1981, Shri Shiv Shankar, the then Law Minister of India, issued a circular addressed to the Governor of Punjab and the Chief Ministers of the other states.

The objective of the circular was to further national integration and to combat narrow parochial tendencies bred by caste, kinship and other local links and affiliations. In order to achieve this, the circular suggested that one-third of the Judges of the High Court should as far as possible be from outside the state in which that High Court is situated.

However, the circular generated heated controversy. Several resolutions were passed by bar associations across the country condemning the circular letter as subversive of judicial independence and asking the Government of India to withdraw the circular letter.

Eight writ petitions were filed in different High Courts across the country, challenging the constitutional validity of the circular, a practice followed by the Central Government in appointing additional Judges in various High Courts, and transfer of judges of the High Courts.

S. P. Gupta was an advocate practicing in the High Court of Allahabad and one of the petitioners in the case.

In the petition filed in the Bombay High Court, the Law minister of India was respondent No. 1 and the Government of India was respondent No. 2. Both of them filed Transfer Petition for transfer of the writ petitions from the Bombay High Court to the Supreme Court under Article 139A of the Constitution.

Other petitions were withdrawn and transferred to itself by the Supreme Court.

That is how these writ petitions came up for hearing before the seven Judges Bench of the Supreme Court.

Upon hearing the arguments, they declared the 'primacy' of the CJI's recommendation on judicial appointments and transfers can be refused for 'cogent reasons'. The ruling gave the Executive primacy over the Judiciary in judicial appointments.

However, this judgment was resented by many on the grounds that it violated the independence of Judiciary, which itself is a 'Basic feature' of the Constitution as held in *Keshavananda Bharati case.*

In 1993, again writ petitions were filed in the Supreme Court for filling the vacancies in the higher Judiciary. This writ petition brought into reconsideration the controversial judgment in *S. P Gupta case.* This is known as *Supreme Court Advocates on Record Association v. Union of India* or *Second Judges Case.*

The case considered two questions:

1. The primacy of the opinion of the Chief Justice of India (CJI) with regard to the appointments of Judges to the Supreme Court and the High Court, and with regard to the transfers of High Court Judges/ Chief Justices, and
2. Justiciability of these matters, including the matter of fixation of the Judge strength in the High Courts.

In *Second Judges case,* the Supreme Court held that *'In the matters of appointment and transfers of Judges, the role of the Chief Justice of India is primal in nature. The Chief Justice of India must take into account the views of two senior-most Judges of the Supreme Court...'.*

However, doubts arose about the interpretation of the law laid down by the Supreme Court. The President was reduced to only an approver. Therefore, exercising his power under Article 143 of the Constitution of India, the President of India made a special reference to the Supreme Court in 1998.

ARGUMENTS IN *S. P. GUPTA CASE*

The petitioners challenged against the validity of the circular letter which required the additional Judges of the High Courts to give their consent for being appointed as Judges outside the state. They argued that such consent in advance would reduce the consultation with the CJI, the Chief Justice of the High Court and the Governor of the state to an illusory and empty formality.

They contended that the circular letter held out a veiled threat to the additional Judges that if they do not consent to their appointment as Judges in a High Court other than their own, they may not be appointed as permanent Judges at all and may be dropped on the expiration of their term of office.

It was argued that to require a person whose name is to be recommended for initial appointment as a Judge to give her/his consent for being appointed as a Judge in another High Court would be to introduce an irrelevant qualification for the appointment of a Judge.

On the other hand, the respondents contended that the petitioners have no *locus standi* in the case.

It was argued that the transfer of a Judge from one High Court to another results in the vacation of his office, and therefore must be construed to be a fresh appointment. In other words, he could be transferred only if he gives his consent as when he is first appointed to the High Court.

It was argued that it is not possible for a person to function as a Judge unless the oath is operative. If a transferred Judge has to take a fresh oath, then it is urged that the order of transfer would become a fresh appointment for which his consent would be required by necessary implication, as it is necessary in the case of the first appointment under Article 217(1).

THE JUDGMENT IN *S. P. GUPTA CASE*

While allowing the Writ Petitions, the Supreme Court quashed and struck down the Circular letter dated 18 March 1981 as impinging on judicial independence and as being violative of Articles 222(1) and 14.

The Supreme Court gave a literal meaning to the word 'consultation' appearing in Articles 124 and 217 of the Constitution. The Court took the view that the opinion of the CJI is merely consultative and the final decision in the matter of appointment of judges is left to the Executive.[1]

ARGUMENTS IN ADVOCATE ON RECORD ASSOCIATION CASE

Petitioners submitted that *S. P. Gupta case* paid no attention to the mandate of Article 50 and its implications and effect on the interpretation of Articles 124 and 217. Article 50 is the culmination of a long drawn-out movement and struggle for judicial independence.

Petitioners submitted that to save the basic feature of Independence of Judiciary, the court through its decision must construe the word 'Consultation' as equivalent to 'Concurrence'.

On the other hand, the Union of India argued that Article 50 cannot be availed of with regard to the appointment of Judges to the Supreme Court and High Courts, especially in the context of independence of the judiciary.

It was contended that if the primacy is given to the opinion of the Chief Justice expressed during the consultation, then Article 124(2) will become redundant.

---

1. https://www.livelaw.in/judges-appointment-executive-primacy-to-judicial-primacy-and-road-ahead/

The Constitution provides several safeguards for the independence of Judiciary. Therefore, the Parliament or Executive can neither impair Independence of Judiciary, which is the basic structure of the Constitution, nor can they make an amendment in these constitutional provisions.

THE JUDGMENT IN *ADVOCATE ON RECORD ASSOCIATION CASE*

The nine-judge bench of the Supreme Court overruled the *S. P. Gupta judgment.*

It held that, '*in issues regarding the appointment of judges in higher judiciary the opinion of CJI must be given primacy in order to minimize the executive influence in the judicial functions*'.

The court expanded the scope of the word 'Consultation' by construing it in equivalent terms with 'Concurrence'.

The Supreme Court held that '*In the matters of appointment and transfers of Judges, the role of the Chief Justice of India is primal in nature. The Chief Justice of India must take into account the views of two senior-most Judges of the Supreme Court...*'.

CONSTITUTIONAL QUESTIONS ASKED IN SPECIAL REFERENCE CASE OF 1998

Exercising his power under Article 143 of the Constitution of India, the President of India referred the following questions to the Supreme Court:

1. Whether the expression 'consultation with the Chief Justice of India' in Articles 217(1) and 222(1) requires consultation with a plurality of Judges in the formation of the opinion of the CJI or does the sole individual opinion of the CJI constitute consultation within the meaning of the said Articles?
2. Whether the transfer of judges is judicially reviewable in light of the observation of the Supreme Court in the Advocate on Record Association case?
3. Whether Article 124(2) requires the CJI to consult only the two senior-most Judges or whether there should be wider consultation according to past practice?
4. Whether the CJI is entitled to act solely in his individual capacity, without consultation with other Judges of the Supreme Court in respect of all materials and information conveyed by the Government of India for non-appointment of a judge recommended for an appointment?

5. Whether the requirement of consultation by the CJI with his colleagues, who are likely to be conversant with the affairs of the concerned High Court, refers to only those Judges who have that, High Court as a parent High Court and excludes Judges who had occupied the office of a Judge or Chief Justice of that Court on transfer?
6. Whether any recommendations made by the CJI without complying with the norms and consultation process are binding upon the Government of India?

THE JUDGMENT IN SPECIAL REFERENCE CASE OF 1998

The Supreme Court held that:

1. The expression 'consultation with the Chief justice of India' in Articles 217(1) and 222(1) of the Constitution of India requires consultation with a plurality of Judges in the formation of the opinion of the Chief Justice of India. The sole, individual opinion of the Chief Justice of India does not constitute 'consultation' within the meaning of the said Articles.
2. The transfer of Judges is judicially reviewable only to this extent: that the recommendation that has been made by the Chief Justice of India in this behalf has not been made in consultation with the four senior-most Judges of the Supreme Court and/or that the views of the Chief Justices of the concerned High Courts have not been obtained.
3. The CJI must make a recommendation to appoint a Judge of the Supreme Court and to transfer a Chief Justice or Judge of a High Court in consultation with the four senior-most Judges of the Supreme Court. As far as an appointment to the High Court is concerned, the recommendation must be made in consultation with the two senior-most Judges of the Supreme Court.
4. The Chief Justice of India is not entitled to act solely in his individual capacity, without consultation with other Judges of the Supreme Court, in respect of materials and information conveyed by the Government of India for non-appointment of a judge recommended for appointment.
5. The requirement of consultation by the Chief Justice of India with his colleagues who are likely to be conversant with the affairs of the concerned High Court does not refer only to those Judges who have that High Court as a parent High Court. It does not exclude Judges

who have occupied the office of a Judge or Chief Justice of that High Court on transfer.

6. The views of the Judges consulted should be in writing and should be conveyed to the Government of India by the Chief Justice of India along with his views to the extent set out in the body of this opinion.
7. The Chief Justice of India is obliged to comply with the norms and the requirement of the consultation process in making his recommendations to the Government of India.
8. Recommendations made by the Chief Justice of India without complying with the norms and requirements of the consultation process are not binding upon the Government of India.

IMPORTANCE

Through these cases, by a process of 'judicial invention', the 'collegium' system for the appointment of judges came into existence.

IMPACT

Doubts are raised that even the collegium of judges are prone to irrelevant considerations in the matter of selection and more so in the non-selection of meritorious judges to the Supreme Court.

For example, non-elevation of Justice A. P. Shah and Justice U. L. Bhatt to the Supreme Court are cited as instances of prejudice and unfairness.

The collegium system has been accused of lack of transparency and allegations of unfairness. To correct this, the Government of India introduced the National Judicial Appointments Commission (NJAC) Act and the 99th Constitutional Amendment.

However, they were declared unconstitutional by the Supreme Court as they compromise judicial independence. So, the old collegium system still continues.

22

Prakash Singh v. Union of India (2006)

How should the police do the duty? What are the reforms needed?

Prakash Singh judgment issued seven binding directions on police reforms.

The Supreme Court recalled its observation in ***Vineet Narain case*** regarding the need for police reforms.

INTRODUCTION

In *Prakash Singh v. Union of India* and others case, the Supreme Court of India issued **seven binding directions** on police reforms.

Prakash Singh and others were the petitioners and Union of India and others were respondents in the case.

BACKGROUND

Policing in India is governed by the **Indian Police Act, 1861**. Despite radical changes in the political, social and economic situation in the country, there was the absence of any comprehensive review at the national level of the police system.

On 15th November 1977, the Government of India appointed a **National Police Commission**. The commission was appointed for the examination of the role and performance of the police both as a law-enforcing agency and as an institution to protect the rights of the citizens enshrined in the Constitution. After a detailed examination of various issues related to the police system in the country, the Commission submitted its first report in February 1979, second in August 1979 and three reports each in the years 1980 and 1981, including the final report in May 1981.

However, the recommendations of the National Police Commission were not implemented.

In 1996, **Prakash Singh, Former DGP of Uttar Pradesh and DG of BSF**, filed a writ petition in the Supreme Court under **Article 32** of the Constitution praying for '*issue of directions to Government of India to frame a new Police Act on the lines of the model Act drafted by the National Police Commission in order to ensure that the police is made accountable essentially and primarily to the law of the land and the people*'.[1]

COMMITTEES RELATED TO POLICE REFORMS IN INDIA

- National Police Commission (1977-1981)
- Ribeiro Committee
- Padmanabhaiah Committee
- Malimath Committee on Reforms of Criminal Justice System
- Soli Sorabjee Committee

ARGUMENTS

The petitioners stated that the violation of fundamental and human rights of the citizens are generally because of non-enforcement and discriminatory application of the laws. Those having power are not held accountable even for blatant violations of laws. They are not brought to justice for the violations of the rights of citizens in the form of unauthorised detentions, torture, harassment, fabrication of evidence, malicious prosecutions and so on.

According to the petitioners, the **present distortions and aberrations in the functioning of the police have their roots in the Police Act of 1861**. The structure and organisation of police basically remained unchanged all these years.

They contended that there is an immediate need to re-define the scope and functions of police, provide for its accountability to the law of the land and implement the core recommendations of the National Police Commission.

1. https://indiankanoon.org/doc/1090328/

The petitioners submitted that **the commitment, devotion and accountability of the police have to be only to the Rule of Law**. The supervision and control have to be such that it ensures that the police serve the people without any regard to the status and position of any person while investigating a crime or taking preventive measures.

Accordingly, the petitioners **sought a direction to the Union of India to redefine the role and functions of the police and frame a new Police Act** on the lines of the Model Act drafted by the National Police Commission.

They also sought directions against the Union of India and State Governments to constitute various Commissions and Boards laying down the policies and ensuring that police perform their duties and functions free from any pressure.

The petitioners also called for the **separation of investigation work from that of law and order**.

The Supreme Court issued a notice to all the State Governments and Union Territories. None of the State Governments/Union Territories objected to any of the suggestion put forth by the petitioners and the Solicitor General of India.

THE JUDGMENT

The Supreme Court recalled its observation in the ***Vineet Narain v. Union of India*** (1998). In that case, the Court observed that '*there is an urgent need for the State Governments to set up the requisite mechanism and directed the Central Government to pursue the matter of police reforms with the State Governments and ensure the setting up of a mechanism for selection/appointment, tenure, transfer and posting of not merely the Chief of the State Police but also all police officers of the rank of Superintendents of Police and above*'.[2]

In the discharge of its constitutional duties and obligations under **Article 32 read with Article 142** of the Constitution, the Court issued the following directions to the Central Government, State Governments and Union Territories for compliance till framing of the appropriate legislation:

1. The State Governments are directed to constitute a **State Security Commission** in every state to ensure that the State Government does not exercise unwarranted influence or pressure on the State police. This body shall be headed by the Chief Minister or Home

2. https://main.sci.gov.in/jonew/judis/13548.pdf

Minister as Chairman and have the DGP of the state as its ex-officio Secretary.

2. The **Director-General of Police** of the state shall be selected by the State Government from **amongst the three senior-most officers** of the department who have been empanelled for promotion to that rank by the Union Public Service Commission. He should have a **minimum tenure of at least two years** irrespective of his date of superannuation.
3. Police officers on operational duties in the field like the Inspector General of Police, Deputy Inspector General of Police, Superintendent of Police and Station House Officer shall also have a prescribed **minimum tenure of two years**. This would be subject to promotion and retirement of the officer.
4. The **investigating police shall be separated from the law and order** police to ensure speedier investigation, better expertise and improved rapport with the people.
5. There shall be a **Police Establishment Board** in each state which shall decide all transfers, postings, promotions and other service-related matters of officers of and below the rank of Deputy Superintendent of Police. The Establishment Board shall be a departmental body comprising the Director General of Police and four other senior officers of the department.
6. There shall be a **Police Complaints Authority** at the district level to look into complaints against police officers of and up to the rank of Deputy Superintendent of Police. Similarly, there should be another Police Complaints Authority at the state level to look into complaints against officers of the rank of Superintendent of Police and above.
7. The Central Government shall also set up a **National Security Commission** at the Union level to prepare a panel for being placed before the appropriate Appointing Authority, for selection and placement of Chiefs of the Central Police Organizations (CPO), who should also be given a minimum tenure of two years.

The Supreme Court said, '*the aforesaid directions shall be complied with by the Central Government, State Governments or Union Territories on or before 31st December 2006*'.

IMPORTANCE

It is a landmark judgment aimed at reforming the policing system in the country.

The guidelines issued in the case tried to insulate the police force from excessive political influence and pressure. It also assured the police officers the security of tenure and shielded them from unnecessary transfers and harassment.

IMPACT

Though the Supreme Court issued the guidelines, they are generally not followed by the Central Government, State Governments or Union Territories.

An assessment by Commonwealth Human Rights Initiative (CHRI) about the compliance status of states and union territories with the Supreme Court directives on police reforms has revealed that there has not been 'a single case of full compliance' and that the governments have 'either blatantly rejected, ignored, or diluted significant features of the directives'.

Several states have either failed to comply with or have violated the Supreme Court's directives in dealing with the tenure and selection of the DGP. A **Contempt Petition** was also filed by Prakash Singh and a few others, and for the violation of the Apex Court's direction is ***Prakash Singh case***.

23

M. Nagaraj v. Union of India (2006)

Is it mandatory for the State to make reservations for SC/ST in the matter of promotions?

M. Nagaraj case dealt with a challenge to constitutional amendments aimed at nullifying the impact of ***Indira Sawhney judgments*** of 1992.

The judgment upheld the essence of the ***Indira Sawhney*** judgment. However, it provided flexibility to states to make a reservation for SC/ST in a matter of promotions.

The Supreme Court reiterated that the ceiling-limit of 50 per cent, the concept of creamy layer and the compelling reasons, namely backwardness, the inadequacy of representation and overall administrative efficiency.

Regarding the issue related to the 'extent of reservation', the Court said that the State will have to show in each case the existence of the compelling reasons.

INTRODUCTION

In *M. Nagaraj v. Union of India* case, the Supreme Court dealt with a challenge to constitutional amendments aimed at nullifying the impact of judgments on **reservations in promotions for SC and ST** employees.

M. Nagaraj and others were petitioners and Union of India and others were respondents in the case.

BACKGROUND

Indira Sawhney v. Union of India (Mandal case) judgment in 1992 restricted the benefits of reservation to initial appointment only. It held that '***Reservation in promotion is constitutionally impermissible*** *as once the advantaged and disadvantaged are made equal and are brought in one class then any further* *benefit extended for promotion based on the inequality existing prior to the initial benefits would be like treating equals unequally'.*[1]

This affected SC and ST employees, and in order to ensure that reservations in promotions continued, **Clause 4A** was inserted under Article 16.

The ***Indira Sawhney judgment*** also held that '*the reservations contemplated in Clause (4) of Article 16 should not exceed 50 per cent*'. To negate this, **Clause 4B** was inserted under **Article 16**. It aimed to ensure that while calculating the quota for a particular year, the unfilled vacancies or backlogs from the previous year was not clubbed with the regular quota of that year.

The Supreme Court in ***Indira Sawhney case*** and ***S Vinod Kumar case (1996)*** held that relaxation of qualifying marks and standards of evaluation for reservation in the promotion were not permissible under Article 16(4) in view of the command contained in **Article 335**.

To restore the relaxations, the 82nd Amendment added a proviso to Article 335 that allowed '*relaxation in qualifying marks in any examination or lowering the standards of evaluation, for reservation in matters of promotion to any class or classes of services or posts in connection with the affairs of the Union or of a State*'.

The Supreme Court judgments in ***Virpal Singh Chauhan case (1995)*** and ***Ajit Singh Januja case (1996)*** had affected the SC/ST employees in the matter of seniority on promotion to the next higher grade. So, the government enacted 85th Amendment to provide **'consequential seniority'** after the promotion under Article 16(4)(A).

ARTICLE 16: EQUALITY OF OPPORTUNITY IN MATTERS OF PUBLIC EMPLOYMENT[2]

ARTICLE 16(1): There shall be equality of opportunity for all citizens in matters relating to employment or appointment to any office under the State.

ARTICLE 16(2): No citizen shall, on grounds only of religion, race, caste, sex, descent, place of birth, residence or any of them, be ineligible for, or discriminated against in respect of, any employment or office under the State.

1. https://indiankanoon.org/doc/1363234/
2. The Constitution of India, Ministry of Law and Justice (Legislative Department)

ARTICLE 16(3): Nothing in this Article shall prevent Parliament from making any law prescribing, in regard to a class or classes of employment or appointment to an office under the Government of, or any local or other authority within, a State or Union territory, any requirement as to residence within that State or Union territory prior to such employment or appointment.

ARTICLE 16(4): Nothing in this Article shall prevent the State from making any provision for the reservation of appointments or posts in favour of any backward class of citizens which, in the opinion of the State, is not adequately represented in the services under the State.

ARTICLE 16(4A): Nothing in this Article shall prevent the State from making any provision for reservation in matters of promotion, with consequential seniority, to any class or classes of posts in the services under the State in favour of the Scheduled Castes and the Scheduled Tribes which, in the opinion of the State, are not adequately represented in the services under the State.

ARTICLE 16(4B): Nothing in this Article shall prevent the State from considering any unfilled vacancies of a year which are reserved for being filled up in that year in accordance with any provision for reservation made under Clause (4) or Clause (4A) as a separate class of vacancies to be filled up in any succeeding year or years and such class of vacancies shall not be considered together with the vacancies of the year in which they are being filled up for determining the ceiling of 50 per cent reservation on total number of vacancies of that year.

ARTICLE 16(5): Nothing in this Article shall affect the operation of any law which provides that the incumbent of an office in connection with the affairs of any religious or denominational institution or any member of the governing body thereof shall be a person professing a particular religion or belonging to a particular denomination.

Petitioners challenged the constitutional validity of these constitutional amendments that were aimed at negating the effects of various judgments of the Supreme Court.

ARGUMENTS

Petitioners contended that the Constitution (85th Amendment) Act, 2001, reverses the decisions of the Supreme Court in the case of ***Union of India v. Virpal Singh Chauhan, Ajit Singh Januja v. the State of Punjab, Indira Sawhney v. Union of India***.

They argued that the Parliament has appropriated the judicial power to itself and has acted as an appellate authority by reversing the judicial pronouncements by the use of the power of amendment. It is violative of the basic structure of the Constitution.

It was submitted that the limited power of amendment cannot become an unlimited one. A **limited amendment power is one of the basic features** of our Constitution.

Petitioners submitted that the Parliament cannot under Article 368 expand its amending power so as to acquire for itself the right to abrogate the Constitution.

Petitioners pleaded that, the amendment also seeks to alter the fundamental right of equality which is part of the basic structure of the Constitution. They said, '*by attaching consequential seniority to the accelerated promotion, the 85th amendment violates equality in Article 14 read with Article 16(1)*'.

They further said that there will be impairment of efficiency if reservation in the matter of promotion is provided with consequential seniority.

They argued that the 85th Amendment which provides for reservation in promotion with consequential seniority would result in reverse discrimination in the percentage of representation of the reserved category officers in the higher cadre.

The reservation in promotion also runs contrary to the judgment of the Supreme Court in ***Indira Sawhney case.*** So, they challenged the constitutional validity of the 77th Amendment Act.

In **summary**, the **substance of the arguments** of the petitioners was that:

- **Equality is a part of the basic structure** and it is impossible to conceive of the Constitution without equality as one of its central components.

- **Article 16 is integral to equality** and it has to be read with Article 14 and with several Articles in Part-IV.
- The Constitution places an **important significance on public employment** and the rule of equality as much as a specific guarantee is given under Article 16 protecting equality principles in public employment.
- **Equality of opportunity cannot be overruled by affirmative action**. A balance has to be evolved to promote equal opportunities while protecting individual rights.

On the question of balancing of fundamental rights vis-à-vis directive principles, it was submitted that the *'directive principles cannot be used to undermine the "basic structure" principles underlying fundamental rights including principles of equality, fundamental freedoms, due process, religious freedom, and judicial enforcement'.*[3]

On the other hand, respondents argued that the **power of amendment under Article 368 is a 'constituent' power and not a 'constituted power'.** In other words, there are no implied limitations on the constituent power under Article 368.

They also contended that the interpretation placed on the Constitution by the Court becomes part of the Constitution and therefore, it is open to amendment under Article 368.

Respondents further argued that the amendments which may abrogate individual rights but which promote Constitutional ideal of 'justice, social, economic and political' and the idea of 'equality of status' are not liable to be struck down under Article 14 or Article 16(1) and consequently, such amendments cannot violate the basic structure of the Constitution.

It was submitted that the principle of balancing of rights of the general category and reserved category in the context of Article 16 has no relation to the basic feature of the Constitution.

They also contended that **power under Article 16(4) overrides Article 16(1)**. The only limitation on this power is that it should act within four corners of Article 16(4), namely backward classes, which in the opinion of the State are not adequately represented in public employment.

It was urged that **jurisprudence relating to public services do not constitute a basic feature of the Constitution**. The right to consideration for promotion in service matters is not a basic feature.

The respondents contended that **Articles 16(4A) and 16(4B) and the changes to Article 335 are merely enabling provisions**. If the action

---

3. https://main.sci.gov.in/jonew/judis/28160.pdf

taken by the appropriate Government under these provisions found to be arbitrary, then the Supreme Court will set it right.

Respondents submitted that the maximum of 50 per cent limit set by the Supreme Court for reservation can be reserved in such manner as the 'appropriate Government may deem fit'. Article 16(4B) makes an exception to 50 per cent ceiling limit imposed by ***Indira Sawhney*** by providing that the vacancies of previous years will not be considered with the current year's vacancies. This is an enabling power and cannot be rendered invalid.

For these reasons, respondents submit that there is no infirmity in the constitutional amendments that are in question.

LEGAL ISSUES INVOLVED

The petitioners challenged the constitutional validity of:

- The Constitution (77th Amendment) Act, 1995, which inserted Clause 4A in Article 16
- The Constitution (81st Amendment) Act, 2000, which inserted Clause 4B in Article 16
- The Constitution (82nd Amendment) Act, 2000, which inserted a proviso to Article 335
- The Constitution (85th Amendment) Act, 2001, which changed the wording of Article 16(4A).

THE JUDGMENT

After hearing the arguments of the petitioners and the respondents, the Supreme Court held that the **constitutional amendments insert Articles 16(4A) and 16(4B) flow from Article 16(4)**.

They do not alter the structure of Article 16(4). They retain the controlling factors 'backwardness and inadequacy of representation which enables the States to provide for reservation keeping in mind the overall efficiency of the State administration under Article 335'.

These **amendments are confined only to SCs and STs**. They **do not dilute any of the constitutional requirements**, namely the ceiling limit of 50 per cent (quantitative limitation), the concept of the creamy layer (qualitative exclusion), the sub-classification between OBC on one hand and SCs and STs on the other hand as held in ***Indira Sawhney case***.

The Supreme Court **reiterated that the ceiling limit of 50 per cent**, the **concept of creamy layer** and the **compelling reasons**, namely backwardness, the inadequacy of representation and overall administrative efficiency are all constitutional requirements without which the structure of equality of opportunity in Article 16 would collapse.

Regarding the **issue related to the 'extent of reservation'**, the Court said that the **State will have to show in each case the existence of the compelling reasons**, namely backwardness, the inadequacy of representation and overall administrative efficiency before making provision for reservation.

The court accepted the argument that the impugned provision is an enabling provision. **The State is not bound to make a reservation for SC/ST in a matter of promotions**. However, **if States wish to exercise their discretion** and make such provision, **they have to collect quantifiable data showing backwardness of the class** and inadequacy of representation of that class in public employment in addition to compliance of Article 335.

Court further held that even if the State has compelling reasons, they will have to see that its reservation provision does not lead to excessiveness so as to breach the ceiling limit of 50 per cent or obliterate the creamy layer or extend the reservation indefinitely.

Subjected to these conditions, the Supreme Court **upheld the constitutional validity** of the Constitution (77th Amendment) Act, 1995, the Constitution (81st Amendment) Act, 2000, the Constitution (82nd Amendment) Act, 2000, and the Constitution (85th Amendment) Act, 2001.

IMPORTANCE

The judgment upheld the essence of the ***Indira Sawhney*** judgment. However, it provided flexibility to states to make a reservation for SC/ST in a matter of promotions. In trying to balance the interests of different sections of the population, the judgment put certain conditions in making a reservation for SC/STs.

IMPACT

The union government considered the **verdict not implementable**.

Recently, the Centre and various state governments had **sought reconsideration** of the ***M. Nagaraj judgment*** on various grounds, including that the members of the SC/ST communities were presumed to be backward and considering the stigma attached to their caste, they should be given reservation even in job promotions.

24

Lily Thomas v. Union of India (2013)

Should not criminals be kept away from politics?

Should not MPs, and MLAs be disqualified on the date of a criminal conviction?

Lily Thomas judgment was aimed at freeing the political setup from criminal elements.

The Supreme Court held subsection (4) of Section 8 of the Representation of Peoples Act is *ultra vires* the Constitution.

INTRODUCTION

Lily Thomas v. Union of India is an attempt by the Supreme Court to free the political setup from the criminal elements.

Lily Thomas was the petitioner and Union of India and others were respondents in the case.

BACKGROUND

The Constituent Assembly of India intended to lay down some disqualifications for persons being chosen as and for being a member of either Houses of Parliament as well as a member of the Legislative Assembly or Legislative Council of the State.

Accordingly, the Constitution under **Article 102** and **Article 191** provides for the disqualifications for membership of either Houses of Parliament and disqualifications for membership of the Legislative Assembly or Legislative Council of the State, respectively.

ARTICLE 102 AND ARTICLE 191

Article 102(1): Disqualifications for membership - A person shall be disqualified for being chosen as and for being a member of either House of Parliament:

(a) If he holds any office of profit under the Government of India or the Government of any State other than an office declared by Parliament by law not to disqualify its holder
(b) If he is of unsound mind and stands so declared by a competent court
(c) If he is an undischarged insolvent
(d) If he is not a citizen of India, or has voluntarily acquired the citizenship of a foreign State or is under any acknowledgement of allegiance or adherence to a foreign State
(e) If he is so disqualified by or under any law made by Parliament

Article 191(1): Disqualifications for membership - A person shall be disqualified for being chosen as and for being a member of the Legislative Assembly or Legislative Council of a State:

(a) If he holds any office of profit under the Government of India or the Government of any State specified in the First Schedule, other than an office declared by the Legislature of the State by law not to disqualify its holder;
(b) If he is of unsound mind and stands so declared by a competent court
(c) If he is an undischarged insolvent
(d) If he is not a citizen of India, or has voluntarily acquired the citizenship of a foreign State, or is under any acknowledgement of allegiance or adherence to a foreign State
(e) If he is so disqualified by or under any law made by Parliament.

In addition to the disqualifications mentioned in the Constitution, Article 102(1)(e) and Article 191(1)(e) empowers the Parliament to make any law to lay down disqualifications for membership of Parliament and State Legislatures.

Exercising its power under these Articles, the Parliament in Chapter-III of the **Representation of the People Act, 1951,** provided for certain disqualifications.

Section 8, under Chapter-III of the Representation of the People Act, 1951, provides for disqualification on conviction for certain offences. Sections 8(1) and 8(2) list out the offences and the duration of punishment, for which a person attracts disqualification.

Section 8(3) states that '*A person* ***convicted of any offence*** *and sentenced to imprisonment for* ***not less than two years****, other than any offence referred to in Sub-section (1) or Sub-section (2), shall be disqualified from the date of such conviction and shall continue to be disqualified for a further period of six years since his release*'.

However, **Section 8(4)** states that '*Notwithstanding anything in Sub-section (1), Sub-section (2) or Sub-section (3), a disqualification under either subsection shall not, in the case of a person who on the date of the conviction is* ***a member of Parliament or the Legislature of a State****, take effect until three months have elapsed from that date or, if within that period an appeal or application for revision is brought in respect of the conviction or the sentence, until that appeal or application is disposed of by the court*'.

In other words, a Member of Parliament or the Legislature of a State cannot be disqualified under Sections 8(1), 8(2) and 8(3) until three months have elapsed from the date of the conviction or until the appeal is disposed of by the court if he/she filed an appeal within that three months period against the conviction or the sentence.

Lily Thomas filed a petition in the Supreme Court and challenged the constitutional validity of the 'protection' provided in Subsection (4) of Section 8 of the Representation of the People Act, 1951, for a Member of Parliament or the Legislature of a State.

ARGUMENTS

The petitioners contended that the **same disqualifications** are provided for a **person being chosen as a member** of either House of Parliament, or the State Assembly or Legislative Council of the State and for a **person being a member** of either the House of Parliament or of the Legislative Assembly or the Legislative Council of a State. Therefore, the disqualifications for a person to be elected as a member of either House of the Parliament or a member of the State Legislature and for a person to continue as a member of either House of Parliament or a member of the state legislature cannot be different.

To support their submission, they cited *Election Commission of India v. Saka Venkata Rao (1953)* judgment which held that Article 191 lays down the same set of disqualifications for election as well as for continuing as a member.

So, they submitted that Subsection (4) of Section 8 of the Act, which provides an opportunity for the sitting member to file an appeal against the conviction or sentence within three months from the date of conviction, is in contravention of the provisions of Clause (1) of Articles 102 and 191 of the Constitution.

They also submitted that during the Constituent Assembly debate, an amendment, moved by one of its member Mr. Shibban Lal Saksena, to insert the similar protection was rejected. Despite this, the Parliament has enacted Subsection (4) of Section 8 of the Representation of the People Act, 1951.

They contended that in the absence of a provision in Articles 102 and 191 of the Constitution conferring power on Parliament to make a provision protecting sitting members of either House of Parliament or a member of State legislature, the **Parliament lacks legislative powers to enact Section 8(4)** of the Act and therefore, it is *ultra vires* the Constitution.

They also submitted that Subsection (4) of Section 8 of the Act is **arbitrary and discriminatory and is violative of Article 14 of the Constitution**, as it classifies the sitting members of Parliament and State Legislatures into a separate category and protected them from disqualifications.

Thus, the petitioners argued that as soon as a person is convicted of any of the offences mentioned in Subsections (1), (2) and (3) of Section 8 of the Act, he becomes disqualified from continuing as a Member of Parliament or of a State Legislature notwithstanding the fact that he has filed an appeal or a revision against the conviction.

On the other hand, respondents submitted that the validity of Subsection (4) of Section 8 of the Act has been upheld by the Constitution Bench of the Supreme Court in *K. Prabhakaran v. P. Jayarajan.*

They submitted that the purpose of the Subsection (4) of Section 8 of the Act is not to confer an advantage on sitting members of Parliament or of a State Legislature but **to protect the House**. Placing their argument on the ***K. Prabhakaran case*** judgment, petitioners said the disqualification will have two consequences:

- The strength of membership of the House shall stand reduced, so also the strength of the political party to which such convicted member may belong and the Government in power may be surviving on a thin majority where each member counts significantly and disqualification of even one member may have a deleterious effect on the functioning of the Government.

- A bye-election shall have to be held which exercise may prove to be futile, also resulting in complications in the event of the convicted member being acquitted by a superior criminal court.

For these reasons, the Parliament has classified the sitting members of Parliament or a State Legislature in a separate category and provided 'protection' in Subsection (4) of Section 8 of the Act.

The respondents also submitted that the reality of the Indian judicial system is that acquittals in the levels of the Appellate Court such as the High Court are very high.

They argued that the power to legislate on disqualification of members of Parliament and the State Legislature conferred on Parliament carries with it the incidental power to say when the disqualification will take effect. Therefore, the source of legislative power for enacting Section 8(4) of the Act is very much there in Articles 102(1)(e) and 191(1)(e) of the Constitution.

THE JUDGMENT

After hearing the arguments of the petitioners and the respondents, the Supreme Court held that '*the powers of Parliament to make any law providing disqualifications for membership can be located only in Articles 102(1)(e) and 191(1)(e) of the Constitution. A reading of the aforesaid two provisions makes it abundantly clear that Parliament is to make* ***one law for a person to be disqualified for being chosen as, and for being, a member*** *of either House of Parliament or of State Legislature*'.

The Constitution Bench of the Supreme Court in *Election Commission of India v. Saka Venkata Rao* observed that '*...the same set of disqualifications for election as well as for continuing as a member*'. Thus, the **Parliament does not have the power to make different laws** for a person to be disqualified for being chosen as a member and for a person to be disqualified for continuing as a Member of Parliament or the State Legislature.

In other words, due to disqualification, if a person cannot be chosen as a Member of Parliament or State Legislature, he cannot continue as a Member of Parliament or the State Legislature due the same disqualification.

The Court also held that '*once a person who was a member of either House of Parliament or House of the State Legislature becomes disqualified by or under any law made by Parliament, his seat automatically falls vacant by virtue of Articles 101(3)(a) and 190(3)(a) of the Constitution and Parliament cannot make a provision to defer the date on which the disqualification of a sitting member will have effect and prevent his seat becoming vacant'.*

In other words, Articles 101(3)(a) and 190(3)(a) of the Constitution put express limitations on such powers of the Parliament to defer the date on which the disqualifications would have an effect.

The seat of a member, who becomes subject to any of the disqualifications, will fall vacant on the date on which the member incurs the disqualification and cannot await the decision of the President or the Governor under Articles 103 and 192, respectively, of the Constitution. However, the filling of the seat which falls vacant may await the decision of the President or the Governor.

Accordingly, Subsection (4) of Section 8 of the Act which carves out a protection in the case of the disqualifications under Subsections (1), (2) and (3) of Section 8 of the Act or which defers the date on which the disqualification will take effect is **beyond the powers conferred on Parliament** by the Constitution.

Therefore, the Court held that Subsection (4) of Section 8 of the Act is *ultra vires* the Constitution.

The court also made it clear that the sitting members of Parliament and State Legislature who have already been convicted for any of the offences mentioned in subsection (1), (2) and (3) of Section 8 of the Act and who have filed appeals which are pending and are saved from the disqualifications by virtue of Subsection (4) of Section 8 of the Act will not be affected by this judgment. In other words, the judgment will be enforced prospectively, from the date of Judgment.

IMPORTANCE

Criminality in politics or criminals sitting in the Parliament and legislatures is an important issue that has for long been debated.

Previously convicted MPs and MLAs were able to file appeals within the stipulated three months without giving up their membership and managed to remain MPs or MLAs, often for long years. After the Lily Thomas judgment, while convicted MPs and MLAs still have the right to appeal, they immediately cease to be members of the House.

The judgment will have a profound impact on cleansing our political system.

IMPACT

In an attempt to nullify this judgment, the Representation of the People (Second Amendment and Validation) Bill, 2013 was introduced in the Rajya Sabha. It provided that there would be no automatic disqualification of MPs and MLAs upon conviction. However, this was later withdrawn.

Since the judgment, some lawmakers have lost their seats after conviction.

25

T. S. R. Subramanian v. Union of India (2013)

Are Civil Servants bound to follow oral directives?

Should not the services like IAS be free from political interference?

T. S. R. Subramanian case aimed at professionalising the bureaucracy, promote efficiency and good governance.

Taking a cue from Vishaka case, Prakash Singh case and Vineet Narain case, it issued directions to the government to make the bureaucracy free from unnecessary political interference, provide them with the security of tenure, increase the bureaucratic efficiency and thus achieve good governance.

It also sought to fix the accountability for any action taken by requiring that the orders need to be in writing.

INTRODUCTION

T. S. R. Subramanian v. Union of India is a landmark case which was aimed at professionalising the bureaucracy, promote efficiency and good governance.

T. S. R. Subramanian and others were the petitioners and Union of India and others were the respondents in the case.

BACKGROUND

T. S. R. Subramanian, former Cabinet Secretary, along with 82 other retired bureaucrats from different services like, IAS, IPS, and IFS, filed a public interest writ petition in the Supreme Court by invoking Article 32 of the Constitution. The objective of the Writ petition was '*to insulate the bureaucracy from political interference and to put an end to frequent transfers of civil servants by political bosses*'.[1]

1. https://www.thehindu.com/news/national/in-major-reform-sc-orders-fixed-tenure-for-bureaucrats/article5299939.ece

Prayers made in the writ petition were based on various reports and recommendations made by several Committees appointed for improving public administration. Some of the important such committees were:

- Santhanam Committee, 1962
- Jha Commission, 1986
- Central Staffing Scheme, 1996
- Conference of Chief Ministers on Effective and Responsive Administration, 1997
- Hota Committee, 2004
- Second Administrative Reforms Commission, 2008

The petitioners sought relief from the Supreme Court in the following matters:

1. Issue a direction requiring the respondents to create an 'independent' **Civil Service Board or Commission** both at the Centre and the State.
2. Issue a direction requiring the respondents to fixed tenure for civil servants ensuring stability.
3. Issue a direction requiring the respondents to mandate that every civil servant formally record all such instructions/directions/orders/suggestions which he/she receives not only from his/her administrative superiors, but also from political authorities, legislators, commercial and business interests and other persons/quarters having interest, wielding influence or purporting to represent those in authority.

ARGUMENTS

Petitioners referred elaborately to these reports and highlighted the necessity of the creation of a **Civil Service Board (CSB)**, with a degree of independence, so that it can make recommendations on all transfers and postings without sacrificing the executive freedom of the Government.

They suggested that the CSB shall function in a bare advisory capacity and its recommendations will not impose any constraint on the independence of the political authority to effect postings and transfers, including premature transfers.

The petitioners highlighted the necessity for providing a fixed tenure for civil servants **ensuring stability,** which is highly **necessary for implementing various programmes** which will have a social and economic impact on the society.

They also highlighted the reasons for recoding of instructions, directions and orders by the civil servants so that they can function independently and the **possibility of arbitrary and illegal decisions could be avoided**.

On the other hand, the respondents opposed the creation of a CSB at the Centre and the State levels, as it would amount to **interference in the functions of the governments** headed by the political executives, who are directly responsible to the people. They submitted that in the absence of any relevant provision in the Constitution or the laws made by the Centre and the State Governments, the involvement of any person who is not part of the Centre or the State Government is not advisable.

They also said that the creation of the CSB would lead to a dual line of control, creating complexities in managing administrative functions and affecting the efficiency of civil servants.

The Union of India also submitted that for fixing the minimum tenures of cadre post in the Indian Administrative Service was initiated in November 2006 by the Department of Personnel and Training. At the time of the hearing, notification providing for two years minimum tenure for IAS posting was issued for 13 States/Joint Cadres.

THE JUDGMENT

The Supreme Court went through this report in detail. It observed that '*much of the deterioration of the standards of probity and accountability, according to the Petitioners, can be traced to the practice of issuing and acting on verbal instructions or oral orders which are not recorded*'.

Rule 3(3) of the All India Services (Conduct) Rules, 1968, also states that the directions of the officials superior shall ordinarily be in writing.

Under the Constitution, UPSC or the State PSCs are to be consulted in all matters relating to the method of recruitment to civil services and on the principles to be followed in making appointments to civil services and posts and in making promotions and transfers from one service to another. However, the Court observed '*the UPSCs and PSCs are being denuded of their powers of consultation while making promotions and transfer from one service to another*'.

The principles governing the roles and responsibilities of the political executive and civil servants are constitutionally defined and also based on the basis of various rules framed by the President and Governor for the conduct of business in the Government. Therefore, the Supreme Court observed that 'Civil servants have to be accountable, of course to their political executive but they have to function under the Constitution, consequently they are also accountable to the people of this country'.

On the question of constituting an independent CSB as recommended by Hota Committee, the Supreme Court observed that '***Retired persons****, howsoever eminent they may be,* ***shall not guide the transfers and postings****, disciplinary action, suspension, reinstatement, etc. of civil servants, unless supported by law enacted by the Parliament or the State Legislature*'.

Instead, the Court suggested an alternative composition for the CSB, consisting of **high-ranking in-service officers**, who are experts in their respective fields, with the Cabinet Secretary at the Centre and Chief Secretary at the State level.

It also suggested that the '*Parliament under Article 309 of the Constitution can enact a Civil Service Act, setting up a CSB, which can guide and advice the political executive transfer and postings, disciplinary action, etc*'.

Therefore, the Supreme Court directed the Centre, State Governments and the Union Territories to **constitute such Boards** with high-ranking serving officers within a period of three months till the Parliament brings in a proper legislation in setting up the CSB.

The Court observed that fixed minimum tenure would not only enable the civil servants to achieve their professional targets, but also help them to function as effective instruments of public policy. Minimum assured service tenure ensures efficient service delivery and also increased efficiency.

Therefore, it directed the Centre, State Governments and the Union Territories to **issue appropriate directions to secure providing of minimum tenure** of service to various civil servants within a period of three months.

The Supreme Court expressed the view that the civil servants cannot function on the basis of verbal or oral instructions, orders, suggestions, proposals and so on, and they must also be protected against wrongful and arbitrary pressure exerted by the administrative superiors, political executive, business and other vested interests.

Recording of instructions and directions are necessary for fixing responsibility and ensuring accountability in the functioning of civil servants and to uphold institutional integrity.

Further, **Section 3 of the RTI Act** confers right to information to all citizens and a corresponding obligation under Section 4 on every public authority to maintain records so that the information sought for can be provided. Oral and verbal instructions, if not recorded, could not be provided.

Therefore, the Supreme Court directed the Centre, State Governments and the Union Territories to **issue directions like Rule 3(3) of the All India Services (Conduct) Rules, 1968,** in their respective States and Union Territories which will be carried out within three months from the date of judgment.

IMPORTANCE

The judgment aims to make the bureaucracy free from unnecessary political interference, provide them with the security of tenure, increase the bureaucratic efficiency and thus to achieve good governance.

It also sought to fix the accountability for any action taken by requiring that the orders need to be in writing.

By bringing in the relevant provision of the RTI Act, the judgment upheld the accountability of civil servants to the public.

IMPACT

In compliance with the Apex Court's directions, amendments in Rule 7 of the IAS, IPS and IFS (Cadre) Rules have been carried out. For other Central Services, the respective Cadre Controlling Authorities were directed to implement the Apex Court's directions.[2]

However, in most of the states, the civil servants are transferred frequently and the CSB has remained only in paper.

2. http://pib.nic.in/newsite/PrintRelease.aspx?relid=124493

26

National Legal Services Authority v. Union of India (2014)

Should transgender people be considered as a third gender?

If yes, should there be a legal recognition for the third gender?

The National Legal Services Authority (NALSA) *case* recognised Hijras/Eunuchs as 'third gender'.

It tried to address the grievances of the members of the Transgender Community in India and extended them all the benefits of the socially and educationally backward classes.

INTRODUCTION

National Legal Services Authority v. Union of India is a landmark case which dealt with the grievances of the members of the Transgender Community in India.

The National Legal Services Authority was the petitioner and the Union of India and others were the respondents in the case.

BACKGROUND

At times, in certain persons, their innate perception of themselves is not in conformity with the sex assigned to them at birth. Countries all over the world, including India, grappled with the question of attribution of gender to persons who believe that they belong to the opposite sex.

When a person acquires gender characteristics of the sex which conform to their perception of gender that is different from the gender assigned at birth, it will lead to legal and social complications since their official record is found to be at variance with the assumed gender identity.

However, as recognised in the Yogyakarta Principles, everyone has the right to recognition everywhere as a person before the law. Persons of diverse sexual orientations and gender identities shall enjoy legal capacity in all aspects of life.

The **Yogyakarta Principles** also recognises fundamental rights such as the right to life, right to privacy, right to freedom of opinion and expression and so on, regardless of sexual orientation or gender identity.

These principles are recognized by the UN bodies, Regional Human Rights Bodies, National Courts and Government Commissions all over the world and considered them as an important tool for identifying the obligations of States to respect, protect and fulfil the human rights of all persons regardless of their gender identity.

Despite recognition of such principles, Transgender Communities in India faced harassment, discrimination, and gender identity problem. The National Legal Services Authority came forward to advocate their cause by filing Writ Petition in 2012.

The Transgender Communities sought a legal declaration of their gender identity than the one assigned to them, male or female, at the time of birth.

The 'Transgender Community' comprises of Hijras, eunuchs, Kothis, Aravanis, Jogappas, Shiv-Shakti and so on.

ARGUMENTS

The petitioners argued that non-recognition of the identity of the Transgender Community as a third gender denies them the right of equality before the law and equal protection of the law guaranteed under **Article 14** of the Constitution and violates the rights guaranteed to them under **Article 21** of the Constitution of India.

They submitted that every person of the Transgender Community has a legal right to decide their sexual orientation and to espouse and determine their identity.

They also contended that, since the Transgender Communities are neither treated as male or female nor given the status of a third gender, they are being deprived of many of the rights and privileges which other persons enjoy as citizens of this country.

They argued that the right to choose one's gender identity is integral to the right to lead a life with dignity, which is guaranteed by Article 21 of the Constitution of India.

Transgender Communities are deprived of social and cultural participation and hence restricted access to education, health care and public places, which deprives them of the Constitutional guarantee of equality before the law and equal protection of laws.

Further, it was also pointed out that the community also faces discrimination to contest the election, right to vote, employment, to get licenses and so on; in effect, treated as an outcast and untouchable.

They also submitted that the State cannot discriminate them on the ground of gender, violating Articles 14 to 16 and 21 of the Constitution of India.

The petitioners also submitted that transgender persons have to be declared 'socially and educationally backward classes' of citizens and must be accorded all benefits available to that class of persons, which are being extended to male and female genders.

On the other hand, the Union of India submitted that the problems highlighted by the transgender community are a sensitive human issue, which calls for serious attention. It was pointed out that, under the aegis of the Ministry of Social Justice and Empowerment, an 'Expert Committee on Issues relating to Transgender' has been constituted to conduct an in-depth study of the problems relating to transgender persons to make appropriate recommendations to the Ministry.

WHAT IS NALSA?

NALSA is a legislative body constituted under the Legal Services Authorities Act, 1987 with the objective to provide free legal services to weaker sections of society. The most important functions of NALSA are:

a. Conduct Lok Adalats for settlement of disputes
b. Provide free legal aid and advice, especially to the marginalized
c. Spread legal awareness
d. Promote alternate mechanisms of dispute resolution

THE JUDGMENT

The Supreme Court observed that the recognition of 'sex identity gender' of persons and 'guarantee to equality and non-discrimination' on the ground of gender identity or expression is increasingly gaining acceptance in international law and therefore, be applied in India as well.

Due to the absence of suitable legislation protecting the rights of the members of the transgender community, they are facing discrimination in various areas and hence the Court said it is necessary to follow the International Conventions to which India is a party and to give due respect to other non-binding International Conventions and principles.

In *Kesavananda Bharati v. State of Kerala* (1973), it was stated that in view of Article 51 of the Constitution, the Court must interpret the language of the Constitution in the light of the UN Charter and the solemn declaration subscribed to it by India.

Article 14 of the Constitution states that '*the State shall not deny any person equality before the law and equal protection of the law*'. Article 14 does not restrict the word 'person' and its application only to male or female.

Therefore, the Supreme Court held that '*transgender persons who are neither male/female fall within the expression 'person' and hence, entitled to legal protection of laws in all spheres of State activity, including employment, healthcare, education as well as equal civil and citizenship rights, as enjoyed by any other citizen of this country*'.

The Court held that '*discrimination on the ground of sexual orientation or gender identity impairs equality before the law and equal protection of the law and violates Article 14 of the Constitution of India*'.

Articles 15 and 16 prohibit discrimination against any citizen on certain enumerated grounds, including the ground of "sex". Both Articles prohibit all forms of gender bias and gender-based discrimination. So, the Supreme Court held that '*the discrimination on the ground of "sex" under Articles 15 and 16 includes discrimination on the ground of gender identity. The expression "sex" used in Articles 15 and 16 is not just limited to the biological sex of male or female, but intended to include people who consider themselves to be neither male or female*'.

It held that '*the Transgender communities are legally entitled and eligible to get the benefits of SEBC. The state is bound to take some affirmative action for their advancement so that the injustice done to them for centuries could be remedied*'.

It also held that '*values of privacy, self-identity, autonomy and personal integrity are fundamental rights guaranteed to members of the transgender community under Article 19(1)(a) of the Constitution of India and the State is bound to protect and recognize those rights*'. Self-determination of gender is an integral part of personal autonomy and self-expression and falls within the realm of personal liberty guaranteed under Article 21 of the Constitution of India. Hijras/Eunuchs, therefore, **have to be considered as the Third Gender** over and above binary genders under our Constitution and the laws.

Thus, the Supreme Court declared that:

1. Hijras and Eunuchs, apart from binary gender, be treated as 'third gender' for the purpose of safeguarding their rights under Part III of our Constitution and the laws made by the Parliament and the State Legislature.
2. Transgender persons' right to decide their self-identified gender is also upheld and the Centre and State Governments are directed to grant legal recognition of their gender identity such as male, female or as a third gender.
3. The Centre and the State Governments to take steps to treat them as socially and educationally backward classes of citizens and extend all kinds of reservation in cases of admission in educational institutions and for public appointments.
4. The Centre and State Governments should take proper measures to provide medical care to Transgenders in the hospitals and also provide them with separate public toilets and other facilities.
5. Centre and State Governments should also take steps for framing various social welfare schemes for their betterment.

IMPORTANCE AND IMPACT

- The judgment tried to redress the grievances of the transgender community in India.
- It recognised the Hijras/Eunuchs as 'third gender' and extended them all the benefits of socially and educationally backward classes.
- It upheld their fundamental rights under Part III of the Constitution.
- The judgment will help in changing the mentality of the people and to accept the transgender community as citizens of our country with equal protection of rights guaranteed by the Constitution same as of other genders like male and female.

27

Shreya Singhal v. Union of India (2015)

Is Section 66A of the Information Technology Act, 2000, unconstitutional?

Shreya Singhal case decided the questions related to the fundamental right of free speech and expression guaranteed by Article 19(1)(a) of the Constitution of India.

The Supreme Court in ***Romesh Thappar case*** stated that freedom of speech lay at the foundation of all democratic organisations.

But Section 66A of the IT Act 2000 authorised the imposition of restrictions on the 'freedom of speech and expression' in language wide enough to cover restrictions both within and without the limits of constitutionally permissible legislative action. Therefore, the Court held that Section 66A is unconstitutional.

INTRODUCTION

The Supreme Court of India in *Shreya Singhal v. Union of India* examined the constitutional validity of various provisions in the **Information Technology Act, 2000**.

Shreya Singhal case raised very important and far-reaching questions related to the fundamental right of free speech and expression guaranteed by Article 19(1)(a) of the Constitution of India.

Shreya Singhal was the petitioner and Union of India was the respondent in the case.

BACKGROUND

There have been many instances in which police have arrested people for broadcasting any information through any communication device, which was 'grossly offensive' or 'menacing' in character or which may cause 'annoyance', 'inconvenience' or 'obstruction'.

The police were empowered to do so under **Section 66A** of the Information Technology Act, 2000. Section 66A says:

'*Any person who sends, by means of a computer resource or a communication device*

(a) *Any information that is grossly offensive or has menacing character; or*
(b) *Any information which he knows to be false, but for the purpose of causing annoyance, inconvenience, danger, obstruction, insult, injury, criminal intimidation, enmity, hatred or ill will, persistently by making use of such computer resource or a communication device,*
(c) *Any electronic mail or electronic mail message for the purpose of causing annoyance or inconvenience or to deceive or to mislead the addressee or recipient about the origin of such messages,*

shall be punishable with imprisonment for a term which may extend to three years and with fine.'

However, terms like *grossly offensive, annoyance, inconvenience and so on,* are very subjective. Interpretation and application of these terms depend on law enforcement officers.

In 2012, two girls - Shaheen Dhada and Rinu Srinivasan - were arrested by the Mumbai police. They posted a certain comment on Facebook, expressing their displeasure at a *bandh* called in the wake of the death of Shiv Sena chief Bal Thackery. They were released later on, but the arrests attracted widespread public protest. It was felt that the police misused its power by invoking Section 66A of the Information Technology Act, 2000.

Section 66A was not in the Act as originally enacted, but came into force by virtue of an Amendment Act of 2009 with effect from 27 October 2009.

Shreya Singhal and others filed a writ petition under Article 32 of the Constitution of India, challenging the constitutional validity of **Section 66A**, **Section 69A** and the **Information Technology** (Procedure and Safeguards for Blocking for Access of Information by Public) **Rules, 2009**, and **Section 79** of the Information Technology Act.

SECTION 69A

SECTION 69A(1): *Where the Central Government or any of its officers specially authorised by it in this behalf is satisfied that it is necessary or expedient so to do, in the interest of sovereignty and integrity of India, defence of India, security of the State, friendly relations with foreign States or public order or for preventing incitement to the commission of any cognizable offence relating to above, it may subject to the provisions of Sub-section (2), for reasons to be recorded in writing, by order, direct any agency of the Government or intermediary to block for access by the public or cause to be blocked for access by the public any information generated, transmitted, received, stored or hosted in any computer resource.*

SECTION 69A(2): *The procedure and safeguards subject to which such blocking for access by the public may be carried out shall be such as may be prescribed.*

SECTION 69A(3): *The intermediary who fails to comply with the direction issued under sub-section (1) shall be punished with an imprisonment for a term which may extend to seven years and shall also be liable to fine.'*

ARGUMENTS

The petitioners contend that the very basis of Section 66A - that a rapid increase in the use of computer and internet has given rise to new forms of crimes - is incorrect and that Sections 66B to 67C and various Sections of the Indian Penal Code are good enough to deal with all such crimes.

The petitioners argued that:

- Section 66A infringes the fundamental right to free speech and expression and is not saved by any of the eight subjects covered in Article 19(2). The causing of annoyance, inconvenience, danger, obstruction, insult, injury, criminal intimidation, enmity, hatred or ill will are all outside the purview of Article 19(2).
- In creating an offence, Section 66A suffers from the vice of vagueness because none of the aforesaid terms is even attempted to be defined.

- It would be open to the authorities to be arbitrary and whimsical in booking any persons under Section 66A. In fact, a large number of innocent persons have been booked under this section.
- The enforcement of Section 66A is a dangerous form of censorship which damages the core value contained in Article 19(1)(a). It has a chilling effect on freedom of speech and expression.
- The rights under Articles 14 and 21 are breached because there is no clear distinction between those who use the internet and those who by words spoken or written use other mediums of communication. To punish somebody because she/he uses a particular medium of communication is itself a discriminatory object and violation of Article 14.

On the other hand, the Union of India defended the constitutional validity of Section 66A.

The respondent argued that:

- The legislature is in the best position to understand and appreciate the needs of the people.
- The mere possibility of abuse of a provision cannot be a ground to declare a provision invalid.
- Loose language may have been used in Section 66A to deal with novel methods of disturbing other people's rights by using the internet as a tool to do so.
- Vagueness is not a ground to declare a statute unconstitutional if the statute is otherwise legislatively competent and non-arbitrary.
- Since the internet as a medium of speech differs from other mediums on several grounds, a relaxed standard of reasonableness of restriction should apply.

The respondents made the **distinction between the Internet and other media of communication** on the following grounds:

1. The reach of print media is restricted to one state or at the most one country, while the Internet has no boundaries and its reach is global.
2. The recipient of the free speech and expression used in a print media can only be literate persons, while the internet can be accessed by literate and illiterate both since just a click is needed to download an objectionable post or a video.
3. In the case of television serials and movies, there is a permitted pre-censorship which ensures the right of viewers not to receive any information which is dangerous to or not in conformity with the social interest, while in the case of Internet, no such pre-censorship is possible.

4. In the case of print media or medium of television and films, whatever is truly recorded can only be published and viewed. While in the case of Internet, morphing of images, change of voices and many other technologically advanced methods to create serious potential social disorder can be applied.
5. By the medium of the internet, rumours having a serious potential of creating a serious social disorder can be spread to trillions of people without any check, which is not possible in the case of other mediums.
6. In the case of mediums like print media, television and films, it is (broadly) not possible to invade the privacy of unwilling persons, while in the case of the Internet, it is very easy to invade the privacy of any individual and thereby violating her/his right under Article 21.
7. By the very nature of the medium, the width and reach of the internet are manifold as against newspaper and films. The said mediums have inbuilt limitations, that is, a person will have to buy/borrow a newspaper and/or will have to go to a theatre to watch a movie while in the case of the Internet, a person abusing the internet can commit an offence at any place at the time of his choice and maintaining his anonymity in almost all cases.
8. In the case of other mediums like newspapers, television or films, the approach is always an institutionalised approach governed by industry-specific ethical norms of self-conduct. As against this, the use of the Internet is solely based on the individualistic approach of each individual without any check, balance or regulatory ethical norms for exercising freedom of speech and expression under Article 19(1)(a).

THE JUDGMENT

The Supreme Court observed that when it comes to democracy, liberty of thought and expression is a cardinal value that is of paramount significance under our constitutional scheme.

As early as in 1950, the Supreme Court in *Romesh Thappar v. the State of Madras* stated that freedom of speech lay at the foundation of all democratic organisations.

The Court held that there are three concepts which are fundamental in understanding the expression 'freedom of speech and expression'. They are discussion, advocacy and incitement.

Mere discussion or even advocacy of a particular cause, howsoever unpopular, is at the heart of Article 19(1)(a). Only when the discussion or advocacy reaches the level of incitement, restrictions under Article 19(2) can be invoked. Only at this stage, a law may be made to curtail the speech or expression.

Section 2(v) of the Information Technology Act, 2000, defines information as:

'2. *Definitions–(1) In this Act, unless the context otherwise requires,–*

(v) 'Information' includes data, message, text, images, sound, voice, codes, computer programmes, software, and databases or micro film or computer generated micro fiche.'

However, it does not refer to what the content of information can be. It only refers to the medium through which such information is disseminated. There is no distinction made between mere discussion or advocacy of a particular point of view, which may be annoying or inconvenient or grossly offensive to some and incitement by which such words lead to an imminent causal connection with public disorder, the security of State and so on Therefore, the Court held that the **public's right to know is directly affected by Section 66A**.

Based on the distinction made between the Internet and other media of communication, the court held that there can be the creation of offences which are applied to free speech over the Internet alone as opposed to other mediums of communication. Thus, the **contention that Section 66A is violative of Article 14 was rejected** by the Supreme Court.

The Court observed that the expressions used in 66A are completely open-ended and undefined. Even 'criminal intimidation' is not defined - and the definition clause of the Information Technology Act (Section 2) does not say that words and expressions that are defined in the Penal Code will apply to this Act.

Section 66A purports to authorise the imposition of restrictions on the fundamental right contained in Article 19(1)(a), in language wide enough to cover restrictions both within and without the limits of constitutionally permissible legislative action. Therefore, the Court held that '***the Section 66A is unconstitutional*** *on the ground that it takes within its sweep protected speech and speech that is innocent in nature and therefore, is liable to be used in such a way as to have a chilling effect on free speech*'.

The Supreme Court upheld the constitutionality of Section 69A and the Information Technology (Procedure & Safeguards for Blocking for Access of Information by Public) Rules 2009 on the grounds that '*...merely because* *certain additional safeguards such as those found in Section 95 and 96 CrPC are not available does not make the Rules constitutionally infirm*'.

The Court held that Section 79 is valid subject to '*Section 79(3)(b) being read down to mean that an intermediary upon receiving actual knowledge from a court order or on being notified by the appropriate government or its agency that unlawful acts relatable to Article 19(2) are going to be committed then fails to expeditiously remove or disable access to such material*'.

IMPORTANCE

Freedom of speech and expression is the bedrock of any democratic setup. It is a fundamental right of the citizen. By striking down Section 66A, the Court upheld this fundamental right.

It also put a restriction on the arbitrary power of the government to curb Freedom of speech and expression.

IMPACT

Even without Section 66A, there exist enough provisions under the Indian Penal Code and the Information Technology Act to prosecute many forms of online abuse and harassment.

However, even after the Supreme Court struck down Section 66A, police departments across the country continue to arrest and detain citizens under this draconian provision.

28

Shayara Bano v. Union of India (2016)

Is triple talak unconstitutional?

The *Shayara Bano judgment* set aside the practice of *talaq-e-bidat*, which allowed Muslim men to divorce their wives instantaneously and irrevocably.

Along with ***Shah Bano case***, it is one of the landmark judgments in protecting the rights of Muslim women in India.

INTRODUCTION

In *Shayara Bano v. Union of India and others,* the Supreme Court of India set aside the practice of *talaq-e-bidat,* which allowed Muslim men to divorce their wives instantaneously and irrevocably.

Shayara Bano was the petitioner and Union of India and others were the respondents in the case.

BACKGROUND

Rizwan Ahmad married Shayara Bano on 11 April 2001 as per 'Shariat' at Allahabad. The matrimonial relationship between them resulted in two children.

On 10 October 2015, Shayara Bano was divorced by her husband Rizwan Ahmad, wherein he affirmed '*...in the presence of witnesses saying that I gave "talak, talak, talak", hence like this I divorce from you from my wife. From this date, there is no relation between husband and wife. From today I am "haraam", and I have become "naamharram". In future, you are free for using your life...*'.

Shayara Bano filed a petition in the Supreme Court and sought a declaration that the 'talaq-e-biddat' pronounced by her husband be declared as *void ab initio.*

ARGUMENTS

The petitioner, Shayara Bano, submitted that the 'talaq-e-biddat' (triple talaq) pronounced by her husband is not valid as it is not a part of 'Shariat' (i.e. Muslim personal law).

She argued that divorce of the instant nature cannot be treated as 'rule of decision' under the Shariat Act.

It was submitted that the practice of 'talaq-e-biddat' is violative of the fundamental rights guaranteed to citizens in India, under Articles 14, 15 and 21 of the Constitution.

'Talaq-e-biddat' could be pronounced in the absence of the wife and even without her knowledge. It vests an arbitrary right in the husband and therefore violates Article 14.

She also argued that the practice of 'talaq-e-biddat' cannot be protected under the rights granted to religious denominations under Articles 25(1), 26(b) and 29 of the Constitution.

It was submitted that the practice of 'talaq-e-biddat' is denounced internationally (a large number of Muslim theocratic countries have forbidden the practice of 'talaq-e-biddat'), and therefore it cannot be considered sacrosanct to the tenets of the Muslim religion.

According to the petitioner, there is no mention of 'talaq-e-biddat' in the Quran. It is recognised only by a few Sunni schools.

Hence, Shayara Bano sought in her petition that '*...such a divorce which abruptly, unilaterally and irrevocably terminates the ties of matrimony, purportedly under Section 2 of the* ***Muslim Personal Law (Shariat) Application Act, 1937*** *be declared unconstitutional*'.

On the other hand, Rizwan Ahmad submitted that Shayara Bano left her matrimonial home to live in her parental home. Despite his many requests, she refused to accompany him and therefore, refused to return to the matrimonial home. He was informed by her father that the petitioner was not inclined to live with Rizwan Ahmad.

Rizwan Ahmad further said that he felt that his wife was not ready for reconciliation and hence, divorced her by serving a 'talaq-nama'.

Rizwan Ahmad argued that he had pronounced 'talaq' in consonance with the prevalent and valid mode of dissolution of Muslim marriages. He also submitted that the present writ petition filed by the petitioner under Article 32 of the Constitution of India is not maintainable as the questions raised in the petition are not justiciable under Article 32 of the Constitution.

It was pointed out that it was not the role of a court to interpret the Muslim 'personal law' - the Shariat.

According to the Union of India, the fundamental question for determination by the Court was that whether in a secular democracy religion can be a reason to deny equal status and dignity to Muslim women.

The Union of India contended that freedom of religion was subservient to the fundamental rights. The words employed in Article 25(1) of the Constitution, which conferred the right to practice, preach and propagate religion, were subjected to Articles 14 and 15. It was necessary to draw a line between religions per se and religious practices. It was submitted that the latter were not protected under Article 25.

It was also contended that the Constitution undoubtedly accords guarantee of faith and belief to every citizen, but every practice of faith could not be held to be an integral part of religion and belief.

AIMPLB contended that the expression 'custom and usage' in Article 13 of the Constitution would not include faith of religious denominations embedded in their 'personal law'.

WHAT IS TALAQ?

Talaq is a means of a divorce, at the instance of the husband. There are three kinds of Talaq, namely 'talaq-e-ahsan', 'talaq-e-hasan' and 'talaq-e-biddat'.

Other modes of divorce are Khula and mubaraat.

Khula is a divorce at the instance of the wife. The mubaraat is divorce by mutual consent.

THE JUDGMENT

The Supreme Court gave its judgment with 3:2 majority, holding that the triple Talaq is unconstitutional.

The majority bench of the Supreme Court observed that all forms of Talaq recognised and enforced by Muslim personal law are recognised and enforced by the Muslim Personal Law (Shariat) Application Act, 1937.

This would necessarily include Triple Talaq when it comes to the Muslim personal law applicable to Sunnis in India. The 1937 Act is a law made by the legislature before the Constitution came into force. Therefore, it would fall squarely within the expression 'laws in force' in Article 13(3)(b) and would be hit by Article 13(1), if found to be inconsistent with the provisions of Part III of the Constitution

The Court observed that Triple Talaq is instant and irrevocable; any attempt at reconciliation between husband and wife by two arbiters from their families, which is essential to save the marital tie, cannot ever take place. This form of Talaq is manifestly arbitrary, in the sense that the marital tie can be broken capriciously and whimsically by a Muslim man without any attempt at reconciliation so as to save it.

The Supreme Court also observed that **Triple Talaq is not an essential religious practice**. If a practice which is arbitrary and not an essential religious practice it will be hit by the exception laid down under Article 25.

Therefore, the court held **Triple Talaq to be violative of the fundamental right** contained under Article 14 of the Constitution of India.

IMPORTANCE AND IMPACT

The Triple Talaq judgment provides a protective shield against gender discrimination in the name of religious practice.

Women's rights groups and other human rights and social justice organisations in India have widely celebrated this historic judgment, which advances the essential constitutional values of equality, dignity and secularism.

Justice K. S. Puttaswamy (Retd.) v. Union of India (2017)

Is 'Right to Privacy' a fundamental right?

Puttaswamy case dealt with the question of whether privacy is a constitutionally protected value under the Indian Constitution.

It held that 'right to privacy' emerges primarily from the guarantee of life and personal liberty in Article 21 of the Constitution.

By holding 'Right to Privacy' as a fundamental right, the court overruled its earlier judgments in ***M. P. Sharma case*** and ***Kharak Singh case***.

The Supreme Court relied on this ruling to declare Section 377 of the IPC unconstitutional in ***Navtej Singh Johar case***; decriminalise adultery in ***Joseph Shine case***; and in ***Indian Young Lawyers Association case*** which dealt with the entry of women into the Sabarimala temple in Kerala.

INTRODUCTION

In *Justice K. S. Puttaswamy (Retd.) v. Union of India and others* case, the Supreme Court dealt with the question whether privacy is a constitutionally protected value under the Indian Constitution.

Justice K. S. Puttaswamy (Retd.) and another were the petitioners and Union of India and others were the respondents in the case.

BACKGROUND

The Aadhaar Scheme, a biometric-based 12-digits unique identification number issued to all Indian residents, is considered as a technology-enabled tool for efficient public service delivery and root out the corruption from it.

Under the Aadhaar Scheme, the Government of India collects and compiles both the demographic and biometric data of the residents of this country to be used for various purposes.

However, the scheme has been opposed by several people. One of the grounds of attack on the scheme is that the collection of biometric data is violative of the 'right to privacy'.

In 2012, Justice K. S. Puttaswamy, a former judge of the High Court of Karnataka, filed the petition in the Supreme Court against the introduction of Aadhaar for access to government schemes. The petitioner contended that it violates the right to privacy.

The question of 'right to privacy' came before the Supreme Court in several cases. The judgment of the Court varied from case to case. This has created a legal confusion regarding this.

In *M. P. Sharma v. Satish Chandra, District Magistrate, Delhi,* and in *Kharak Singh v. State of Uttar Pradesh,* the Supreme Court observed that the Indian Constitution does not specifically protect the right to privacy.

On the other hand, in *Gobind v. State of Madhya Pradesh, R. Rajagopal v. State of Tamil Nadu* and in *People's Union for Civil Liberties v. Union of India* cases, the Supreme Court held that the right to privacy is a constitutionally protected fundamental right.

However, these decisions which affirmed the existence of a constitutionally protected right of privacy were rendered by Benches of a strength smaller than those in ***M. P. Sharma*** and ***Kharak Singh***.

Hence, having due regard to the far-reaching questions of importance involving interpretation of the Constitution, a three-judge bench of the Supreme Court, in an order dated 11 August 2015, referred the petition filed by Justice K. S. Puttaswamy to a constitution bench of nine judges.

LEGAL ISSUES INVOLVED

1. Whether there is a constitutionally protected right to privacy?
2. If there is a constitutionally protected right, whether this has the character of an independent fundamental right or whether it arises from within the existing guarantees of protected rights such as life and personal liberty?
3. The doctrinal foundations of the claim to privacy.
4. The content of privacy.
5. The nature of the regulatory power of the state.

ARGUMENTS

The petitioners asserted that the right to privacy emanates not only from Article 21, but also from various other articles embodying the fundamental rights guaranteed under Part III of the Constitution of India.

According to them, this right is found in Articles 14, 19, 20, 21 and 25 when read with the Preamble of the Constitution.

They argued that the judgments contained in *M. P. Sharma* and *Kharak Singh* should be overruled as they do not reflect the correct position in law.

It was also argued that several international covenants have stated that the right to privacy is fundamental to the development of the human personality and that these international covenants need to be read into the fundamental rights chapter of the Constitution.

The Attorney General for India, on behalf of the Union of India, opposed the recognition being given to a general right of privacy on the following grounds:

1. There is no general or fundamental right to privacy under the Constitution;
2. No blanket right to privacy can be read as part of the fundamental rights and where some of the constituent facets of privacy are already covered by the enumerated guarantees in Part III, those facets will be protected in any case;
3. Where specific species of privacy are governed by the protection of liberty in Part III of the Constitution, they are subject to reasonable restrictions in the public interest;
4. Privacy is a concept which does not have any specific meaning or definition and the expression is inchoate;
5. The framers of the Constitution specifically did not include such a right as part of the chapter on fundamental rights and even the ambit of the expression liberty which was originally sought to be used in the draft Constitution was cut back to personal liberty.

The respondents contended that there is a statutory regime by virtue of which the right to privacy is adequately protected and hence, it is not necessary to read a constitutional right to privacy into the fundamental rights.

The Union of India also argued that the right to privacy must be forsaken in the interest of welfare entitlements provided by the State.

THE JUDGMENT

The Supreme Court observed that the privacy of the individual is an essential aspect of dignity. Privacy enables the individual to retain the autonomy of the body and mind. The autonomy of the individual is the ability to make decisions on vital matters of concern to life.

Further, it said that 'life and personal liberty are not creations of the Constitution. These rights are recognized by the Constitution as inhering in each individual as an intrinsic and inseparable part of the human element which dwells within'.

The Court held that '*Privacy is a constitutionally protected right which emerges primarily from the* ***guarantee of life and personal liberty in Article 21*** *of the Constitution. Elements of privacy also arise in varying contexts from the* ***other facets of freedom and dignity*** *recognized and guaranteed by the fundamental rights contained in Part III*'.

While not going into to the exhaustive entitlement under the privacy, the court said: 'the Constitution must evolve with the necessities of time to meet the challenges thrown up in a democratic order governed by the rule of law'. Giving indicative elements of privacy, it said: '*privacy includes at its core the preservation of personal intimacies, the sanctity of family life, marriage, procreation, the home, and sexual orientation*'.

Privacy has both positive and negative content. The negative content restrains the State from committing an intrusion on the life and personal liberty of a citizen. Its positive content imposes an obligation on the State to take all necessary measures to protect the privacy of the individual.

It was observed by the court that '*no legal right can be absolute. Every right has limitations. Therefore, even a fundamental right to privacy has limitations. The limitations are to be identified on the case to case basis depending upon the nature of the privacy interest claimed*'.

By holding that **'Right to Privacy' as a fundamental right**, the court overruled its earlier judgments in ***M. P. Sharma*** and ***Kharak Singh***.

IMPORTANCE

It is a landmark judgment which held 'Right to privacy' as a fundamental right under Part III of the Constitution.

IMPACT

Some of the petitioners made attempts to attack the legality and correctness of Aadhar Scheme in their submissions. But the Court did not entertain this on the grounds that the Bench is constituted to answer only specific questions.

The question of Constitutionality of Aadhaar was considered **separately in a judgment delivered on 26 September 2018**. In that, the Supreme

Court held that '*the requirement under Aadhaar Act to give one's demographic and biometric information does not violate the fundamental right of privacy*'.

The Supreme Court upheld the constitutional validity of Aadhaar, but struck down certain provisions, including its linking with bank accounts, mobile phones and school admissions.

The Supreme Court relied on this ruling to declare Section 377 of the IPC unconstitutional in ***Navtej Singh Johar case***, decriminalise adultery in ***Joseph Shine case*** and in ***Indian Young Lawyers Association case*** which dealt with the entry of women into the Sabarimala temple in Kerala.

30

Indian Young Lawyers Association v. State of Kerala (2018)

Should women be allowed entry to the Sabarimala temple in Kerala?

Indian Young Lawyers Association case allowed the entry of women aged between 10 and 50 to the Sabarimala temple in Kerala.

It held that the devotees of Lord Ayyappa are Hindus and do not constitute a separate religious denomination. The exclusionary practice followed at the Sabarimala temple cannot be treated as an essential practice.

It upheld the women's right to profess practice and propagate a religion.

The judgment reaffirms the Constitution's transformative character and derives strength from the centrality it accords to fundamental rights.

While upholding the rights of women, the court also referred to the ***Puttaswamy judgment***.

INTRODUCTION

Indian Young Lawyers Association v. State of Kerala is a landmark judgment of the Supreme Court that allowed the entry of women aged between 10 and 50 to the Sabarimala temple in Kerala.

Indian Young Lawyers Association and others were the petitioners and the State of Kerala and others were the respondents in the case.

BACKGROUND

The Sabarimala Temple, devoted to Lord Ayyappa, is a temple of great antiquity situated in the State of Kerala.

In 1955 and 1956, two notifications were issued by the Travancore Devaswom Board, prohibiting entry of women aged between 10 and 50 years.

In 1965, the Kerala Hindu Places of Public Worship (Authorization of Entry) Act, 1965, was enacted. Rule 3(b) of the Kerala Hindu Places of Public Worship (Authorization of Entry) Rules, 1965, framed in exercise of the powers conferred by Section 4 of the 1965, Act, legally banned the entry of women above the age of 10 and below the age of 50 to offer worship at the Sabarimala shrine.

Constitutionality of this ban was challenged in the Kerala High Court in *Mahendran v. the Secretary, Travancore Devaswom Board (1992).*

In 2006, the ban was once again challenged in the Supreme Court by the Indian Young Lawyers Association and others. They filed writ petition under Article 32 of the Constitution, seeking issuance of directions against the Government of Kerala, Devaswom Board of Travancore, Chief Thanthri of Sabarimala Temple and the District Magistrate of Pathanamthitta to ensure entry of female devotees between the age group of 10 to 50 years to the Lord Ayyappa at the Sabarimala temple in Kerala.

The three-Judge Bench of the Supreme Court, keeping in view the gravity of the issues involved, referred the matter to the Constitution Bench.

LEGAL ISSUES INVOLVED

The following questions were framed for the purpose of the reference to the Constitution Bench:

1. Whether the exclusionary practice which is based on a biological factor exclusive to the female gender amounts to 'discrimination' and thereby violates the very core of Articles 14, 15 and 17 and not protected by 'morality' as used in Articles 25 and 26 of the Constitution?
2. Whether the practice of excluding such women constitutes an 'essential religious practice' under Article 25 and whether a religious institution can assert a claim in that regard under the umbrella of the right to manage its own affairs in the matters of religion?
3. Whether the Ayyappa Temple has a denominational character, and if so, is it permissible on the part of a 'religious denomination' managed by a statutory board and financed under Article 290-A of the Constitution of India out of the Consolidated Fund of Kerala and Tamil Nadu to indulge in such practices violating constitutional principles/morality embedded in Articles 14, 15(3), 39(a) and 51-A(e)?
4. Whether Rule 3 of the Kerala Hindu Places of Public Worship (Authorization of Entry) Rules permits 'religious denomination' to ban entry of women between the ages of 10 to 50 years? And if so, would it not play foul of Articles 14 and 15(3) of the Constitution by restricting the entry of women on the grounds of sex?

5. Whether Rule 3(b) of the Kerala Hindu Places of Public Worship (Authorization of Entry) Rules, 1965, is *ultra vires* the Kerala Hindu Places of Public Worship (Authorization of Entry) Act, 1965, and, if treated to be *intra vires*, whether it will be violative of the provisions of Part III of the Constitution?

ARGUMENTS

The petitioners and Interveners in the case contended that:

1. For the purpose of constituting a 'religious denomination', not only the practices followed by that denomination should be different, but its administration should also be distinct and separate. Since the administration of the temples attached to the Devaswom Board is centralised, it cannot attain a distinct identity of a separate religious denomination.
2. The mere difference in practices carried out at Hindu Temples cannot accord to them the status of separate religious denominations.
3. The Sabarimala temple is not a separate religious denomination, because the religious practices performed in the temple at the time of Puja and other religious ceremonies are similar to any other practice performed in any Hindu temple.
4. Before any religious practice is examined on the touchstone of constitutional principles, it has to be ascertained positively whether the said practice is, in pith and substance, really the 'essence' of the said religion.
5. Discrimination in matters of entry to temples is neither a ritual nor a ceremony associated with the Hindu religion, as this religion does not discriminate against women.
6. The exclusionary practice of preventing women between the ages of 10 to 50 years, based on physiological factors exclusively to be found in female gender, violates Article 14 of the Constitution of India.
7. The exclusionary practice violates Article 15(1) of the Constitution, which amounts to discrimination on the basis of sex, as the physiological feature of menstruation is exclusive to women alone.
8. The exclusionary practice has the impact of casting a stigma on women of menstruating age, for it considers them polluted, and leads to violation of Article 17 as the expression 'in any form' under the Article 17 includes untouchability based on social factors.
9. The exclusionary practice violates the rights of Hindu women under Article 25 of the Constitution, as they have the right to enter Hindu temples dedicated to the public.

On the other hand, respondents contended that:

1. The Kerala Hindu Places of Public Worship (Authorization of Entry) Act, 1965, and the Rules framed thereunder are in consonance with Article 25(2)(b) of the Constitution.
2. The custom of young women aged between 10 to 50 years not being allowed to enter the Sabarimala temple has its traces in the basic tenets of the establishment of the temple, the deification of Lord Ayyappa and His worship.
3. The Sabarimala pilgrimage was to be undertaken after observing 'Vrutham' for 41 days, during which either the woman leaves the house or the man resides elsewhere in order to separate himself from all family ties. The problem with women is that they cannot complete the 41 days Vruthum, as their periods would eventually fall within the period of 41 days Vruthum.
4. Even men who cannot observe the 41 days Vruthum due to births and deaths in the family, which results in breaking of Vruthum, are also not allowed to take the pilgrimage that year.
5. It is for the sake of pilgrims who practice celibacy that young women are not allowed in the Sabarimala pilgrimage.
6. The prohibition is not social discrimination, but is only a part of the essential spiritual discipline related to this particular pilgrimage.
7. The exclusion of women is not based on gender and satisfies the test of intelligible differentia and nexus to the object sought to be achieved.
8. The deity at Sabarimala is in the form of 'Naishtika Brahmachari', and that is also a reason why young women are not allowed inside the temple so as to prevent even the slightest deviation from celibacy and austerity observed by the deity.

Amicus Curiae in the case submitted that:

1. The right of a woman to visit and enter a temple as a devotee of the deity and as a believer in the Hindu faith is an essential aspect of her right to worship without which her right to worship is significantly denuded. Article 25 pertinently declares that all persons are equally entitled to freely practice religion.
2. Article 17 proscribes untouchability 'in any form' as prohibited, and the exclusion of menstruating women from religious spaces and practices is no less a form of discrimination than the exclusion of oppressed castes.
3. The exclusionary practice in its implementation results in involuntary disclosure by women of both their menstrual status and age, which amounts to forced disclosure that consequently violates the right to dignity and privacy embedded in Article 21 of the Constitution of India.

4. The exclusionary practice in the present case cannot be justified either on the grounds of health, public order or morality for the term 'morality' used in Articles 25 or 26.
5. The respondents have failed to prove that the devotees of Lord Ayyappa form a denomination within the meaning of Article 26. None of the three tests for determination of denominational status, that is (i) common faith, (ii) common organisation and (iii) designation by a distinctive name, have been established by the respondents.

WHAT IS ESSENTIAL RELIGIOUS PRACTICE?

'Essential religious practice' means any ritual/practice fundamentally associated with the religion. Any changes in such a practice would result in changing the religion itself.

This doctrine was developed by the Supreme Court and it has vested itself with the duty to determine what constitutes an essential practice within a religion.

There is no set of guidelines or definite rules to determine the essentiality of any practice but it is dependent upon the facts and circumstances of each case.

THE JUDGMENT

After hearing the petitioners, respondents and Amicus Curiae, the Supreme Court held that:

1. The devotees of Lord Ayyappa are Hindus and **do not constitute a separate religious denomination**. For a religious denomination, there must be new methodology provided for a religion. Mere observance of certain practices, even though from a long time, does not make it a distinct religion on that account.
2. The notions of public order, morality and health cannot be used as colorable device to restrict the freedom to freely practice religion and discriminate against women of the age group of 10 to 50 years by denying their right to enter and offer their prayers at the Sabarimala temple for the simple reason that **public morality must yield to constitutional morality**.
3. The restriction of entry for women was only during Mandalam, Makaravilakku and Vishnu days. Prior to 1950, women of all age groups used to visit the Sabarimala temple for the first rice feeding ceremony of their children. There is no continuity in the exclusionary practice followed at the Sabarimala temple and therefore, it **cannot be treated as an essential practice**.

4. The exclusionary practice being followed at the Sabarimala temple by virtue of Rule 3(b) of the **1965 Rules violates the right of Hindu women** to practice their religion and exhibit their devotion towards Lord Ayyappa and in consequence, makes their fundamental right of religion under Article 25(1) a dead letter. Therefore, Rule 3(b) is *ultra vires* the 1965 Act.

The lone woman in the constitution bench, Justice Indu Malhotra, gave a dissenting judgment. She held that:

1. The petition does not deserve to be entertained. It is not for courts to determine which religious practices are to be struck down, except in issues of social evil like 'Sati'.
2. The equality doctrine enshrined under Article 14 does not override the Fundamental Right guaranteed by Article 25 to every individual to freely profess, practice and propagate their faith, in accordance with the tenets of their religion.
3. The limited restriction on the entry of women during the notified age group does not fall within the purview of Article 17 of the Constitution.
4. Rule 3(b) of the 1965 Rules is not *ultra vires* Section 3 of the 1965 Act, since the proviso carves out an exception in the case of public worship in a temple for the benefit of any religious denomination or sect thereof to manage their affairs in matters of religion.

IMPORTANCE

- The judgment upheld the women's right to profess practice and propagate religion.
- The judgment reaffirms the Constitution's transformative character and derives strength from the centrality it accords to fundamental rights.[1]

IMPACT

Following the Supreme Court judgment, some women tried to enter the temple.

But such attempts were strongly resisted by the devotees of the temple. On 14 November 2019, the Supreme Court Constitution Bench referred the review petitions on this case to a larger bench.

1. https://www.thehindu.com/opinion/editorial/freedom-to-pray/article25074443.ece

31

Joseph Shine v. Union of India (2018)

Is adultery a criminal offence?

Joseph Shine case struck down Section 497 of the Indian Penal Code which criminalised adultery.

It expanded the horizons of individual liberty and gender parity.

The court referred to the ***Puttaswamy judgment*** in decriminalising adultery.

INTRODUCTION

In *Joseph Shine v. Union of India* case, the Supreme Court delivered a landmark verdict, striking down Section 497 of the Indian Penal Code which criminalised adultery.

Joseph Shine was the petitioner and the Union of India was the respondent in the case.

BACKGROUND

Section 497 of the Indian Penal Code, 1860, makes adultery a punishable offence against '*whoever has sexual intercourse with a person who is and whom he knows or has reason to believe to be the wife of another man, without the consent or connivance of that man*'.

It goes on to state that '*in such case, the wife shall not be punishable as an abettor*'.

The stated objective of the law is to protect the 'institution of marriage'.

The offence applies only to the man committing adultery. A woman committing adultery is not considered to be an 'abettor' to the offence.

The power to prosecute for adultery rests only with the husband of the woman.

The act which constitutes the offence under Section 497 of the IPC is a man engaging in sexual intercourse with a woman who is the wife of another man. For the offence to arise, the man who engages in sexual intercourse must either know or have reason to believe that the woman is married. Though a man has engaged in sexual intercourse with a woman who is married, the offence of adultery does not come into being where he did so with the consent or connivance of her husband.

The constitutionality of the section was challenged for the first time in 1954. However, the scope of the challenge was limited then, as it was based on the exclusion of women from punishment.

The section was again challenged in *Sowmithri Vishnu v. Union of India* case and *Yusuf Abdul Aziz v. State of Bombay* case. However, the Supreme Court upheld its constitutional validity.

Joseph Shine, a hotelier from Kerala residing in Italy, filed a petition under Article 32 of the Constitution of India, challenging the constitutional validity of Section 497 of the IPC and Section 198(2) of the Code of Criminal Procedure (CrPC).

SECTION 497 OF IPC: ADULTERY

Section 497: *'Whoever has sexual intercourse with a person who is and whom he knows or has reason to believe to be the wife of another man, without the consent or connivance of that man, such sexual intercourse not amounting to the offence of rape, is guilty of the offence of adultery, and shall be punished with imprisonment of either description for a term which may extend to five years, or with fine, or with both. In such case, the wife shall not be punishable as an abettor.'*

SECTION 198(2)

Section 198(2): *'For the purpose of Sub-section (1), no person other than the husband of the woman shall be deemed to be aggrieved by any offence punishable under Section 497 or Section 498 of the said Code.*

Provided that in the absence of the husband, some person who had the care of the woman on his behalf at the time when such offence was committed may, with the leave of the Court, make a complaint on his behalf.'

ARGUMENTS

The petitioner contended that:

1. Section 497 is manifestly arbitrary and amounts to a violation of the constitutional guarantee of substantive equality.
2. The operation of Section 497 is a denial of equality to women in marriage. It places a husband and wife on a different footing in a marriage.
3. Though adultery is considered to be an offence relating to marriage, the legislature did not penalise sexual intercourse between a married man and a single woman.
4. Section 497 is destructive and deprives a woman of her agency, autonomy and dignity. It is founded on the notion that a woman by entering upon marriage loses, so to speak, her voice, autonomy and agency.
5. Section 497, based on the patriarchal conception of the woman as property, entrenches gender stereotypes.
6. Section 497 is violative of the fundamental right to privacy under Article 21, since the choice of a partner with whom she could be intimate, falls squarely within the area of autonomy over a person's sexuality.

On the other hand, the respondents contended that:

1. Adultery must be retained as a criminal offence in the IPC, as it has the effect of breaking up the family which is the fundamental unit in society.
2. An act which outrages the morality of society, and harms its members, ought to be punished as a crime. Adultery falls within this definition.
3. Adultery is not an act that merely affects just two people; it has an impact on the aggrieved spouse and children as well as society.
4. Adultery is essentially violence perpetrated by an outsider, with complete knowledge and intention, on the family which is the basic unit of society.
5. Section 497 is valid on the grounds of affirmative action. All discrimination in favour of women is saved by Article 15(3) and hence, was exempted from punishment.
6. The sanctity of family life and the right to marriage are fundamental rights comprehended in the right to life under Article 21. An outsider who violates and injure, these rights must be deterred and punished in accordance with criminal law.

THE JUDGMENT

Section 497 exempts a woman from being punished as an abettor. The underlying exemption is the notion that a woman is a victim of being seduced into a sexual relationship with a person who is not her husband. The exemption seeks to be justified on the grounds of being a provision that is beneficial to women and protected under Article 15(3) of the Constitution.

However, the Supreme Court held that constitutional guarantee in Article 15(3) cannot be employed in a manner that entrenches paternalistic notions of 'protection'. This latter view of protection only serves to place women in a cage. **Discrimination which is grounded in paternalistic and patriarchal notions cannot claim the protection of Article 15(3)**.

The court observed that the principle on which Section 497 rests is the preservation of the sexual exclusivity of a married woman - for the benefit of her husband, the owner of her sexuality. Such **patriarchal underpinnings of Section 497 render the provision manifestly arbitrary**. It violates the non-discrimination principle embodied in Article 15 of the Constitution.

The Supreme Court held that Section 497 is **a denial of substantive equality,** in that it reinforces the notion that w**omen are unequal participants in a marriage**, incapable of freely consenting to a sexual act. Thus, Section 497 violates Article 14 of the Constitution.

The Court held that Section 497 is a denial of the constitutional guarantees of dignity, liberty, privacy and sexual autonomy which are intrinsic to Article 21 of the Constitution.

Therefore, the Supreme Court held **Section 497 is unconstitutional**. Accordingly, the decision in *Sowmithri Vishnu case* was overruled.

The Court also held Section 198(2) of the CrPC, which contains the procedure for prosecution, shall be unconstitutional only to the extent that it is applicable to the offence of adultery under Section 497.

IMPORTANCE AND IMPACT

By overruling earlier judgments, the Supreme Court showed that it will not remain a passive prisoner to its earlier judgments.

The judgment is in tune with the expanding horizons of individual liberty and gender parity.

In the words of the then Chief Justice Dipak Misra, 'It is time to say that the husband is not the master of a wife'.

32

Navtej Singh Johar v. Union of India (2018)

Is homosexual sex a crime?

Navtej Singh Johar case partially struck down Section 377 of the Indian Penal Code (IPC).

It upheld the right of the LGBT community to have intimate relations with people of their choice, their inherent right to privacy and dignity and the freedom to live without fear.

It corrected the judicial error committed by a two-member Bench in ***Suresh Kumar Koushal case*** (2013).

The court referred to the ***Puttaswamy judgment*** extensively in striking down Section 377.

INTRODUCTION

Navtej Singh Johar and others v. Union of India is one of the finest judgments of the Supreme Court, which discarded societal prejudice.

The Supreme Court partially struck down Section 377 of the IPC.

Navtej Singh Johar and others were the petitioners and the Union of India was the respondent in the case.

BACKGROUND

Section 377 of the IPC is an act that criminalises homosexuality. It was introduced in 1861 during the British rule of India.

It reads that:

377. Unnatural offences – '*Whoever voluntarily has carnal intercourse against the order of nature with any man, woman or animal, shall be punished with 1[imprisonment for life], or with imprisonment of either description for a term which may extend to ten years, and shall also be liable to fine*'.

'Explanation. – Penetration is sufficient to constitute the carnal intercourse necessary to the offence described in this section'.[1]

Suresh Kumar Koushal v. Naz Foundation and ***Naz Foundation v. Government of NCT of Delhi*** cases dealt with the Constitutionality of Section 377 of the IPC.

In the ***Naz Foundation judgment*** (2009), the High Court of Delhi held that *'Section 377 IPC, insofar it criminalizes consensual sexual acts of adults in private, is violative of Articles 21, 14 and 15 of the Constitution. The provisions of Section 377 IPC will continue to govern non-consensual penile non-vaginal sex and penile non-vaginal sex involving minors...'.*[2]

This judgment was overturned by a two-Judge Bench of the Supreme Court in the ***Suresh Kumar Koushal judgment*** (2013). The Bench held that *'Section 377 IPC does not suffer from the vice of unconstitutionality and the declaration made by the Division Bench of the High court is legally unsustainable'.*[3]

In 2016, Navtej Singh Johar and others filed a new writ petition for declaring 'right to sexuality', 'right to sexual autonomy' and 'right to choice of a sexual partner' to be part of the right to life guaranteed under Article 21 of the Constitution of India and to declare Section 377 of the Indian Penal Code to be unconstitutional.

A three-Judge Bench of the Supreme Court expressed the opinion that the issues raised should be answered by a larger Bench and accordingly, referred the matter to the larger Bench.

ARGUMENTS

The petitioners submitted before the Court that individuals belonging to the LGBT group suffer discrimination and abuse throughout their lives due to the existence of Section 377 IPC, which is a manifestation of a mindset of societal values prevalent during the Victorian era where sexual activities were considered mainly for reproduction.

The petitioners and the interveners contended that:

1. Homosexuality, bisexuality and other sexual orientations are equally natural and reflective of expression of choice and inclination founded on the consent of two persons who are eligible in law to express such consent.

---

1. https://indiankanoon.org/doc/1836974/
2. https://indiankanoon.org/doc/100472805/
3. https://indiankanoon.org/doc/58730926/

2. Homosexuality is neither a physical nor a mental illness; rather, they are natural variations of expression and free thinking process and making it a criminal offence destructs the individual dignity, decisional autonomy and right to privacy which is a pivotal facet of Article 21 of the Constitution.
3. The phrase 'order of nature' is limited to the procreative concept that may have been conceived as natural by a systemic conservative approach and such limitations do not really take note of inborn traits or developed orientations or consensual acts.
4. The American Psychological Association has opined that sexual orientation is a natural condition and attraction towards the same sex or opposite sex are both naturally equal, the only difference being that the same-sex attraction arises in far lesser numbers.
5. Section 377 has a chilling effect on Article 19(1)(a) of the Constitution which protects the fundamental right of freedom of expression, including that of LGBT persons to express their sexual identity and orientation. It also violates the rights of LGBT persons under Article 19(1)(c) and denies them the right to form associations.
6. Sexual minorities in societies need protection more than the heterosexuals, so as to enable them to achieve their full potential and to live freely without fear in such a manner that they are not discriminated against by the society or by the State in matters such as employment, choice of partner, testamentary rights, insurability and medical treatment in hospitals.
7. In ***NALSA case***, transgenders have been recognised as a third gender apart from male and female and have been given certain rights. Yet, in view of the existence of Section 377 in the IPC, consensual activities amongst transgenders would continue to constitute an offence.
8. Section 377, if retained in its present form, would involve the violation of several fundamental rights of the LGBTs, namely right to privacy, right to dignity, equality, liberty and right to freedom of expression.
9. Sexual autonomy and the right to choose a partner of one's choice is an inherent aspect of the right to life and the right to autonomy.
10. The Indian Constitution mandates that we must promote fraternity amongst the citizens and Section 377 is an anathema to the concept of fraternity as enshrined in the Preamble to our Constitution.
11. Section 377 is violative of Article 14 of the Constitution as it is vague, in the sense that carnal intercourse against the order of nature is neither defined in the Section nor in the IPC or any other law.
12. Section 377 violates Article 15 of the Constitution since there is discrimination inherent in it based on the sex of a person's sexual

partner. Same-sex partner is criminalised even if the partner consents, which is not the case with an opposite-sex partner.

On the other hand, some of the respondents and interveners contended that:

1. Homosexuality is against the order of nature and Section 377 rightly forbids it.
2. There is no uncanalised and unbridled right to privacy and the said right cannot be abused. Further, there is no personal liberty to abuse one's organs and such offensive acts committed by abusing the organs are forbidden by Section 377 IPC.
3. Section 377 makes certain acts punishable after taking note of the legal systems and principles which prevailed in ancient India, and now in 2018, the Section 377 is more relevant legally, medically, morally and constitutionally.
4. Persons indulging in unnatural sexual acts are more susceptible and vulnerable to contracting HIV/AIDS and the percentage of prevalence of AIDS in homosexuals is much greater than heterosexuals. The right to privacy may not be extended to such persons, in order to enable people to indulge in unnatural offences and thereby contact AIDS.
5. If Section 377 is declared unconstitutional, then the family system which is the bulwark of social culture will be in shambles, the institution of marriage will be affected detrimentally.
6. Since fundamental rights are not absolute, there is no unreasonableness in Section 377 of the IPC and decriminalising the same would run foul to all religions practised in the country, and while deciding the ambit and scope of constitutional morality, Article 25 also deserves to be given due consideration.
7. In the event consenting acts between two same-sex adults are excluded from the ambit of Section 377 IPC, then a married woman would be rendered remediless under the IPC against her bi-sexual husband and his consenting male partner indulging in any sexual acts.
8. Section 377 criminalises an act irrespective of gender or sexual orientation of the persons involved. The universal application of the said provision without any gender bias is the touchstone of Part III of the Constitution and is not arbitrary, as there is no intentional or unreasonable discrimination in the provision.
9. Section 377 of the IPC is not violative of Article 15 of the Constitution as the said Article prohibits discrimination on the grounds of only religion, race, caste, sex, place of birth or any of them but not sexual orientation. The word 'sexual orientation' is alien to our Constitution.

If the word 'sex' has to be replaced by 'sexual orientation', it would require a constitutional amendment.

10. Decriminalisation of Section 377 of the IPC will open a floodgate of social issues which the legislative domain is not capable of accommodating, as same-sex marriages would become social experiments with an unpredictable outcome. It will also have a cascading effect on the existing laws.

The Union of India submitted that:

1. As far as the constitutional validity of Section 377 of the IPC, to the extent it applies to 'consensual acts of adults in private', is concerned, the same to the wisdom of the Supreme Court.
2. In the event Section 377 of the IPC so far as 'consensual acts of adults in private' is declared unconstitutional, other ancillary issues or rights may not be dealt with by the Bench. If other issues are considered, the Union of India expressed its wish to file a detailed affidavit in reply.

THE JUDGMENT

The Supreme Court observed that '*Our Constitution is a living and organic document capable of expansion with the changing needs and demands of the society... The role of the Courts gains more importance when the rights which are affected belong to a class of persons or a minority group who have been deprived of even their basic rights since time immemorial.*'

After hearing the arguments and submission made by the petitioners, interveners and the Union of India, the Supreme Court held that:

- Sexual orientation is one of the many biological phenomena which is natural and inherent in an individual and is controlled by neurological and biological factors. Any discrimination on the basis of one's sexual orientation would entail a violation of the fundamental right of freedom of expression.
- After the privacy judgment in ***Puttaswamy case***, the right to privacy has been raised to the pedestal of a fundamental right. The existence of Section 377 of the IPC abridges the fundamental rights of the LGBT community.
- Under the autonomy principle, the individual has sovereignty over his/her body. He/she can surrender his/her autonomy willfully to another individual and their intimacy in privacy is a matter of their choice. Section 377 of the IPC does not give due recognition to the absence of 'wilful and informed consent' to criminalise carnal

intercourse. This results in criminalising even voluntary carnal intercourse between homosexuals, heterosexuals, bisexuals and transgenders.

- Section 377 of the IPC subjects the LGBT community as societal pariah and dereliction and therefore, is manifestly arbitrary. Thus it violates Article 14 of the Constitution.
- Section 377 IPC amounts to an unreasonable restriction because public decency and morality cannot be amplified beyond a rational limit and cannot be accepted as reasonable grounds for curbing the fundamental rights of freedom of expression and choice of the LGBT community. Thus, it violates Article 19(1)(a) of the Constitution.

Thus, the Supreme Court held that '*Section 377 IPC, so far as it penalizes any consensual sexual relationship between two adults, be it homosexuals (man and a man), heterosexuals (man and a woman) or lesbians (woman and a woman), cannot be regarded as constitutional*'.

In other words, the Court held that Section 377 of the Penal Code is unconstitutional, to the extent that it criminalises **consensual sexual conduct between adults of the same sex**.

Persons who are homosexual have a fundamental right to live with dignity, which in the larger framework of the Preamble of India will assure the cardinal constitutional value of fraternity. Hence, the court overruled the decision in ***Suresh Kaushal case***.

IMPORTANCE AND IMPACT

The dilution of Section 377 marks a welcome departure from centuries of heteronormative thinking. The judgment is a step in the direction that expands the frontiers of personal freedom.[4]

It corrected the judicial error committed by a two-member Bench in the ***Suresh Kumar Koushal*** (2013).

It upheld the right of the LGBT community to have intimate relations with people of their choice, their inherent right to privacy and dignity and the freedom to live without fear.

As Justice Chandrachud observed, this judgment will help sexual minorities 'confront the closet' and realise their rights.

4. https://www.thehindu.com/opinion/editorial/the-right-to-love/article24885401.ece

33

Anuradha Bhasin v. Union of India (2020)

Is the Government of India empowered to impose a complete shutdown of internet services?

If yes, can the shutdown go on 'indefinitely'?

Further, if a government imposes a ban on internet services, can that Order be subjected to judicial review?

Anuradha Bhasin v. Union of India case is associated with the challenging of law-and-order restrictions and orders passed by the Executive in light of the abrogation of Article 370.

In this case, the Supreme Court declared the right to practice profession and trade over the internet as a fundamental right under Article 19(1)(g).

INTRODUCTION

The right to shut down the internet as a whole has been granted to the government by Suspension Rules passed under the Telegraph Act.

However, these rules provide certain safeguards for citizens as any ban on the internet also results in curtailment of the fundamental rights of citizens as a whole.

In *Anuradha Bhasin v. Union of India,* the Supreme Court held that any ban on telecommunication services of any kind is a drastic measure and should only be used in grave necessity or unavoidable circumstances.

BACKGROUND

The constitutional order abrogating Article 370 in the then State of Jammu and Kashmir was accompanied by restrictions on movement, shutting down of mobile, internet and other such services.

In light of such circumstances, journalists claimed that restrictions on movement and unavailability of internet facilities hamper their right to freedom of speech and expression, and freedom to carry out any trade and profession.

Therefore, a writ petition was filed before the Supreme Court challenging the same under Article 32.

LEGAL ISSUES INVOLVED

1. Whether the Government can claim exemption from producing all the orders passed under Section 144 of CrPC and other orders under the suspension rules?
2. Whether the freedom of speech and expression and freedom to practice any profession, or to carry on any occupation, trade or business over the internet is a part of the fundamental rights under Part III of the Constitution?
3. Whether the Government's action of prohibiting internet access is valid?
4. Whether the imposition of restrictions under Section 144 of CrPC was valid?
5. Whether the freedom of the press of the petitioner was violated due to the restrictions?

SECTION 144 OF CrPC

Section 144 in the Code of Criminal Procedure, 1973 deals with the power to issue orders in urgent cases of nuisance or apprehended danger. It is an emergency measure to tackle the law-and-order situation.

The power to invoke the same is entrusted to the district magistrate, sub-divisional magistrate or any other executive magistrate empowered by the State. There are seven sub-sections provided in Section 144 dealing with–when the order should be proclaimed, what should be its ground, what should be its duration and what are the procedures that need to be contemplated by invoking the same.

ARGUMENTS

The petitioner argued that the ban on the internet has resulted in bringing press and media to a grinding halt.

The orders passed under Section 144 of CrPC are not accompanied by valid reasoning from the government. It was pointed out that the order of the Magistrate under Section 144 of CrPC cannot be passed to the public generally, and must be specifically targeted against the group which is likely to disturb the peace.

Further, the petitioner argued that the orders are passed only on the apprehension of danger to law and order. There is no concrete evidence of any such risk; hence a balancing of measures is required between national security and curbing terrorism.

It was also argued that the procedure that is to be followed for restricting internet services is provided under the Temporary Suspension of Telecom Services (Public Emergency or Public Service) Rules, 2017 which were notified under the Telegraph Act and cannot be done under Section 144 of CrPC.

It was emphasized that the orders unreasonably restrict the fundamental rights of citizens. Hence they fail to justify the test of proportionality.

TEST OF PROPORTIONALITY

The doctrine of proportionality is a legal method adopted by the court, especially by the constitutional court, in balancing the rights which collide with each other due to administrative action.

The doctrine mandates that there must be a reasonable nexus between the desired result and measures taken to achieve the goal. There should not be anything shockingly disproportionate to the consciousness of the court.

The court will analyze the advantages and disadvantages of the said administrative action for testing proportionality. It is adopted from Europe jurisprudence and is adopted in India through *Om Kumar v. Union of India*[1] case.

The respondents argued that the state of Jammu and Kashmir suffers from both physical and digital cross-border terrorism. Hence, drastic measures are required to ensure that no issues of public disturbance arise. The Magistrates passed orders under Section 144 of CrPC, as they were the ones present on the ground and had the best knowledge of the situation at hand.

Concerning newspapers and other forms of communication, there was no general clampdown, but restrictions were specifically imposed on the internet because it provides two-way communication.

Internet can act as a comfortable medium to exchange messages and spread fake news. This different context should be kept in mind by the Court while dealing with the restrictions concerning the two media.

1. https://indiankanoon.org/doc/1285195/

THE JUDGMENT

The Hon'ble Supreme Court declared that the freedom of speech and expression and the freedom to practice any profession or carry on any trade, business or occupation over the medium of the internet enjoys constitutional protection under Article 19(1)(a) and Article 19(1)(g).

The restriction upon the exercise of these fundamental rights should align with the mandate under Article 19 (2) and (6) of the Constitution. The restrictions should also justify the test of proportionality.

An order suspending internet services for an indefinite period is not permissible under the Temporary Suspension of Telecom Services (Public Emergency or Public Service) Rules, 2017.

Suspension can be utilized for a temporary duration only and it must adhere to the principle of proportionality.

Since these Rules do not provide for a definite period, the Court stated that until an appropriate amendment is made by the legislature, Review Committee constituted under the Rules should conduct a periodic review of such orders within seven working days and ensure that suspension is not extended beyond the necessary duration.

Any order suspending the internet under the Suspension Rules is subject to judicial review based on the parameters set out herein.

The Court also highlighted that any ban on telecommunication services of any kind is a drastic measure and should only be used in grave necessity or unavoidable circumstances.

The Supreme Court said that the power under Section 144 of CrPC is remedial as well as preventive and is exercisable not only when there exists present danger, but also when there is an apprehension of danger. However, the danger contemplated should be in the nature of an 'emergency' and to prevent obstruction and annoyance or injury to any person lawfully employed. The Court held that the power under Section 144 of CrPC cannot be used to suppress the legitimate expression of opinion or grievance or exercise of any democratic rights.

IMPORTANCE AND IMPACT

In this case, the Supreme Court highlighted the importance of the internet in today's information technology world. The fundamental right to use the internet for freedom of speech and expression and to carry on trade, business or profession was also recognized by the Court.

The recognition of this right can have many more implications in the upcoming future and may also change the way internet services are provided to every individual.

The government's right to reasonably restrict the internet has been recognized in the case. This may prove to be a contentious issue in future as instances of internet bans have been on the rise.

Rambabu Singh Thakur v. Sunil Arora (2020)

Elections are the core processes upon which most democracies are based.

However, the criminalization of politics is a serious threat to the efficient functioning of democratic nations like India.

According to Section 8 of the Representation of People Act, 1951 an electoral candidate convicted of criminal charges is disqualified from contesting elections in India.

However, what about political parties giving tickets to candidates with a criminal background?

What about candidates undergoing criminal trials contesting in elections?

Should They Also Be Banned?

The Supreme Court in *Rambabu Singh Thakur v. Sunil Arora* case ensured that the general public will be properly aware of the criminal background of candidates contesting elections so that they can exercise their right to vote judiciously.

However, the Supreme Court resisted banning candidates undergoing criminal trials to contest elections.

INTRODUCTION

Indian Constitution is silent concerning what disqualifies a person from contesting elections to the Parliament, Legislative Assembly or any other Legislature. This is dealt with by the **Representation of People Act, 1951** which mentions the criteria for disqualifying a person from contesting an election of the legislature.

It is well established that the right to contest in elections is not a fundamental right but instead a statutory right which is dependent on legislative actions. By the judgment in this case, the Supreme Court offered directions in the exercise of constitutional powers under Article 129 and

Article 142 of the Constitution of India for a cemented democratic spirit that upholds transparency.

> **Article 129** - The Supreme Court shall be a court of record and shall have the powers of such a court including the power to punish for contempt of itself.
>
> **Article 142** deals with the discretionary power of the Supreme Court. It states that the Supreme Court can pass any order or decree necessary for doing complete justice in any matter pending before it.

BACKGROUND

In a previous case, ***People's Union for Civil Liberties v. Union of India***, the Supreme Court had held that for a democracy to survive, the best available men must be chosen as the people's representatives for the proper governance of the country.

The best available persons, as is expected by the democratic system should not have criminal antecedents and the voters have a right to know about their antecedents and assets.

Keeping the aforementioned view, the Supreme Court appropriated the following directions in the ***Public Interest Foundation v. Union of India*** case:

1. Each candidate shall fill up the Form as provided by the Election Commission and the Form must contain all the particulars as required therein.
2. The Form also should state criminal cases pending against the candidate in bold letters.
3. If a candidate is contesting an election on the ticket of a particular party, he/she is required to inform the party about the criminal cases pending against him/her.
4. The concerned political party shall be obligated to put up on its website the aforesaid information about candidates having criminal antecedents.
5. The candidate and the concerned political party shall issue a declaration in the widely circulated newspapers in the locality about the antecedents of the candidate and also give wide publicity in the electronic media.

Rambabu Singh Thakur v. Sunil Arora case was a contempt petition regarding the pertinent criminalization of politics. This case also in its rights called for attention concerning disregard towards the directions laid down by a Constitutional Bench of the Supreme Court in ***Public Interest Foundation v. Union of India***.

CONTEMPT OF COURT

In India contempt of court is provided under the **Contempt of Courts Act, 1971**. It defines contempt of court as civil contempt and criminal contempt. Civil contempt is defined as wilful disobedience of any judgment, decree, writ, direction, order or other processes of a court or wilful breach of an undertaking given to a Court. Criminal contempt means publication of any matter or the doing of any act whatsoever which -

(i) scandalises or tends to scandalise, or lowers or tends to lower the authority of any court,
(ii) prejudices, or interferes or tends to interfere with, the due course of any judicial proceeding.
(iii) interferes or tends to interfere with, or obstructs or tends to obstruct, the administration of justice in any other manner.

LEGAL ISSUES INVOLVED

1. Whether Article 102 of the Constitution of India mentions instances where disqualification of Members of Parliament is possible?
2. Whether the Supreme Court can make new laws which would be beyond the scope of Article 102?
3. Whether making laws regarding such disqualification by the court will act as a violation of the principle of separation of powers?

ARTICLE 102 OF THE INDIAN CONSTITUTION

1. A person shall be disqualified for being chosen as, and for being, a member of either House of Parliament –
   a. if he holds any office of profit under the Government of India or the Government of any State, other than an office declared by the Parliament by law not to disqualify its holder;

b. if he is of unsound mind and stands so declared by a competent court;
c. if he is an undischarged insolvent;
d. if he is not a citizen of India, has voluntarily acquired the citizenship of a foreign State, or is under any acknowledgement of allegiance or adherence to a foreign State;
e. if he is so disqualified by or under any law made by the Parliament.

Explanation: For the purposes of this clause a person shall not be deemed to hold an office of profit under the Government of India or the Government of any State by reason only that he is a Minister either for the Union or for such State.

2. A person shall be disqualified for being a member of either House of Parliament if he is so disqualified under the Tenth Schedule.

ARGUMENTS

The petitioner stressed the interest of the people at large and therefore a candidate having criminal antecedents should be disqualified from contesting the elections. The petitioner also prayed to the court to direct the Election Commissioner to prevent political parties from giving tickets to candidates having criminal backgrounds.

The petitioner urged the court to invoke the powers under Article 142 of the Constitution of India to pass a decree which is necessary for ensuring complete justice.

In the contour of the petitioner's arguments seeking laws against the criminalisation of politics, respondents highlighted the **principle of presumption of innocence, if a person is considered innocent until and unless he is proven guilty**. Therefore, according to respondents disqualifying a candidate because there are pending criminal cases against him/her would be unjust. Respondents also argued based on the **doctrine of colourable legislation that states "what cannot be done directly cannot be done indirectly".**

WHAT IS DOCTRINE OF COLOURABLE LEGISLATION?

The maxim implies that 'whatever legislature cannot do directly, it cannot do indirectly'. This doctrine is also called as 'fraud on the Constitution'. It comes into play when a legislature does not possess the power to make law upon a particular subject but it tries to overcome the limitation by indirectly making one.

THE JUDGMENT

The Supreme Court after considering the above-mentioned issues framed an observation of the incapability of the court to issue the writ of mandamus to the Election Commission of India in the matters related to laws on disqualification on grounds of criminal proceedings against the candidates. The Supreme Court abstained itself from crossing the *Lakshmanrekha* but provided six guidelines to ensure fairness and decriminalization coupled with efficiency. They are:

1. It shall be mandatory for both the central and state-level political parties to provide detailed information about the selected candidates including the pending criminal cases. The information about pending criminal cases should contain–the nature of the offence, whether charges have been framed or not, the concerned court, the case number, etc. The political party shall also provide reasons for such selection along with the reasons as to why the other candidates with no criminal antecedence could not be selected.
2. The reasons for selection have to be based upon the qualification, achievements, and merits of the candidate and not just their winning ability at the polls.
3. The detailed information about the candidate shall be published in one local vernacular newspaper and one national newspaper along with the social media platforms of the political party concerned, including Facebook and Twitter.
4. This information shall be published in either of the two-time frames, whichever is earlier –
   a. Within 48 hours of the selection of the candidate.
   b. Within not less than two weeks before the first date of filing for nomination.

5. The political party concerned shall submit a report of compliance with the Election Commission by following all the aforesaid directions and such submission has to be done within 72 hours of the selection of the concerned candidate.
6. In case of failure of submission of such compliance, the Election Commission shall put forward non-compliance by the political party to the Supreme Court of India by way of contempt of this court's orders/directions.

IMPORTANCE AND IMPACT

The Hon'ble Supreme Court in ***Rambabu Singh Thakur v. Sunil Arora*** case ensured that the general public will be aware of the election candidates in a loud and clear manner so that they can exercise their right to vote judiciously. The judgment was delivered without diluting the established principles of separation of powers.

The Division Bench also expressed their growing concerns on statistics which shows as many as 43% of Members of Parliament had criminal cases pending against them.

Even though the petitioner's prayers were not fulfilled in their entirety, the Supreme Court by its judgment substantiated many procedures which were given earlier by the Apex Court itself.

35

Internet and Mobile Association of India v. Reserve Bank of India (2020)

The Reserve Bank of India (RBI) is the regulator of the entire banking sector in India.

However, does RBI possess the power to regulâte Cryptocurrencies?

Reserve Bank of India in 2018 instructed entities regulated by the Central Bank to terminate any relationship with individuals or business entities dealing with virtual currencies.

Many cryptocurrency enthusiasts questioned this order. Questions were raised about whether the powers of RBI as regulatory authority were exercised properly in a manner prescribed by law while dealing with cryptocurrencies.

In the *Internet and Mobile Association of India v. Reserve Bank of India* case, the Supreme Court decided in favour of cryptocurrency transactions in India after using the doctrine of proportionality.

As a result, the RBI's circular to regulate cryptocurrencies was declared illegal and set aside. This paved the way for facilitating the exchanges of crypto traders not only in India but around the world.

INTRODUCTION

Throughout history, various mediums of exchange have been used to meet people's needs, beginning with the barter system and progressing to coins, currency notes, and so on.

However, in the twenty-first century, with technological progress, we have arrived at an intangible medium of exchange. It is known as cryptocurrency, also known as virtual currency.

What distinguishes cryptocurrency from traditional currency is that it is decentralised, which means that it is not regulated by any central authority in the world. However, cryptocurrencies are protected by blockchain, which ensures their security and the augmentation of their price in the future.

The rise of crypto-asset funds demonstrates that these new financial products have the potential to replace traditional currencies-if the governments approve their use globally.

VIRTUAL CURRENCY

'Virtual Currency' is a digital representation of value that can be traded digitally. It should perform the functions of money such as (1) a medium of exchange; and/or (2) a unit of account; and/or (3) a store of value. However, they may not have a legal tender status.

'Cryptocurrency' is defined as a math-based, decentralised convertible virtual currency protected by cryptography. It relies on public and private keys to transfer value from one person to another and is signed cryptographically each time it is transferred.

BACKGROUND

In his budget statement on January 31, 2018, the Minister of Finance stated that the government did not view cryptocurrencies as legal tender and that it would take all necessary steps to prevent their use for funding illegal activities or as a component of the payment system. He did add, though, that the government would actively look into using blockchain technology to usher in the digital economy.

On April 5, 2018, the RBI issued a "Statement on Development and Regulatory Policies", instructing entities regulated by the RBI to not deal with services to any individual/business dealing with virtual currencies; and to terminate any existing relationship with such individuals/business entities dealing with virtual currencies.

The Internet and Mobile Association of India which represents the interests of the online and digital services industries have filed a writ petition to challenge this prohibition.

One of the main grounds for the challenge was that virtual currencies are not legal tender but tradable commodities or digital goods, not falling within the regulatory framework of the RBI Act, 1934 or the Banking Regulation Act, 1949.

According to Section 2(h) of the Foreign Exchange Management Act (FEMA), 1999, and an examination of the definition of currency, they may fall under the category of 'other similar instruments'. Furthermore, it was argued that these services could not be classified as a 'payment system', resulting in their exclusion from the Payment Settlement and Systems Act of 2007.

Hence, the Internet and Mobile Association of India took a stand that the RBI cannot regulate virtual currencies in India.

LEGAL ISSUES INVOLVED

1. Whether the RBI possess the power to deal with, regulate or even ban virtual currencies?
2. Whether the exercise of powers of regulatory authority was exercised properly in a manner prescribed by law?

ARGUMENTS

The petitioners argued that the RBI lacks the authority to prohibit virtual currencies from trading through virtual currency exchanges because virtual currencies are not legal tender. As commodities or digital goods, virtual currencies do not fall under the purview of the regulatory framework of the RBI or the Banking Regulation Act, 1949.

The Indian government's Department of Economic Affairs, the Securities and Exchange Board of India, the Central Stock Exchange of India, and the Board of Direct Taxes were just a few of the parties the petitioners cited as examples of changing mindsets. The petitioners pointed out that in contrast to the RBI, which has adopted a different approach without any justification, these parties have recognized the benefits and advantages of cryptocurrencies as digital assets.

The petitioners drew attention to the RBI's deliberate concealment of the fact that not all cryptocurrencies are anonymous. They presented a study from the European Parliament that divided virtual currencies into anonymous and pseudo-anonymous groups. Therefore, in their opinion, RBI should have forbidden only anonymous virtual currencies if the issue sought to be addressed was the anonymity of transactions. They also argued that the virtual currencies do not fall within the credit system of the country and therefore enabling the RBI to decide its mode is questionable.

The petitioners also expressed their surprise at the RBI's dichotomy that cryptocurrency is illegal but blockchain technology is accepted.

The petitioners further argued that the benefit of the rule of judicial deference to economic policies of the State is not available to the RBI, as the circular by the RBI is an exercise of power by a statutory body and is neither legislation nor an exercise of executive power.

The petitioners stated that a total prohibition, especially through subordinate legislation such as a directive from the RBI, of an activity not declared by law to be unlawful, and is violative of Article 19(1)(g) of the Indian Constitution.

In this case, the RBI took a stance that virtual currencies do not satisfy the criteria required for being acknowledged as currency such as store of value, medium of payment and unit of account.

The Central Bank pointed out that the virtual currency exchanges do not have any formal or structured mechanism for handling consumer grievances.

Virtual currencies are capable of being used for illegal activities due to their anonymity/pseudo-anonymity.

The RBI highlighted that the increased use of virtual currencies would eventually erode the monetary stability of the Indian currency and the credit system.

In the opinion of the RBI, the impugned decisions were necessitated because, virtual currency transactions cannot be termed as a payment system, but only peer-to-peer transactions which do not involve a system provider under the Payments and Settlement Systems Act. Also, no one has an unfettered fundamental right to do business on the network of the entities regulated by the RBI.

Despite this, virtual currency transactions have the potential to develop as a parallel system of payment.

THE JUDGMENT

The Supreme Court acknowledged that the RBI has not found, in the last five years or more, that the activities of Virtual Currency Exchanges (VCEs) have impacted negatively the way entities were regulated by the RBI function. The Supreme Court also observed that the RBI's consistent stance has not prohibited virtual currencies in the country.

The Supreme Court cited the case of the Inter-Ministerial Committee which thought that a ban might be an extreme tool and that the same objectives can be achieved through regulatory measures.

The Supreme Court stated that the concern of the RBI should be about the entities regulated by it. However, the RBI has not come out with any stand that any of the entities regulated by it have suffered any loss, directly or indirectly, on account of the interface that the VCEs had with any of them.

In the *State of Maharashtra v. Indian Hotel and Restaurants Association* case, the Supreme Court held that there must have been at least some empirical data about the degree of harm suffered by the regulated entities.

The Apex Court determined that the RBI had failed to meet the aforementioned stand before the restriction and did not comply with Article 19(6) of the Indian Constitution.

The European Union's July 2018 report, suggesting a complete ban on cryptocurrencies was not necessary to govern the banking industry, was another source the Court cited. Before enforcing a total ban, the Court noted that the RBI had not taken into account less intrusive options.

Finally, the Court decided in favour of cryptocurrencies after using the doctrine of proportionality. As a result of these prominent interpretations, the RBI's circular was declared illegal and set aside, paving the way for facilitating the exchanges of crypto traders not only in India but around the world.

THE DOCTRINE OF PROPORTIONALITY

To achieve the desired outcome, an administrative measure must be proportionate to the situation at hand. This theory seeks to balance means and ends.

IMPORTANCE AND IMPACT

The Supreme Court's ruling highlights the value of judicial scrutiny about choices made on economic policy. The RBI circular was overruled by the Supreme Court because it was disproportionate to its intended goal. It should also be noted that Supreme Court had not made any comments on whether virtual currency is genuinely legitimate or not. This judgment, therefore, does not eliminate the ongoing dangers connected with trading in virtual currencies, which are still not subject to regulation in India.

The judgment resulted in the boom of the virtual currency industry in India and abroad. A notable increase in the trading of virtual currencies has been observed in India since the relaxation of this ban. While this judgment marks a positive step toward the growth of cryptocurrencies and exchange technology nationwide, there are still lingering concerns about possible misuse of virtual currencies for money laundering, terrorist financing, etc.

36

Laxmibai Chandaragi v. State of Karnataka (2021)

Is consent of the family needed when two adults decide to marry?

Do the parents have a say in their child's right to choose a life partner who has attained the legal age for contracting marriage?

Can society exert any influence over the matrimonial choices of any person?

Hon'ble Supreme Court in *Laxmibai Chandaragi* case ruled that in India when two adult individuals agree to marry, consent of family, community or clan is not required.

The Court has also stated that the choice of an individual to select a partner for marriage is an integral part of 'dignity'.

INTRODUCTION

In India, culturally, marriages are often solemnized with the consent of families. The decision of the youngsters to marry based on their choice often results in resistance from the family members.

It is a common occurrence that when two individuals marry against the will of the family, the girl's family registers a complaint against the boy and his family and alleges abduction.

The harassment of young couples by their families to the extent of 'honour killings' are prevalent in many states in India.

BACKGROUND

Father of Ms. Laxmibai Chandaragi filed an FIR in a police station in Karnataka reporting that his daughter is missing. Upon investigation, it came to the light that she has travelled on her own and married Mr. Santosh Singh Yadav without informing her parents. Later she sent a marriage certificate to her parents through WhatsApp and revealed to them the factum of marriage.

Laxmibai also informed the Investigation Officer (IO) about her marriage and stated that she was residing with him. The IO insisted on her appearance before the police station where the complaint was filed to record her statement to close the case. She refused to comply with the same and stated that there was an imminent threat from her parents. However, the IO threatened to register a case of kidnapping against Santosh unless she visited the police station.

It is in the aforesaid circumstances, that the present petition was filed under Article 32 of the Constitution of India.

LEGAL ISSUES INVOLVED

1. Can the Investigating Officer compel someone to travel to a specifically designated Police station to record a statement?
2. Can the police threaten someone by pursuing false charges against them in case the person fails to comply with the Police Officer's dictates?
3. Do the parents have a say in their child's right to choose a life partner who has attained the legal age for contracting marriage?
4. Can society exert any influence over the matrimonial choices of any person?
5. Whether the FIR should be quashed as both the parties married on their own will and with consent?

ARGUMENTS

The petitioner asserted that she was subject to dual jurisdiction since she shared a residence with Petitioner No. 2 in Uttar Pradesh while being a resident of Karnataka when they filed their petition with the Supreme Court of India under Article 32 of the Indian Constitution.

She claimed that their uncle, Petitioner No. 1, was threatening them. They also requested protection from the Allahabad High Court, but despite repeated requests for a prompt hearing over the course of a month, the petition could not be delivered to the board.

THE JUDGMENT

In this case, Hon'ble Supreme Court quashed the complaint filed and reprimanded the Investigation Officer for his callous behaviour. The Court recommended that the concerned officer should be sent for counselling and other Investigation Officers should be trained to deal with such sensitive issues arising in future.

The Apex Court also stated that the right of choice is an important part of dignity and this right cannot be compromised on the pretext of 'class honour'. It made the following important observations on the right to choose one's partner for marriage:

1. The norms of society are changing. Educated boys and girls now have started to express the freedom in choosing their partners.
2. The consent of family or community or clan is not necessary once two adult individuals agree to enter into a wedlock.
3. 'Intimacies of Marriage' lie within the core zone of privacy and hence the right to marry a person of choice is an integral part of Article 21 of the Constitution of India.
4. The Court also cited *K. S. Puttaswamy v. Union of India,* where the autonomy of a person in relation to family and marriage, should be considered as an integral component of the dignity of an individual.

IMPORTANCE AND IMPACT

The *Laxmibai Chandaragi* case should be read in the backdrop of Dr. B. R. Ambedkar's words about 'Annihilation of Caste':

> "*I am convinced that the real remedy is inter-marriage. Fusion of blood can alone create the feeling of being kith and kin, and unless this feeling of kinship, of being kindred, becomes paramount, the separatist feeling–the feeling of being aliens–created by caste will not vanish. Where society is already well-knit by other ties, marriage is an ordinary incident of life. But where society is cut asunder, marriage as a binding force becomes a matter of urgent necessity. The real remedy for breaking caste is inter-marriage. Nothing else will serve as the solvent of caste*".

Hundreds of honour killings had happened in different states in India. It continues to shatter the dreams of many youngsters. However, the *Laxmibai Chandaragi* judgment comes to the aid of many young couples who are harassed by family members for marrying against their choices.

Mohammad Salimullah v. Union of India (2021)

How should the Government of India deal with refugees who come to India seeking shelter?

Can the Government of India force refugees to return to the country in which they are liable to be subjected to persecution?

As Article 21 (Right to Life) of the Indian Constitution applies even to non-citizens, do refugees have the right not to be deported?

INTRODUCTION

The Supreme Court in the case of *Mohammad Salimullah v. Union of India* dealt with an application filed for the release of detained Rohingya refugees. The Court tried to answer the question of whether the detained refugees could be deported to their country of origin by the Government of India.

The Apex Court considered the view that the fundamental right to reside and settle in India guaranteed under Article 19(1)(e) of the Indian Constitution is available only to the citizens.

The Court ruled that the right not to be deported is ancillary (secondary) to the right to reside or settle in any part of the territory of India.

BACKGROUND

Since 2011, Rohingya refugees had been arriving in India from Myanmar because of ethnic conflicts there and were being housed in various refugee camps.

According to Indian government sources, as of 2017, an estimated 10,000 Rohingya Muslims are living in Jammu and 40,000 living in other parts of the country after entering India illegally.

In 2017, the Ministry of Home Affairs issued a letter to the Chief Secretaries of all the State Governments and Administrators of Union Territories advising them to sensitize all law enforcement and intelligence agencies to take prompt action to deport the Rohingya refugees.

In 2021, about 150 Rohingya refugees were detained in a sub-jail in Jammu. They faced deportation back to Myanmar. To alleviate this situation, the petitioner, Mohammad Salimullah, approached the Supreme Court seeking the provision of basic human amenities to the refugees and to prevent their deportation.

LEGAL ISSUES INVOLVED

1. Is India bound by the Principle of 'Non-Refoulement'?
2. Does the deportation of Rohingya Muslims violate their rights granted under the Indian Constitution Articles 14 and 21?
3. Whether the fundamental right mentioned in Article 19(1)(e) available to non-citizens of India as well?

NON-REFOULEMENT

This principle is mentioned under Article 33 of the U.N. Convention for Refugees, 1951. The principle of non-refoulement states that no refugees should be returned to any place where there are chances of their persecution. This principle emerged during World War II for the protection of refugees.

ARGUMENTS

The petitioner, in this case, tried to argue that -

1. The principle of non-refoulement (the practice of not forcing refugees to return to the country in which they are liable to be subjected to persecution) is a right that is guaranteed under Article 21 of the Constitution;
2. The rights guaranteed under Articles 14 and 21 are available to non-citizens;

3. Though India is not a signatory to the United Nations Convention on the Status of Refugees 1951, it is still a party to the Universal Declaration of Human Rights, 1948, the International Covenant on Civil and Political Rights, 1966 and the Convention on the Rights of the Child, 1992, it still has a binding obligation towards non-refoulement.

The Government of India in its reply stated that the persons whose protection is sought against deportation are 'foreigners' within the meaning of Section 2(a) of the Foreigners Act, 1946,[1].

India is not a signatory to the United Nations Convention on the Status of Refugees 1951. The principle of non-refoulement applies to only 'contracting states' of the 1951 Convention.

Further, it was argued by the Government that though rights guaranteed under Articles 14 and 21 may be available to non-citizens, the fundamental right to reside and settle in India is guaranteed under Article 19(1)(e) and is available only to the citizens.

The Government stated that India's porous borders allow for an influx of immigrants who may enter the country for various reasons other than seeking refuge and hence pose a threat to national security. Hence the Government has to retain the unlimited and absolute right to expel any foreigner as needed.

THE JUDGMENT

The Apex Court stated that India is not bound by the Principle of 'Non-Refoulement' as India is not a signatory to the 1951 Refugee Convention.

Given the non-application of this Convention, the application of Article 51(c) of the Constitution was considered in the present case.

Article 51(c) is a directive principle of state policy. Article 51(c) says that the State shall endeavour to foster respect for international law and treaty obligation in the dealings of organized people with one another.

In addressing this question, the Court held that domestic courts can draw inspiration from International Conventions and Treaties as long as they are not in conflict with municipal and domestic laws.

The Court agreed that the rights under Articles 14 and 21 are available to all persons. However, the right to not be deported is ancillary (secondary)

1. Section 2(a), Foreigners Act, 1946- In this Act, 'foreigner' means a person who is not a citizen of India.

to the right to reside or settle in any part of the territory of India which is guaranteed under Article 19(1)(e). The Apex Court held that Article 19(1)(e) cannot be guaranteed to all persons.

IMPORTANCE AND IMPACT

In India, until now, there is no clear distinction between an illegal immigrant and a refugee because there is no legislation created explicitly regarding concerns involving refugees.

However, with respect to refugees, non-refoulement is often considered a rule of customary international law.

Having said that, any sovereign country has to balance national interest and national security with respect to humanitarian considerations.

The Supreme Court held that India is not bound by the Principle of 'Non-Refoulement' as India is not a signatory to the 1951 Refugee Convention.

The judgment made an important distinction with respect to the application of Articles 14, 19 and 21 of the Constitution to refugees seeking asylum in the country.

The judgment also clarified that, with respect to borrowing principles from international conventions and treaties, domestic courts can take inspiration from them as long as they are not in conflict with local laws.

38

Farzana Batool v. Union of India (2021)

Article 21-A obligates the government to provide free and compulsory education to all children in the age group of six to fourteen years only.

The right to professional education is not a fundamental right under Part III of the Constitution of India.

However, is the government of India obligated to provide professional education to the citizens?

Farzana Batool v. Union of India is a case that deliberates upon the obligation of the government under Article 21-A, that is, the right to education.

It pondered upon the fact that whether higher education up to the professional level comes under the fundamental right to education or not.

The Hon'ble Supreme Court held that the right to pursue higher education is not explicitly mentioned as a fundamental right in Part III of the Constitution and thus access to professional education is not a governmental obligation.

INTRODUCTION

Article 45 of the Constitution provided that the State shall endeavour to provide free and compulsory education to all children up to the age of fourteen years. But being a Directive Principles of State Policy (DPSP), this provision had its limitations. Hence, a change was needed to improve the level of education in India.

Ramamurti Committee Report, 1990 was a pioneer to recommend that the Right to Education should be included as a fundamental right under Part III along with other rights. The Supreme Court in the cases of *Mohini Jain v. State of Karnataka*[1] and *Unnikrishnan JP v. State of Andhra Pradesh*[2] recognized the right to education as a part of the Right to Life and Personal Liberty

1. https://indiankanoon.org/doc/40715/
2. https://indiankanoon.org/doc/1775396/

under Article 21. Finally, in 1999, the Tapas Majumdar Committee was set up, which recommended the insertion of Article 21A in the Constitution.

The 86th Constitutional Amendment Act, 2002 added Article 21A to the Constitution of India, which aims to provide free and compulsory education to children in the age group of six to fourteen years as a Fundamental Right.

The 86th Amendment also added a new fundamental duty under Article 51A which states that it is the duty of every citizen of India to provide opportunities for education to his/her child or ward between the age of six and fourteen years.

BACKGROUND

Two students from Ladakh named Ms. Farzana Batool and Mr. Mohammed Mehdi Waziri were nominated by the Administration of the Union Territory of Ladakh for admission to the MBBS degree programme through the Union Ministry of Health and Family Welfare's 'central pool' seats.

One of them was allocated a seat at Lady Hardinge Medical College (LMHC) and the other was assigned Maulana Azad Medical College (MAMC).

Unfortunately, these students were not admitted to their respective course of studies even though there was due nomination by the Administration of the Union Territory of Ladakh and in terms of the seats notified by the Union Government. Hence, they filed this writ petition under Article 32 to the Supreme Court.

LEAGAL ISSUES INVOLVED

1. Whether right to higher education is a fundamental right?
2. Whether access to quality education is infringed here on account of caste, class, religion or geographical region?
3. Whether it is correct to deprive students of pursuing professional education even after the allocation is made?

ARGUMENTS

The petitioners contended that their denial of admission to their allotted colleges was a violation of fundamental rights under Article 21A. They stated that their denial of admission was based on caste, class, place of birth, etc. Hence, the petitioners argued that even though the Right to

Professional Education is not stated explicitly in the Constitution, it should be considered as part of the Fundamental Right of the citizens.

The respondents were of the view that the Right to Higher Education is not a Fundamental Right and the Constitution only makes provision for free and compulsory 'elementary' education as a fundamental right. It was also put forth that the financial instability of students was the reason for the denial of their admission.

THE JUDGMENT

The Hon'ble Supreme Court held that the right to pursue higher education is not explicitly mentioned as a fundamental right in Part III of the Constitution. Thus access to professional education is not a governmental obligation.

However, the Apex Court observed that professional education plays a greater role in a student's life. No student should be denied access to education due to caste, class, gender, religion and geographic location.

The Court held that the State has an affirmative obligation to facilitate access to education, at all levels. The Court commented that such students who face barriers in accessing quality education should be provided with greater opportunities by the State.

The Hon'ble Court directed the respondents to complete the admission formalities of the petitioners within a week of the date of the Supreme Court's order and stated that there was no lawful justification for denying their admission to the respective colleges.

IMPORTANCE AND IMPACT

This judgment by the Supreme Court can be debated in both positive and negative light. The positive aspect of the decision lies in the fact that now providing quality professional education has been spelt out as an affirmative obligation. This precedence can act as a harbinger of change for many institutes run by the government which face a myriad of problems.

The negative aspect is that the burden of government has increased up to the professional level when it is struggling to even provide quality education at the elementary level. The sad state of government schools, high dropout rate, inefficient staff, etc. are a few problems that the education system in India is currently facing. For a system which is already facing financial crunches, ensuring quality professional education will create more challenges for the government.

39

Kerala Union of Working Journalists v. Union of India (2021)

What are the rights available to undertrial prisoners?

Does being an undertrial take away the fundamental right to life that accrues to every person in the country?

Are undertrial prisoners eligible to be provided with health and medical care as needed?

The Supreme Court of India in *Kerala Union of Working Journalists v. Union of India* case held that the fundamental right to life is available to undertrial prisoners.

This case established that undertrial prisoners are eligible to be provided health and medical care.

INTRODUCTION

A traditional rule of Indian criminal law is the presumption of innocence. In general, a person accused of a crime is assumed to be innocent unless proven guilty by the State. However, several Indian laws deviate from this tenet.

There are several media reports citing misuse of laws like the Unlawful (Activities) Prevention Act and Section 124A of IPC (Sedition law) by the state machinery.

There are lakhs of undertrials in various Indian prisons. Some of them may be innocent. In some cases, due process may not be followed in arrest. Further, there are numerous instances where undertrials are denied even basic human needs.

The Supreme Court in the *Kappan case*[1] checked whether due process was followed in his arrest. The Apex Court in this case upheld the right of undertrials in the country.

1. https://main.sci.gov.in/judgments

BACKGROUND

Kerala journalist Sidhique Kappan was arrested in Uttar Pradesh while going to Hathras to report a case of rape and murder of a girl.

A writ petition was filed in the Supreme Court seeking a writ of *habeas corpus* for the release of Kappan.

The petition alleged that Kappan had been taken into illegal custody in October 2020 without serving any notice or order as required under Section 107 of the Code of Criminal Procedure.[2]

The Uttar Pradesh state government claimed that Kappan was arrested lawfully under Sections 107 and 151 of the Code of Criminal Procedure and an FIR was registered against him under Section 153A (Promoting enmity between different groups on grounds of religion, race, place of birth, residence, language, etc., and doing acts prejudicial to maintenance of harmony), 295A (Deliberate and malicious acts, intended to outrage religious feelings of any class by insulting its religion or religious beliefs) and 124A (Sedition).

LEGAL ISSUES INVOLVED

The matter contested in this case was regarding the validity of the arrest of Kappan and whether the proper procedure established for arrest under the Code of Criminal Procedure was followed in this case.

2. Section 107. Security for keeping the peace in other cases.

(1) When an Executive Magistrate receives information that any person is likely to commit a breach of the peace or disturb the public tranquillity or to do any wrongful act that may probably occasion a breach of the peace or disturb the public tranquillity and is of opinion that there is sufficient ground for proceeding, he may, in the manner hereinafter provided, require such person to show cause why he should not be ordered to execute a bond, 1 with or without sureties,] for keeping the peace for such period, not exceeding one year, as the Magistrate thinks fit.

(2) Proceedings under this section may be taken before any Executive Magistrate when either the place where the breach of the peace or disturbance is apprehended is within his local jurisdiction or there is within such jurisdiction a person who is likely to commit a breach of the peace or disturb the public tranquillity or to do any wrongful act as aforesaid beyond such jurisdiction.

The petitioner sought directions from the court and the release of Kappan on bail due to his deteriorating health condition. With this as the central point of issue, the Court had to determine the matter of providing adequate health care to the detainee.

While there were larger factual and circumstantial matters to be discussed regarding the arrest of Kappan, the Supreme Court refused to comment on the factual matters and decided to adjudicate only on the matter of whether Kappan was receiving medical attention as his health conditions were rapidly deteriorating while under arrest.

ARGUMENTS

The petitioner argued that the arrest is illegal and is done without any prior information.

The petitioner requested that he be granted bail due to his serious medical issues, and the court was also shown a report that revealed the accused was Covid Positive and had also sustained a brain injury.

Additionally, the appellant pleaded for permission to travel to Kerala to see his mother, who was reportedly in serious health condition and had little prospect of long survival.

The state of Uttar Pradesh stated that it is evident from the records that the accused was brought before the jurisdictional court following his arrest, and only then was an FIR filed.

The state of Uttar Pradesh presented another set of medical records corresponding to the next morning that showed the accused tested to be Covid Negative.

The state also emphasized that the accused would be given much-needed medical treatment. The respondent further stated that the right to life is given to all, even to an undertrial.

THE JUDGMENT

The Apex Court, in this case, observed that the accused was legally detained and hence, did not intervene with the facts of the case.

The Court, however, gave instructions and orders about medical care.

The Court added that Sidhique Kappan is at liberty to avail appropriate remedy in accordance with law before the concerned courts for the grant of bail or to challenge the proceedings or for quashing the charge sheet.

The Court held that due to the precarious health condition of the detainee, it was necessary to provide adequate and effective medical assistance and treatment to him.

In doing so, the Court stated that the most precious fundamental right, that is the fundamental right to life, is unconditionally available to undertrials and detainees too.

The Court also permitted Sidhique Kappan to visit Kerala for five days to see his ailing mother.

IMPORTANCE AND IMPACT

This case is yet another judgment in the long line of cases that have reiterated the importance of preserving the human rights and dignity of detainees and prisoners.

Quite often undertrial prisoners are not aware of the rights and remedies available to them. It is important to note that even when in prison, detainees and arrestees do not lose their fundamental right with respect to the right to life and are very much eligible to receive adequate medical and health care as required by them.

There cannot be a denial of human rights just because a person has been potentially accused of a crime.

The criminal procedure code and the criminal justice system have been designed in a way that ensures that human rights are not violated. However, the onus is on the government to ensure that procedural safeguards are followed to prevent the violation of the rights guaranteed.

Barun Chandra Thakur v. Master Bholu (2022)

Can a child be treated like an adult if he is an offender?

How fair is the current system when a child between the ages of 16 to 18 years may be treated as an adult when he/she has committed a heinous offence?

Is it mandatory for the Juvenile Justice Board to take opinions or assistance from experts before passing any preliminary order?

What are the parameters the Juvenile Justice Board should look at while considering a child as an adult?

Section 15 of the Juvenile Justice (Care and Protection of Children) Act, 2015 (JJ Act) states that a child between the ages of 16 to 18 years may be treated as an adult when he/she has committed a heinous offence.

However, this decision will depend on a preliminary assessment done by Juvenile Justice Board.

In *Barun Chandra Thakur v. Master Bholu and Another* case, the Supreme Court ruled that the Board was required to consult with experts before making any preliminary decisions.

INTRODUCTION

Juvenile Justice Act was enacted to protect children in conflict with the law and children in need of care and protection.

Before the Amendment of 2015, all children below 18 years of age were treated as juveniles (children) and were sent to social reform centres for their development and care.

However, after the Amendment of the Act in 2015, if a child between the ages of 16 to 18 years possesses an appropriate level of maturity and he/she can understand the acts committed, then such a child will be treated like an adult and the proceedings will be conducted in a normal court of law.

> **Important Note:** When proceedings are conducted under the JJ Act, the identity of the accused and the victim are never revealed to safeguard the future of children. Hence, in this present case, the child in conflict of law is referred to Bholu and the victim is referred to as Prince.

BACKGROUND

In this case, Prince (Class II student) was found dead in the school bathroom, upon investigation it was found that Bholu was involved in the incident. Hence, he was arrested by the police and sent to the social reform centre.

Since Bholu was above 16 years of age, the Board conducted the preliminary assessment as per Section 15 of the Act and concluded that he should be treated like an adult. However, this assessment was challenged in the High Court.

The High Court ordered for fresh assessment by the Board. This order was challenged in the Supreme Court by a Special Leave Petition.

The Supreme Court ordered to maintain a *status quo* in the case for more than three years before expediting the case and finally delivering an important judgment.

LEGAL ISSUES INVOLVED

1. Should a child be treated like an adult if he commits serious crimes?
2. What are the parameters the Juvenile Justice Board should look at while considering a child as an adult?

ARGUMENTS

The appellants argued that the provisions of the law under the JJ Act are not to provide cover or shelter to the accused.

They argued that the principle of 'best interest of child' or 'presumption of innocence' does not mean that every child will get immunity from criminal charges. If the child understands his acts, then he should be treated like an adult.

The Board conducted their inquiry under Section 15 of the Act. It followed all the due requirements. Section 15 states that the Board 'may' take the help of experienced psychologists, psychosocial workers or other experts. As the word used is 'may', the appellants argued that it is not mandatory for the Board to take such advice.

The appellants also said that the High Court has widened its jurisdiction by questioning the authenticity of the report of the medical board. Hence the decision of the Board should be retained and Bholu should be tried like an adult.

The respondents argued that the amendment in the JJ Act was not done to treat all children who have committed heinous crimes as an adult but only those who have the required level of mental maturity.

While interpreting Sections 14 and 15, the Board should always consider that the object is to protect the interests of children.

They also stated that the child was kept in police lock-ups and a confession was drawn out from him which was relied upon by the Board when concluding their preliminary assessment.

Secondly, the Board did not allow respondents sufficient opportunity to present their cases at different instances.

Thirdly, the word 'may' under Section 15 and Section 101 should be treated as 'shall' for the welfare of children.

THE JUDGMENT

The Hon'ble Supreme Court made the following important observations:

1. The preliminary assessment done by the Board can affect the entire life of the child hence proper opportunity to be heard should be provided while conducting the assessment under Section 15.
2. Section 15 lays down the criteria under which the Board is required to make an assessment but how that assessment is made by the Board depends upon their discretion.
3. The words 'may' under the Section should be read as 'shall' and it should be mandatory for the Board to take opinion or assistance from such experts before passing any preliminary order.
4. While considering a child as an adult, the Board should look at his/her physical maturity, cognitive abilities, and social and emotional competencies.
5. The words 'ability to understand the consequence' under Section 15 should not be narrowly interpreted by the Board but they should

mean whether the child can understand far-reaching effects on family and his/her future.

IMPORTANCE AND IMPACT

This judgment of the Supreme Court comes at a very important time when increasing criminality by children is a rising concern for the government and law enforcement agencies.

The Amendment of 2015 in the JJ Act has always been under contentions because of the provision of treating children as adults based on an assessment and nature of the crime committed.

Child activists and social workers were always against this provision but it was still added to the lawbooks because of the uproar after the *Nirbhaya case*.

The problem is not treating children as adults but the way these inquiries are conducted.

Many discrepancies have been highlighted in the process and hence such an intervention by the Apex Court is expected to improve the process.

Appendix-1: Landmark Supreme Court Judgments in Brief

Sl. No.	Case	Related with
1.	*Romesh Thappar v. State of Madras* (1950)	Freedom of speech
2.	*A. K. Gopalan v. State of Madras* (1950)	Preventive Detention Act, 1950
3.	*Brij Bhushan v. The State of Delhi* (1950)	Pre-censorship of media
4.	*State of Madras v. Smt. Champakam Dorairajan* (1951)	Caste-based reservation in admission to the educational institutions
5.	*Shankari Prasad v. Union of India* (1951)	Power of the Parliament to amend Fundamental Rights
6.	*The Commissioner, Hindu Religious Endowments, Madras v. Sri Lakshmindra Thirtha Swamiar of Shirur Mutt* (1954)	The test of Essential Religious Practices
7.	*M. P. Sharma v. Satish Chandra* (1954)	Right to Privacy
8.	*K. M. Nanavati v. the State of Maharashtra* (1959)	Pardoning power of the Governor; Jury Trial
9.	*Berubari Union v. Unknown* (1960)	Cession of a part of the territory of India; Exchange of enclaves with Pakistan
10.	*Kharak Singh v. The State of U.P.* (1962)	Whether Privacy is a guaranteed constitutional right?
11.	*Sajjan Singh v. State of Rajasthan* (1965)	Power of the Parliament to amend the Constitution

Sl. No.	Case	Related with
12.	*I. C. Golaknath v. State of Punjab* (1967)	Power of the Parliament to amend the Fundamental Rights under Part III of the Constitution
13.	*H. H. Maharajadhiraja Madhav Rao Jiwaji Rao Scindia v. Union of India* (1970)	Abolition of Privy Purse by the Presidential Order
14.	*Kesavananda Bharati v. State of Kerala* (1973)	Power of the Parliament to amend the Constitution; The 'Doctrine of Basic Structure'
15.	*E. P. Royappa v. State of Tamil Nadu*	Definition of Article 14 and protection against arbitrary action by the government.
16.	*Indira Nehru Gandhi v. Raj Narain* (1975)	Election of Indira Gandhi; Election malpractice
17.	*ADM Jabalpur v. Shivkant Shukla* (1976)	Right to move writ petitions before High Courts under Article 226, during the Emergency
18.	*Maneka Gandhi v. Union of India* (1978)	Personal liberty under Article 21; 'Procedure established by law' and 'Due process of law'
19.	*Hussainara Khatoon v. Home Secretary, State of Bihar* (1979)	The rights of the undertrial prisoners
20.	*Bachan Singh v. State of Punjab* (1980)	Capital punishment (death penalty); the doctrine of 'rarest of rare case'
21.	*Minerva Mills Ltd v. Union of India* (1980)	Harmony and balance between fundamental rights and directive principles
22.	*Waman Rao v. Union of India* (1980)	Whether the doctrine of the basic structure be applied retrospectively? Whether the laws placed under Ninth Schedule before April 24, 1973, are valid and constitutional?

Sl. No.	Case	Related with
23.	*S. P. Gupta v. President of India* (1981)	Appointment of judges of the Supreme Court and High Courts
24.	*Sheela Barse v. State of Maharashtra* (1983)	Guidelines for prisoners, especially women prisoners
25.	*Bandhua Mukti Morcha v. Union of India* (1984)	Whether a person to whom the legal injury is caused by reason of the violation of a fundamental right is unable to approach the court, any member of the public acting bona fide can move the court for relief under Article 32 and Article 226?
26.	*Indian Express Newspapers v. Union of India* (1984)	Freedom of press under Freedom of speech and expression
27.	*Mohd Ahmad Khan v. Shah Bano Begum* (1985)	Providing maintenance to a divorced Muslim woman
28.	*Olga Tellis v. Bombay Municipal Corporation* (1985)	Whether Article 21 includes the right to livelihood? Whether the eviction of pavement dwellers using unreasonable force without giving them a chance to explain violates Article 21?
29.	*Dr. D. C. Wadhwa v. State of Bihar* (1986)	Re-Promulgation of Ordinances
30.	*M. C. Mehta v. Union of India* (1986)	Responsibility of industries in an accident; compensation; scope and ambit of the jurisdiction of the Supreme Court under Article 32
31.	*Bijoe Emmanuel v. State of Kerala* (1986)	Whether forcing the children to sing the National Anthem violated their fundamental right to religion?

Sl. No.	Case	Related with
32.	*Kehar Singh v. Union of India* (1988)	Pardoning the power of the President
33.	*Mohini Jain v. State of Karnataka* (1989)	Right to education
34.	*Subhash Kumar v. State of Bihar*	Whether Article 21 includes the right to a wholesome environment?
35.	*Indira Sawhney v. Union of India* (1992)	Reservation for backward classes in Government jobs
36.	*Kihoto Hollohan v. Zachillhu* (1992)	The constitutional validity of Anti-defection law
37.	*Advocate on Record Association v. Union of India* (1993)	Appointment of judges of the Supreme Court and High Courts
38.	*Unni Krishnan, J. P. v. State of Andhra Pradesh* (1993)	Right to education
39.	*S. R. Bommai v. Union of India* (1994)	Proclamation of emergency under Article 356 of the Constitution
40.	*R. Rajagopal v. State of Tamil Nadu* (1994)	Freedom of Speech and expression - right to publish an autobiography
41.	*Sarla Mudgal v. Union of India* (1995)	Principles against the practice of solemnizing second marriage by conversion to Islam, with first marriage not being dissolved
42.	*T. N. Godavarman Thirumulkpad v. Union of India* (1996)	Forest Conservation
43.	*Bodhisattwa Gautam v. Subhra Chakraborty* (1996)	Whether rape is violative of Right to Life under Article 21?
44.	*Indian Council of Enviro-Legal Action v. Union of India*	Application of polluters-pay principle for the first time.
45.	*Vishakha v. State of Rajasthan* (1997)	Sexual Harassment at the workplace; the Supreme Court laid out Vishaka guidelines

Sl. No.	Case	Related with
46.	*Vineet Narain v. Union of India* (1997)	Curbing political influence in the functioning of the CBI
47.	*L. Chandra Kumar v. Union of India* (1997)	Power of High Courts and the Supreme Court to review the legislative action
48.	*Samatha v. State of Andhra Pradesh* (1997)	Granting of mining licenses in the Scheduled Area to non-tribals
49.	*D. K. Basu v. State of West Bengal*	Whether the rights granted under Article 21 be denied to convicts or undertrials in custody?
50.	Special Reference case of 1998	Appointment of judges of the Supreme Court and High Courts
51.	*People's Union For Civil Liberty v. Union of India* (2001)	Right to food
52.	*T. M. A. Pai Foundation v. State of Karnataka* (2002)	Rights of minority educational institutions
53.	*Union of India v. Association for Democratic Reforms* (2002)	Right to know about public functionaries and candidates for office
54.	*Pradeep Kumar Biswas v. Indian Institute of Chemical Biology* (2002)	Whether, under Article 12, 'other authorities' include those bodies upon which government has deep and pervasive control, i.e, controlled by the government financially, functionally and administratively?
55.	*People's Union of Civil Liberties v. Union of India* (2003)	Right of the voters to know about the candidates contesting the election
56.	*John Vallamattom v. Union of India* (2003)	Section 118 of the Indian Succession Act; Advocated a Common Civil Code for the cause of national integration

Sl. No.	Case	Related with
57.	*Zee Telefilms Ltd. v. BCCI* (2005)	Definition of state; Whether a body mere regulated by the government or which performs public duties brings it within the ambit of State under Article 12?
58.	*P. A. Inamdar v. State of Maharashtra* (2005)	Reservation policy on minority and non-minority unaided private colleges, including professional colleges
59.	*Prakash Singh v. Union of India* (2006)	Police reforms
60.	*M. Nagaraj v. Union of India* (2006)	Reservations in promotions for Scheduled Caste and Scheduled Tribe employees
61.	*Jaya Bachchan v. Union of India* (2006)	Disqualification on the ground of office of profit
62.	*Kuldip Nayar v. Union of India* (2006)	Requirement of 'domicile' in the State Concerned for getting elected to the Council of States; Principle of Federalism is a basic structure of the Constitution
63.	*I. R. Coelho (Dead) By Lrs v. State of Tamil Nadu* (2007)	Interpretation of the doctrine of the basic structure of the Constitution; Ninth Schedule is not immunized from the Judicial Review of the Constitution
64.	*Ashoka Kumar Thakur v. Union of India* (2008)	Reservations to OBCs in central educational institutions
65.	*Selvi v. State of Karnataka* (2010)	Whether the use of neuro-scientific investigative techniques violates Article 20(3) (Right against self-incrimination)?

Sl. No.	Case	Related with
66.	*Aruna Ramchandra Shanbaug v. Union of India* (2011)	Recognition of passive euthanasia-permitted withdrawal of life-sustaining treatment from patients not in a position to make an informed decision
67.	*Gian Singh v. State of Punjab* (2012)	Settlements and quashing of criminal proceedings
68.	*Medha Kotwal Lele v. Union of India* (2012)	Court repeated the Vishaka guidelines (1997) and stressed additional measures for their enforcement
69.	*Ramlila Maidan v. Home Secretary, Union of India*	Whether the right to sleep is a fundamental right under Article 21?
70.	*Lily Thomas v. Union of India* (2013)	Disqualifications for membership of Parliament and State Legislatures, if convicted of any offence and sentenced to imprisonment for not less than two years
71.	*T. S. R. Subramanian v. Union of India* (2013)	Professionalizing the Bureaucracy, promoting efficiency and good governance
72.	*Suresh Kumar Koushal v. Naz Foundation* (2013)	Section 377 of the Indian Penal Code, which criminalized homosexuality
73	*National Legal Services Authority v. Union of India* (2014)	Rights of the members of the Transgender Community in India
74.	*Shabnam Hashmi v. Union of India* (2014)	Whether the right to adopt and to be adopted is a fundamental right under Part-III of the Constitution?
75.	*Subramaniam Swamy v. Union of India* (2014)	The constitutionality of the criminal offence of defamation

Sl. No.	Case	Related with
76.	*Pramati Educational and Cultural Trust v. Union of India* (2014)	The constitutional validity of the RTE Act
77.	*Shreya Singhal v. Union of India* (2015)	The fundamental right of free speech and expression; whether the Section 66A of IT Act, 2000 is unconstitutional?
78.	*Supreme Court Advocates-on-Record-Association v. Union of India* (2015)	The constitutional validity of the National Judicial Appointments Commission (NJAC) Act
79.	*Rajbala v. State of Haryana* (2015)	Right to vote and Contest Election
80.	*Shayara Bano v. Union of India* (2016)	Triple Talak or talaq-e-bidat
81.	*Abhiram Singh v. C. D. Commachen* (2017)	Whether asking for votes in elections in the name of religion, caste or community will amount to corrupt practice?
82.	*Krishna Kumar Singh v. State of Bihar* (2017)	Re-Promulgation of Ordinances against the spirit of Constitutionalism
83.	*Justice K. S. Puttaswamy (Retd) v. Union of India* (2017)	Whether the right to privacy is a fundamental right?
84.	*Independent Thought v. Union of India* (2017)	The exception to the Marital Rape; whether sex with minor wife is rape?
85.	*Rajesh Sharma v. State of U.P.* (2017)	Directions to Prevent Misuse of Section 498A of the IPC
86.	*Common Cause (A Regd. Society) v. Union of India* (2018)	Whether the right to die with dignity is a fundamental right?
87.	*Tehseen S. Poonawalla v. Union of India* (2018)	Guidelines against Mob lynching
88.	*Government of NCT of Delhi v. Union of India* (2018)	Power tussle between Delhi Government and Lt. Governor

Sl. No.	Case	Related with
89.	*Dr. Subhash Kashinath Mahajan v. The State of Maharashtra* (2018)	Directions to prevent misuse of SC/ST Act
90.	*Shafin Jahan v. Asokan K.M.* (2018)	Right of a girl to marry a person of her own choice
91.	*Indian Young Lawyers Association v. the State of Kerala* (2018)	The entry of women aged between 10 and 50 to the Sabarimala temple in Kerala
92.	*Joseph Shine v. Union of India* (2018)	Section 497 of the Indian Penal Code which criminalized adultery
93.	*Navtej Singh Johar v. Union of India* (2018)	Section 377 of the IPC, which criminalizes homosexuality
94.	*Jarnail Singh v. Lachhmi Narain Gupta* (2018)	The reservation in promotion for the SC/ST communities
95.	*M. Ismail Faruqui v. Union of India* (2018)	Ram Janmabhoomi-Babri Masjid land title case
96.	*Justice Puttaswamy (Retd) v. Union of India* (2018)	The constitutional validity of Aadhaar; The Aadhaar Act 2016
97.	*Shakti Vahini v. Union of India* (2018)	Honour Killings
98.	*Ashwini Kumar Upadhyay v. Union of India* (2018)	Legislators practising as advocates
99.	*Swapnil Tripathi v. Supreme Court of India* (2018)	Video recording or live streaming of the court proceedings in the public interest
100.	*B. K. Pavitra v. Union of India* (2019)	Reservations in promotions for SCs/STs and issues of seniority
101.	*Wildlife First v. Ministry of Environment and Forest* (2019)	The implementation of the Forest Rights Act (FRA) of 2006
102.	*Anuradha Bhasin v. Union of India* (2020)	The shutdown of internet services
103.	*Rambabu Singh Thakur v. Sunil Arora* (2020)	Criminalization of politics

Sl. No.	Case	Related with
104.	*Internet and Mobile Association of India v. Reserve Bank of India* (2020)	Regulation of cryptocurrencies
105.	*Laxmibai Chandaragi v. State of Karnataka* (2021)	The choice of an individual selecting a partner for marriage is an integral part of 'dignity'.
106.	*Mohammad Salimullah v. Union of India* (2021)	India's stand regarding refugees
107.	*Farzana Batool v. Union of India* (2021)	Whether the right to professional education is a fundamental right?
108.	*Kerala Union of Working Journalists v. Union of India* (2021)	Rights available to undertrial prisoners
109.	*Barun Chandra Thakur v. Master Bholu* (2022)	The criteria the Juvenile Justice Board should look at while considering a child as an adult

Appendix-2: Famous Cases that Made News Headlines

S. No.	Case Name	Significance
1.	**The A. K. Gopalan Case (1950):** *A. K. Gopalan v. State of Madras*	This case analysed whether the Preventive Detention Act 1950, conforms to the standard of the 'procedure established by law' as laid down in Article 21 of the Indian Constitution. Many critics consider the interpretation of the Court in this case as narrow in nature.
2.	**The Champakam Dorairajan Case (1950):** *Srimathi Champakam Dorairajan v. State of Madras*	In this case, the Supreme Court gave a verdict against the reservation based on religion or caste. The Court also held that whenever there is a conflict between Fundamental Rights and DPSPs, it will always be the Fundamental Rights that will prevail. This judgment led to the amendment in Article 15 by the Indian Parliament, by which Clause 4 that is related to the reservation was added.
3.	**The Raj Narain Case (1975):** *Indira Nehru Gandhi v. Raj Narain*	In this case, the Apex Court held that the 39th Constitutional Amendment violates the principle of separation of powers. The Supreme Court also ruled that Clauses (4) and (5) of Article 329A are unconstitutional.

S. No.	Case Name	Significance
4.	**The Hussainara Khatoon Case (1979):** *Hussainara Khatoon v. Home Secretary, State of Bihar*	In this case which is popularly known as the '*Habeas Corpus* case', the Supreme Court held that prisoners should receive free legal aid and fast hearings.
5.	**The Olga Tellis Case (1985):** *Olga Tellis v. Bombay Municipal Corporation*	In this case, also known as the 'pavement dwellers case', the Supreme Court expanded its interpretation of Article 21. The Apex Court held that the Right to Livelihood is an intrinsic part of Article 21, i.e. Right to Life.
6.	**The D. K. Basu Case (1987):** *D. K. Basu v. State of Bengal*	The case dealt with custodial torture and custodial deaths. The Apex Court specified certain guidelines to be followed at times of arrest to avoid abuse of power by the police.
7.	**The Bhopal Gas Tragedy Case (1989):** *Union Carbide Corporation v. Union of India*	The Supreme Court upheld the out-of-court \$470 million settlement to victims and dismissed any other outstanding petitions. The Court also ordered the Indian Government 'to purchase, out of settlement fund, a group medical insurance policy to cover 100,000 persons who may later develop symptoms' and cover any shortfall in the settlement fund. The Apex Court further requested that UCC and its subsidiary UCIL 'voluntarily' fund a hospital in Bhopal, at an estimated \$17 million, to specifically treat victims of the Bhopal disaster.

S. No.	Case Name	Significance
8.	**The Kilhoto Hollohan Case (1992):** *Kihoto Hollohan v. Zacihillhu*	In this case, the Supreme Court upheld the sweeping discretion available to the Speaker in deciding cases of disqualification of MLAs or MPs.
9.	**The I. R. Coelho Case (2007):** *I.R.Coelho v. State of Tamil Nadu*	In this case, the Apex Court held that even if an Act is put in the Ninth Schedule, its provisions would be open for judicial review. However, the Court ruled that only those amendments to the Constitution placed in Ninth Schedule made on or after 24th April 1973 (date of *Kesavanatha Bharathi* case judgment) will be subjected to judicial review.
10.	**The Aruna Shanbaug Case (2011):** *Aruna Ramachandra Shanbaug v. Union of India*	The Apex Court allowed passive euthanasia in this case. The Court also laid down important guidelines to prevent any misuse of the provision.
11.	**The Nota Case (2013):** *People's Union for Civil Liberties (PUCL) v. Union of India*	The Apex Court, in this case, directed the Election Commission of India to introduce a 'None of the Above (NOTA)' option into the Electronic Voting Machines so that voters can exercise their right not to vote while maintaining their secrecy.
12.	**The Hadiya Case (2017):** *Shafin Jahan v. Ashokan K. M.*	Even though infamous as the 'Love-Jihad' case, the Supreme Court upheld the fundamental right of Hadiya Jahan to marry a person of her own choice.

S. No.	Case Name	Significance
13.	**The Rafale Case (2018):** *Manoharl Lal Sharma v. Narendra Damodardas Modi*	The Supreme Court upheld the Rafale deal concerning the purchase of 36 fighter aircrafts for about Rs.60,000 crore, stating that no irregularities or corruption have been found.
14.	**The Ayodhya Case (2019):** *M Siddiq v. Mahant Suresh Das*	In this controversial case, the Supreme Court pronounced its verdict on the decades-old civil dispute over 2.77 acres of land in the ancient town of Ayodhya. The Apex Court in a unanimous verdict cleared the way for the construction of a Ram Temple at the disputed site at Ayodhya and directed the Centre to allot a 5-acre plot to the Sunni Waqf Board for building a mosque.

Appendix-3: Conflict Areas v. Judgments

Sl. No.	Conflict Area	Related Judgments
1.	Freedom of speech and expression	• *Romesh Thappar v. State of Madras* (1950) • *Brij Bhushan v. State of Delhi* (1950) • *Virendra v. State of Punjab* (1957) • *Hamdard Dawakhana v. Union of India* (1959) • *Bennett Coleman and Co. v. Union of India* (1972) • *Indian Express Newspapers v. Union of India* (1984) • *R. Rajagopal v. State of Tamil Nadu* (1994) • *People's Union for Civil Liberties v. Union of India* (2004) • *Shreya Singhal v. Union of India* (2015)
2.	Reservation in admission to the educational institutions and employment	• *State of Madras v. Smt. Champakam Dorairajan* (1951) • *M R Balaji v. State of Mysore* (1963) • *Indira Sawhney and others v. Union of India* (1992) • *T. M. A. Pai Foundation v. State of Karnataka* (2002) • *P. A. Inamdar v. State of Maharashtra* (2005) • *M. Nagaraj v. Union of India* (2006) • *Ashoka Kumar Thakur v. Union of India* (2008) • *Jarnail Singh v. Lachhmi Narain Gupta* (2018) • *B. K. Pavitra v. Union of India* (2019)

Sl. No.	Conflict Area	Related Judgments
3.	Power of the Parliament to Amend the Constitution	• *Shankari Prasad v. Union of India* (1951) • *Sajjan Singh v. State of Rajasthan* (1965) • *I. C. Golaknath v. State of Punjab* (1967) • *Kesavananda Bharati v. State of Kerala* (1973) • *Indira Nehru Gandhi v. Raj Narain* (1975) • *Minerva Mills Ltd. v. Union of India* (1980) • *L. Chandra Kumar v. Union of India* (1997)
4.	Test of Essential Religious Practices	• *The Commissioner, Hindu religious endowments, Madras v. Sri Lakshmindra Thirtha Swamiar of Shirur Mutt* (1954) • *Durgah Committee, Ajmer v. Syed Hussain Ali* (1961) • *Sardar Syedna Taher Saifuddin v. State of Bombay* (1962) • *S. P. Mittal v. Union of India* (1982) • *Commissioner of Police v. Acharya Jagdishwarananda* (2004) • *Shayara Bano v. Union of India* (2016) • *Indian Young Lawyers Association v. State of Kerala* (2018)
5.	Right to Privacy	• *M. P. Sharma v. Satish Chandra* (1954) • *Kharak Singh v. State of UP* (1962) • *Justice K. S. Puttaswamy (Retd) and Another v. Union of India* (2017)
6.	Basic structure of the Constitution	• *Kesavananda Bharati v. State of Kerala* (1973) • *Indira Nehru Gandhi v. Raj Narain* (1975) • *Minerva Mills Ltd. v. Union of India* (1980)
7.	Right to Life and Personal Liberty	• *Maneka Gandhi v. Union of India* (1978) • *Sunil Batra v. Delhi Administration* (1979) • *Hussainara Khatoon v. State of Bihar* (1979) • *D. K. Basu v. State of West Bengal* (1996) • *Vishakha v. State of Rajasthan* (1997) • *Justice K. S. Puttaswamy (Retd) v. Union of India* (2017)

Sl. No.	Conflict Area	Related Judgments
8.	Capital Punishment	• *Jagmohan Singh v. State of Uttar Pradesh* (1973) • *Rajendra Prasad v. State of Uttar Pradesh* (1979) • *Bachan Singh v. State of Punjab* (1980) • *Machhi Singh v. State of Punjab* (1983) • *T. V. Vatheeswaran v. State of Tamil Nadu* (1983) • *Shashi Nayar v. Union of India* (1991) • *Aloke Nath Dutta v. State of West Bengal* (2007) • *Swamy Shraddhananda v. State of Karnataka* (2008) • *Santosh Kumar Satishbhushan Bariyar v. State of Maharashtra* (2009) • *Shatrughan Chauhan v. Union of India* (2014)
9.	Appointment of Judges of the Supreme Court and High Courts	• *S. P. Gupta v. President of India* (1981) • *Advocate on Record Association v. Union of India* (1993) • Special Reference case of 1998 • *Supreme Court Advocates-on-Record-Association and Another v. Union of India* (2015)
10.	Re-promulgation of Ordinances	• *Dr. D. C. Wadhwa v. State of Bihar* (1986) • *Krishna Kumar Singh and Another v. State of Bihar* (2017)
11.	Pardoning power of the President/ Governor	• *K. M. Nanavati v. State of Maharashtra* (1959) • *Maru Ram v. Union of India* (1980) • *Kehar Singh v. Union of India* (1988) • *Dhananjay Chatterjee Alias Dhana v. State of West Bengal* (1994) • *Swaran Singh v. State of Uttar Pradesh* (1998) • *Epuru Sudhakar v. Government of A.P.* (2006)
12.	Right to Education	• *Mohini Jain v. State of Karnataka* (1989) • *Unni Krishnan, J. P. v. State of Andhra Pradesh* (1993) • *Pramati Educational & Cultural Trust v. Union of India* (2014)

Sl. No.	Conflict Area	Related Judgments
13.	Disqualification of Legislators	• *Kihoto Hollohan v. Zachillhu* (1992) • *Ravi S. Naik v. Union of India* (1994) • *G. Viswanathan v. Speaker Tamil Nadu Legislative Assembly* (1996) • *Jaya Bachchan v. Union of India* (2006) • *Rajendra Singh Rana v. Swami Prasad Maurya* (2007) • *Speaker Haryana Vidhan Sabha v. Kuldeep Bishnoi* (2012)
14.	Proclamation of Emergency under Article 356	• *State of Rajasthan v. Union of India* (1977) • *Minerva Mills Ltd. v. Union of India* (1980) • *S. R. Bommai v. Union of India* (1994) • *Rameshwar Prasad v. Union of India* (2006)
15.	Electoral Reforms	• *Association for Democratic Reforms v. Union of India* (2003) • *People's Union of Civil Liberties v. Union of India* (2003) • *Lily Thomas v. Union of India* (2013) • *Abhiram Singh v. C. D. Commachen* (2017) • *Lok Prahari v. Union of India* (2018)
16.	Euthanasia	• *Aruna Ramchandra Shanbaug v. Union of India* (2011) • *Common Cause (A Regd. Society) v. Union of India* (2018)
17.	Sexual harassment at the workplace	• *Vishakha v. State of Rajasthan* (1997) • *Medha Kotwal Lele v. Union of India* (2012)
18.	Section 377/ Homosexuality	• *Suresh Kumar Koushal v. Naz Foundation* (2013) • *Navtej Singh Johar v. Union of India* (2018)
19.	Right to Vote and Contest Elections	• *Javed v. State of Haryana* (2003) • *People's Union of Civil Liberties v. Union of India* (2003) • *Rajbala v. State of Haryana* (2015)

Sl. No.	Conflict Area	Related Judgments
20.	Right to Livelihood/ Food	• *Olga Tellis v. Bombay Municipal Corporation* (1985) • *Chameli Singh v. State of Uttar Pradesh* (1995) • *People's Union For Civil Liberty v. Union of India* (2001)
21.	Protection of Environment	• *Vellore Citizens' Welfare Forum v. Union of India* (1995) • *T. N. Godavarman Thirumulpad v. Union of India* (1996) • *Indian Council for Enviro-legal Action v. Union of India* (1996) • *Andhra Pradesh Pollution Control Board v. M. V. Nayudu* (1999)
22.	Tribal Rights	• *Samatha v. State of A.P.* (1997) • *Wildlife First v. Ministry of Forest* (2019)
23.	*Fundamental Rights v. DPSP*	• *State of Madras v. Smt. Champakam Dorairajan* (1951) • *The Kerala Education Bill v. Unknown* (1958) • *I. C. Golaknath and Others v. State of Punjab* (1967) • *Kesavananda Bharati v. State of Kerala* (1973) • *Minerva Mills Ltd. v. Union of India* (1980) • *Waman Rao v. Union of India* (1980)
24.	Center-State Relations	• *State of West Bengal v. Union of India* (1962) • *State of Punjab v. Sat Pal Dang* (1968) • *State of Rajasthan v. Union of India* (1977) • *Pradeep Jain v. Union of India* (1984) • *S. R. Bommai v. Union of India* (1994) • *Rameshwar Prasad v. Union of India* (2006)

Appendix-4: Mindmaps Which Help You Understand the Indian Polity

1. MINDMAP – THREE ORGANS OF THE STATE

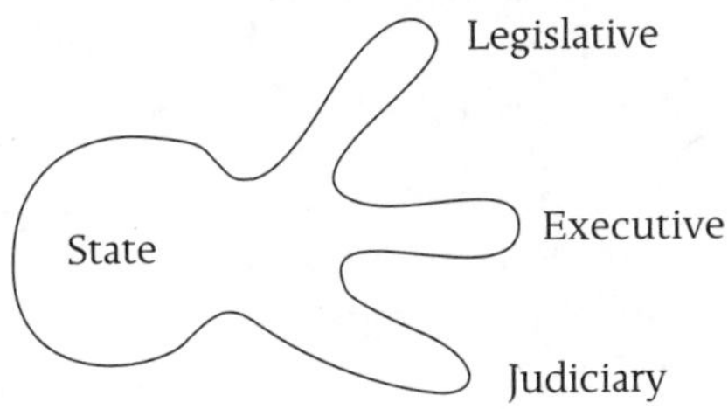

⇒ Also known as 'three pillars of democracy'.
⇒ Fourth pillar of democracy is = Press.

Separation of Powers

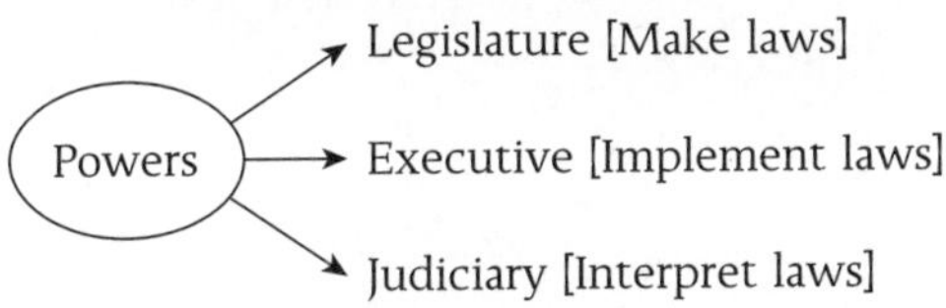

⇒ Concept famously articulated by the French philosopher Montesquieu ("Spirit of laws", 1748)

2. MINDMAP – PARLIAMENTARY FORM OF DEMOCRACY IN INDIA

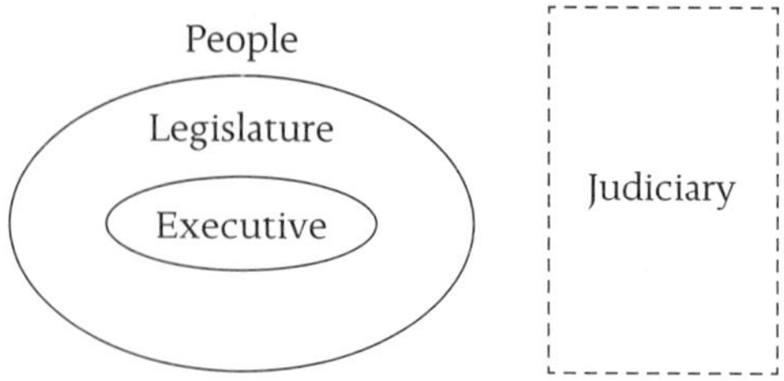

- "Democracy" ⇒ rule by the people.
- People elect their representatives to make laws, rules and policies for better governance of the country.
  - ⇒ The elected representatives (Eg: MPs and MLAs) are responsible (answerable) to the people.
  - ⇒ Executive is a part of Legislature.
  - ⇒ Judiciary is neither a part of the Executive nor the Legislature, it is separate and independent.
  - ⇒ The Council of Ministers (COM) at the Centre is collectively responsible for the Lok Sabha.
  - ⇒ The Council of Ministers (COM) in the States are collectively responsible to the State Legislative Assemblies.

3. MINDMAP – FEDERALISM IN INDIA

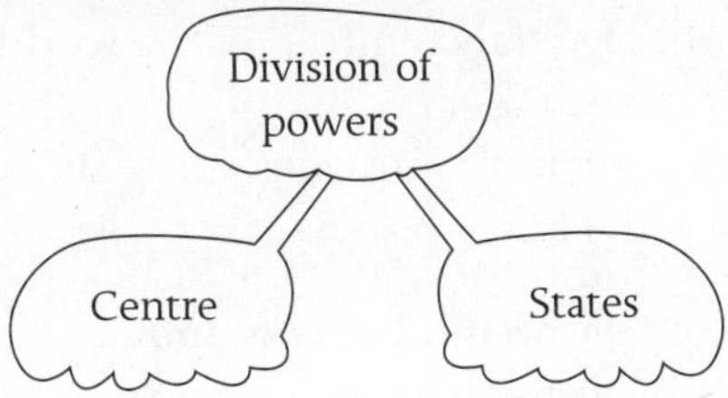

→ Central Executive
→ Central Legislature

→ State Executive
→ State Legislature

Only Executive and Legislature is Federal; Judiciary is integrated

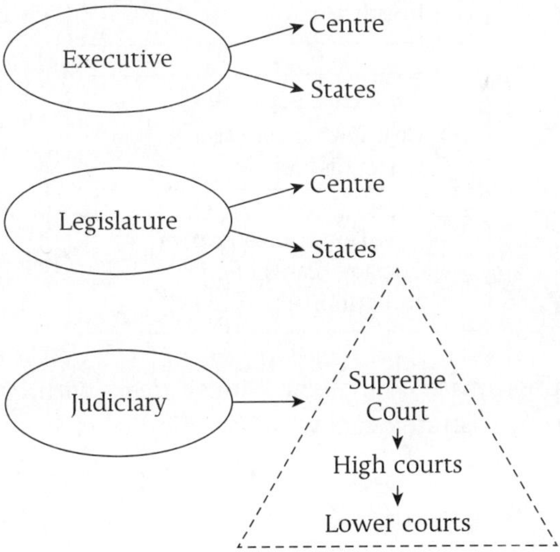

Note: India does not have independent State courts, the decisions of the Supreme Court are binding on all courts.

4. MINDMAP – STRUCTURE OF INDIAN JUDICIARY

⇒ Unlike some other federal countries of the world, India does not have separate state courts.

⇒ The Constitution of India provides for a single integrated judicial system.

Supreme Court of India
→ Its decisions are binding on all courts

↓

High court
→ Can deal with cases within the jurisdiction of the State

↓

District court
→ Deal with cases arising in the district

↓

Subordinate courts
→ Consider cases of civil and criminal nature

Note: In the subordinate courts, the Munsif deals with civil court cases, while the Magistrate hears with the criminal cases.

5. MINDMAP – JUDICIAL REVIEW

⇒ Only the Indian Parliament can amend Indian Constitution.

⇒ However, Judiciary can strike down a law or an amendment to the Constitution by a process called judicial review.

⇒ The Judiciary gets the power of review from:

1. Article 13
2. Article 32 (Right to Constitutional Remedy)
3. Article 136 (Special leave to appeal by the Supreme Court)
4. Article 226 (Power of High courts to issue certain writs)
5. Article 227 (Power of superintendence over all courts by the High courts)

6. MINDMAP – EXAMPLES OF MAJOR AREAS OF LEGAL CONFLICTS

1. *Parliamentary Sovereignty v. Judicial Supremacy*
2. *Rights of the citizens (Fundamental Rights) v. Power of the State (DPSPs)*
3. *Centre v. State*
4. *State v. State*

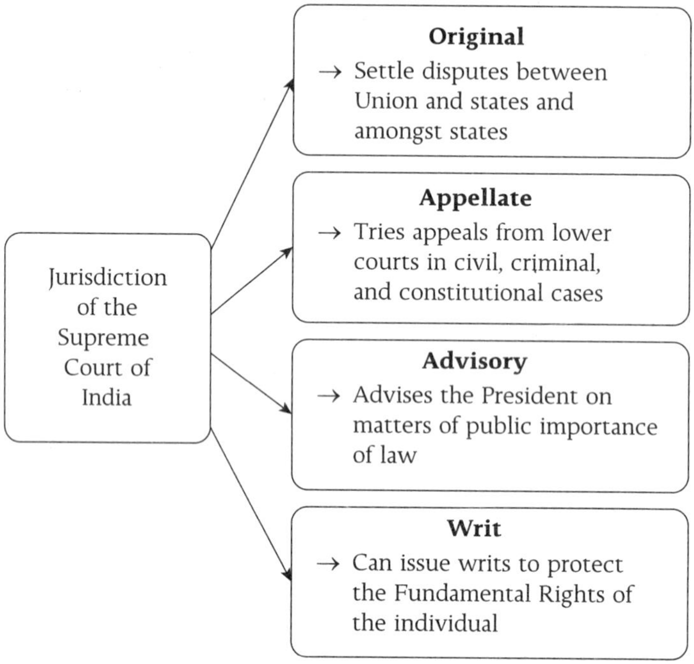

7. MINDMAP – PROCEDURE ESTABLISHED BY LAW v. DUE PROCESS OF LAW

The difference between *procedure established by law* and *due process of law* can be easily studied in the backdrop of Article 21 of the Indian Constitution.

Article 21 in the Constitution of India

Protection of life and personal liberty: No person shall be deprived of his life or personal liberty except according to the **procedure established by law.**

Procedure Established by Law v. Due Process of Law

Due Process of Law

Procedure Established by Law

Due Process of Law = *Procedure Established by Law + The procedure should be fair and just and not arbitrary.*

The term 'Procedure established by law' is used directly in the Indian Constitution. Due process of law has much wider significance, but it is not explicitly mentioned in the Indian Constitution.

The due process doctrine is followed in the United States of America, and Indian constitutional framers purposefully left that out. However, in most of the recent judgments of the Supreme Court, the due process aspect is coming into the picture again.

Due process of law = Procedure established by law + The procedure should be fair and just and not arbitrary.

Procedure Established by Law

It means that a law that is duly enacted by the Legislature or the concerned body is valid if it has followed the correct procedure. As per this doctrine, a person can be deprived of his life or personal liberty according to the **procedure established by law**.

So, if Parliament passes a law, then the life or personal liberty of a person can be taken off according to the provisions and procedures of that law.

This doctrine has a major flaw. What is it?

It does not seek whether the laws made by the Parliament is fair, just, and non-arbitrary.

Blindly following "Procedure established by law" doctrine may lead to a situation where a law duly enacted be valid even if it's contrary to principles of justice and equity. The strict following of the procedure established by law may raise the risk of compromise to life and personal liberty of individuals due to unjust laws made by the law-making authorities. It is to avoid this situation that the Supreme Court stressed the importance of the due process of law.

Due Process of Law

Due process of law doctrine not only checks if there is a law to deprive the life and personal liberty of a person but also see if the law made is fair, just and non-arbitrary.

If the Supreme Court finds that any law is not fair, it will declare it as null and void. This doctrine provides for more fair treatment of individual rights.

Under due process, it is the legal requirement that the state must respect all of the legal rights that are owed to a person and laws that states enact must conform to the laws of the land such as fairness, fundamental rights, liberty, etc. It also gives the Judiciary the right to access fundamental fairness, justice, and liberty of any legislation.

The difference in layman's terms is as follows:

Due process of law = Procedure established by law + The procedure should be fair and just and not arbitrary.

History of Due Process of Law

The due process developed from Clause 39 of the *magna carta* in England. When English and American law gradually diverged, due process was not upheld in England but did become incorporated in the Constitution of the United States.

Change of Situation in India: *Maneka Gandhi v. Union of India* Case (1978)

In India, a liberal interpretation is made by the Judiciary after 1978 and it has tried to make the term 'Procedure established by law' as synonymous with 'Due Process' when it comes to protecting individual rights.

In *Maneka Gandhi v. Union of India case* (1978), the Supreme Court held that 'Procedure established by law' within the meaning of Article 21 must be 'right and just and fair' and 'not arbitrary, fanciful or oppressive' otherwise, it would be no procedure at all and the requirement of Article 21 would not be satisfied. Thus, the 'procedure established by law' has acquired the same significance in India as the 'due process of law' clause in America.

REFERENCE

https://www.clearias.com/procedure-established-by-law-vs-due-process-of-law/

8. MINDMAP – JUDICIAL REVIEW v. JUDICIAL ACTIVISM v. JUDICIAL OVERREACH

Judicial Review, Judicial Activism and Judicial Overreach are terms which are often seen in the news.

	Judicial Review	Judicial Activism	Judicial Overreach
Whether the Power is derived from the Indian Consitution?	YES	NO	NO
Desirable?	YES	YES	NO

Judicial Review

Though the legislature has the power to make laws, this power is not absolute. Judicial Review is the process by which the Judiciary **review the validity of laws** passed by the Legislature.

- ⇒ **From where does the power of Judicial Review come from?** From the Constitution of India itself (Article 13, Article 32, etc.).
- ⇒ The power of judicial review is evoked to protect and enforce the fundamental rights guaranteed in Part III of the Constitution.
- ⇒ Article 13 of the Constitution prohibits the Parliament and the state legislatures from making laws that 'may take away or abridge the fundamental rights' guaranteed to the citizens of the country.
- ⇒ The provisions of Article 13 ensure the protection of the fundamental rights and consider any law 'inconsistent with or in derogation of the fundamental rights' as void.
- ⇒ Under Article 13, the term 'law' includes any 'Ordinance, order, bye-law, rule, regulation, notification, custom or usage' having the force of law in India.
- ⇒ **Examples of Judicial Review:** The striking down of Section 66A of the IT Act as it was against the fundamental rights guaranteed by the Constitution.

Judicial Activism

Judicial activism denotes a more active role taken by Judiciary to dispense social justice. When we speak of Judicial Activism, we point fingers to the invented mechanisms which have no constitutional backing (e.g., Suo moto (on its own) cases, Public Interest Litigations (PIL), new doctrines, etc.).

- ⇒ **From where does the power of Judicial Activism come from:** Judicial Activism has no constitutional articles to support its origin.

Indian Judiciary invented it. There are similar concepts in countries like the United States of America.

⇒ Suo Motto cases and the innovation of the Public Interest Litigation (PIL), with the discontinuation of the principle of Locus Standi, have allowed the Judiciary to intervene in many public issues, even when there is no complaint from the concerned party.

⇒ Although the earlier instances of Judicial Activism were connected with enforcing Fundamental Rights, nowadays, Judiciary has started interfering in the governance issues as well.

⇒ **Examples of Judicial Activism:** Invention of the 'basic structure doctrine' in the 'Keshavananda Bharati case' (1973) by which Supreme Court further extended the scope of Judicial Review, incorporation of due process of law instead of procedure established by law, collegium system, institutionalization of PIL, banning smoking in public places based on PIL, the order by Supreme Court in 2001 to provide mid-day meals to school children, the order passed by the National Green Tribunal (NGT) banning diesel trucks older than 10 years in Delhi, etc.

Judicial Overreach

The line between Judicial Activism and Judicial Overreach is very narrow. In simple terms, when Judicial Activism crosses its limits and becomes Judicial Adventurism, it is known as Judicial Overreach. When the judiciary oversteps the powers given to it, it may interfere with the proper functioning of the Legislative or Executive organs of government.

⇒ **From where does the power of Judicial Overreach come from:** Nowhere. This is undesirable in any democracy.

⇒ Judicial Overreach destroys the spirit of separation of powers.

⇒ **Examples of Judicial Overreach:** What makes any action activism or overreach is based upon the perspective of individuals. But in general, striking down of NJAC bill and the 99th Constitutional Amendment, the order passed by the Allahabad High Court making it compulsory for all Bureaucrats to send their children to a government school, misuse the power to punish for contempt of court, etc. are considered as Judicial Overreach.

REFERENCE

https://www.clearias.com/judicial-review-vs-judicial-activism-vs-judicial-overreach/

Appendix-5: Indian Judicial Doctrines – Principles of Constitutional Law Explained

A doctrine is a belief, principle or position - usually upheld by authorities like courts. Let's see some of the important doctrines followed by the Indian Judiciary.

THE DOCTRINE OF BASIC STRUCTURE

The basic structure doctrine is an Indian judicial principle that the Constitution of India has certain basic features that cannot be altered or destroyed through amendments by the Parliament.

Even though the basic features of the Indian Constitution are not explicitly defined by the Judiciary, it is widely considered that fundamental rights, democracy, federalism, independence of the judiciary, secularism etc. are part of the basic features.

The claim of any particular feature of the Constitution to be a 'basic' feature is determined by the Court on a case-by-case basis.

This doctrine was first expressed in *Kesavananda Bharati v. State of Kerala (1973)* case.

DOCTRINE OF SEVERABILITY

According to this doctrine, if there is any offending part in a statute, then, only the offending part is declared void and not the entire statute.

Article 13 states that the portion that is invalid should be struck off and not the entire one. The valid part can be kept.

However, it should be kept in mind that even after separation; the remaining part should not become ambiguous.

If the remaining part becomes ambiguous, then the whole statute would be declared void and of no use.

Supreme Court in the case of *RMDC v. UOI* states that the doctrine of severability is a matter of substance and not of form.

DOCTRINE OF ECLIPSE

The doctrine states that if any law becomes contradictory to the fundamental rights, then it becomes inactive, but does not die permanently.

When a court strikes out a part of the law, it becomes unenforceable. Hence, an 'eclipse' is said to be cast on it. The law just becomes invalid but continues to exist.

In case, sometime in future, if a fundamental right is omitted from the Constitution, the inactive law may get revived.

The eclipse may also be removed when another (probably a higher level court) makes the law valid again or an amendment is brought to it by way of legislation.

Supreme Court first applied this doctrine in the case of *Bhikaji v. State of Madhya Pradesh* where it applied to pre-constitutional law. The extension to the post-constitutional law was stated in the case of *Dulare Lodh v. ADJ, Kanpur.*

THE DOCTRINE OF HARMONIOUS CONSTRUCTION

This doctrine was brought about to bring harmony between different lists (Union list, State list, and Concurrent list) mentioned in Schedule 7 of the Constitution of India.

There can be situations where an entry of one list overlaps with that of another list. This doctrine comes in picture in such instances.

It is said that the words of the entries should be given wide amplitude and the courts shall bring harmony between different entries and lists.

Supreme Court applied this Doctrine in the case of *Tika Ramji v. State of Uttar Pradesh.*

THE DOCTRINE OF PITH AND SUBSTANCE

Pith and Substance mean the true nature of law.

This doctrine comes into the picture when there is a conflict between the subjects in different lists mentioned in Schedule 7 of the Indian Constitution. To resolve the conflict when the subject of one list touch the subject of another list, this doctrine is applied.

As per this doctrine, only the real subject matter is challenged and not its incidental effect on another field.

The doctrine has been applied in India also to provide a degree of flexibility in the otherwise rigid scheme of distribution of powers.

The reason for the adoption of this doctrine is that if every legislation were to be declared invalid on the grounds that it encroached powers, the powers of the legislature would be drastically circumscribed.

It was applied by the Supreme Court in the case *State of Bombay v. F. N. Balasar*.

THE DOCTRINE OF INCIDENTAL OR ANCILLARY POWERS

This principle is an addition to the doctrine of Pith and Substance.

What it means is that the power to legislate on a subject also includes the power to legislate on ancillary matters that are reasonably connected to that subject.

For example, the power to impose tax would include the power to search and seizure to prevent the evasion of that tax. However, the power relating to banking cannot be extended to include the power relating to non-banking entities.

It should also be noted that, if a subject is explicitly mentioned in a State or Union list, it cannot be said to be an ancillary matter. For example, the power to tax is mentioned in specific entries in the lists and so the power to tax cannot be claimed as ancillary to the power relating to any other entry of the lists.

As held in the case of *State of Rajasthan v. G. Chawla AIR 1959*, the power to legislate on a topic includes the power to legislate on an ancillary matter which can be said to be reasonably included in the topic. Supreme Court has consistently cautioned against such extended construction.

For example, *in R. M. D. Charbaugwala v. State of Mysore, AIR 1962*, the Supreme Court held that betting and gambling is a state subject as mentioned in Entry 34 of State list but it does not include power to impose taxes on betting and gambling because it exists as a separate item as Entry 62 in the same list.

THE DOCTRINE OF COLOURABLE LEGISLATION

The expression 'colourable legislation' simply means what cannot be done directly, cannot be done indirectly too.

It is the substance that matters and not the outward appearance.

There are certain situations when it seems that it is within the power of the legislature enacting the law but actually it is transgressing. This is when this doctrine comes into the picture.

It was applied by the Supreme Court of India in the case *State of Bihar v. Kameshwar Singh* and it was held that the Bihar Land Reforms Act was invalid.

THE DOCTRINE OF TERRITORIAL NEXUS

In simple words, doctrine territorial nexus says that laws made by a state legislature are not applicable outside the state, except when there is a sufficient nexus between the state and the object.

If there is sufficient nexus between a state and the object, then the state law can operate outside that state also.

Such laws cannot be declared invalid on the growth that they are extraterritorial according to Article 245(2).

Supreme Court applied this doctrine in the case of *Tata Iron Steel v. State of Bihar*.

DOCTRINE OF LACHES

Laches means delay. The doctrine of laches is based on the maxim that 'equity aids the vigilant and not those who slumber on their rights' (Black's Law Dictionary).

It is well known that one who wants the remedy must come before the court within a reasonable time.

Supreme Court under the case of *Ravindra Jain v. UOI* stated that remedy under Article 32 can be denied on grounds of unreasonable delay.

A legal right or claim will not be allowed if a long delay in asserting the right or claim has prejudiced the adverse party.

Elements of laches include knowledge of a claim, unreasonable delay, neglect, which taken together hurt the opponent.

Lapse of time violates equity and it is against the concept of justice.

REFERENCE

https://www.clearias.com/indian-judicial-doctrines/

Appendix-6: Common Legal Terms

Plaintiff

The party who initiates a lawsuit (also known as an action) before a court of law.

Respondent

A party against whom a petition is filed. In the case of appeals, the respondent can be the plaintiff or defendant from a lower court.

Petitioner

The party who presents a petition in the court of law.

Litigant

A party to a lawsuit in a court.

Lawyer

A person who practises or studies law.

Advocate

A law graduate entered in any roll under the provisions of the Advocates Act, 1961.

Judge

A public officer authorized to hear and decide cases in a court of law.

Complaint

A group of operative facts giving rise to one or more bases for filing a case.

Dispute

A conflict of claims or rights that has given rise to the subject of litigation.

Issues

The question of fact or law that is in dispute.

Petition

A formal written request presented to a court of law.

Plaint

A written complaint filed in a cause of action stating accusation or charge.

Prayer

A prayer for relief is a portion of a complaint in which the plaintiff describes the remedies that they seek from the court.

Writs

A writ is a formal written order issued by a court asking the addressee to refrain from or perform a specific act.
The following are the five types of writs:

1. *Mandamus*
   An order that is issued by a court of superior jurisdiction to ask a lower court, tribunal, commission, or individual, to perform or refrain from performing an action that is required by law.
2. *Habeas Corpus*
   A court order that commands an individual or a government official who has restrained another to produce the prisoner at a designated time and place so that the court can determine the legality of custody.
3. *Prohibition*
   An extraordinary writ issued by a higher court commanding an inferior court or quasi-judicial body to keep within its jurisdiction.
4. *Quo Warranto*
   A writ issued with a view to restraining a person from holding a civil office to which he/she is not entitled.
5. *Certiorari*
   A writ issued by the Supreme Court or High Court to quash the order already passed by an inferior court, tribunal or quasi-judicial body. It is a type of writ seeking judicial review.

Civil

That part of the law that encompasses business, contracts, estates, domestic (family) relations, accidents, negligence, and everything related to legal issues, statutes, and lawsuits, that is not criminal law.

Criminal

That which pertains to crimes, and requires the administration of penal justice. Involving those cases that deal with a violation of a law in which a citizen inflicts injury upon another citizen or the state. Punishable with the curtailment of liberty, via imprisonment or detention, or fines.

Civil Procedure Code

Codified procedural law related to the administration of Indian civil law.

Criminal Procedure Code

The main legislation on procedure for administration of substantive criminal law in India.

Indian Penal Code

The main criminal code of India that covers all aspects of substantive criminal law in India.

Appeals

Legal proceedings in which a case is brought to or before a higher court for the reconsideration of the decision of a lower court.

Disposal

The resolution of a legal matter. This could either be the dismissal or a charge, or a final judgment. Court records often specify the nature of the resolution.

LIST OF IMPORTANT LATIN LEGAL TERMS

- ***Suo moto***: Meaning - of its own motion. Refers to a court or other official agency taking some action on its own accord (synonyms: ex proprio motu, ex mero motu).
- ***Amicus curiae***: Meaning - a friend of the court. A person who offers information to a court regarding a case before it.
- ***Ex parte***: Meaning - from [for] one party. A decision reached, or case brought, by or for one party without the other party being present.
- ***Status quo***: Meaning - the state in which. In a case of innocent representation, the injured party is entitled to be replaced in the state of affairs that existed previously.
- ***Alibi***: Meaning - In another place. A defence of having been somewhere other than at the scene of a crime at the time the crime was committed.
- ***Actus reus***: Meaning - a guilty act. The wrongful act that makes up the physical action of a crime.

- ***Bona fide***: Meaning - in good faith. Characterized by good faith and lack of fraud or deceit.
- ***Prima facie***: Meaning - after the first view. On first appearance absent other information or evidence.
- ***Pro se***: Meaning - for himself. This term refers to a party who has decided to use no lawyer and represent himself.
- ***De novo***: Meaning - anew. When a higher court reviews the action of a lower court de novo, it means the court reviews it independently without regard to the lower court's determinations.

Appendix-7: Previous Years' UPSC CSE (Prelims) Questions (Solved)

Based on the topic 'Important Judgments and Constitutional Evolution'

1. The Constitution 44th Amendment (renumbered as 43rd Amendment) **(CSE - 1979)**

(a) Ensures the right to property
(b) Ensures the press freedom
(c) Limits the powers of the Government to proclaim internal emergency
(d) Restores to the High Courts and to the Supreme Court their jurisdiction to consider the validity of any central or State law.

Answer: (D) Restores to the High Courts and to the Supreme Court their jurisdiction to consider the validity of any central or State law.

Explanation: 42nd Amendment Act provided for '*Exclusive jurisdiction of the Supreme Court in regard to questions as to constitutional validity of Central laws*' and '*Constitutional validity of Central laws not to be considered in proceedings under Article 226*'. The 43rd Amendment Act repealed this and restored to the High Courts and to the Supreme Court their jurisdiction to consider the validity of any central or State law.

2. The most controversial provision in the 42nd Constitution Amendment is **(CSE - 1979)**

(a) Supremacy of Parliament
(b) Enumeration of ten Fundamental Duties
(c) Term of Lok Sabha and Legislative Assemblies
(d) Primacy to the Directive Principles over the Fundamental Rights

Answer: (D) Primacy to the Directive Principles over the Fundamental Rights.

Explanation: The 42nd Constitution Amendment gave Primacy to the Directive Principles over the Fundamental Rights, by stating that "*no law implementing any of the Directive Principles could be declared unconstitutional on the grounds that it violated any of the Fundamental Rights*".

3. 44th Amendment of the Constitution speaks of **(CSE - 1980)**

(a) Right to property as no longer a Fundamental Right
(b) Suspension of individual liberty during emergency

(c) Barring the courts from interfering in the disputes regarding the election of Prime Minister
(d) Giving more importance to Directive Principles over Fundamental Rights.

Answer: (A) Right to property as no longer a Fundamental Right
Explanation: 44th Amendment of the Constitution removed the Right to property as a fundamental right and inserted a new article 300A making Right to property a legal right.

4. Which famous judgment restricted the authority of the Parliament to amend the Constitution so as to damage or destroy its basic or essential features or its basic structure? **(CSE - 1981)**
   (a) Golaknath case
   (b) Balananda Saraswati case
   (c) Minerva Mills Ltd. and others case
   (d) Keshvanand Bharti case

Answer: (D) Keshvanand Bharti case
Explanation: Keshvanand Bharti case (1973) restricted the authority of the Parliament to amend the Constitution so as to damage or destroy its basic or essential features.

5. Which Amendment of the Constitution gave priority to Directive Principles over Fundamental Rights? **(CSE - 1981)**
   (a) 36th Amendment
   (b) 38th Amendment
   (c) 40th Amendment
   (d) 42nd Amendment

Answer: (D) 42nd Amendment
Explanation: The 42nd Constitution Amendment gave Primacy to the Directive Principles over the Fundamental Rights, by stating that '*no law implementing any of the Directive Principles could be declared unconstitutional on the grounds that it violated any of the Fundamental Rights*'.

6. By which Amendment to the Constitution, the Fundamental Duties of the citizens were specified? **(CSE - 1981)**
   (a) 38th Amendment
   (b) 40th Amendment
   (c) 42nd Amendment
   (d) 44th Amendment

Answer: (C) 42nd Amendment
Explanation: The Fundamental Duties of the citizens under Part IV-A (Article 51A) were inserted in the Constitution by the 42nd Amendment Act.

7. The 45th Amendment to the Indian Constitution relates to **(CSE - 1982)**

(a) Minorities Commission
(b) Commission for Scheduled Castes and Scheduled Tribes
(c) Extension of reservation of seats for Scheduled Castes and Scheduled Tribes
(d) None of the above

Answer: (C) Extension of reservation of seats for Scheduled Castes and Scheduled Tribes

Explanation: The Constitution (45th Amendment) Act, 1980 extended the period of reservation of seats for the Scheduled Castes and Scheduled Tribes.

8. 'The original structure of the Indian Constitution cannot be changed'. In which of the following cases, the Supreme Court of India gave this verdict? **(CSE - 1985)**

(a) The Golak Nath case
(b) The Minerva Mills case
(c) The Kesavananda Bharati case
(d) None of the above

Answer: (C) The Keshvanand Bharti case

Explanation: In Keshvanand Bharti case (1973), the Supreme Court ruled that 'The original structure of the Indian Constitution cannot be changed' and thus restricted the authority of the Parliament to amend the Constitution so as to damage or destroy its basic or essential features.

9. The Directive Principles of State Policy have been given precedence over Fundamental Rights in the __Constitutional Amendment **(CSE - 1986)**

(a) 41st
(b) 42nd
(c) 43rd
(d) 45th

Answer: (B) 42nd

Explanation: The 42nd Constitution Amendment gave Primacy to the Directive Principles over the Fundamental Rights, by stating that '*no law implementing any of the Directive Principles could be declared unconstitutional on the grounds that it violated any of the Fundamental Rights*'.

10. The 42nd Amendment to the Indian Constitution is notable because it gives **(CSE - 1989)**

(a) Primacy to Fundamental Rights over Directive Principles
(b) Primacy to Directive Principles over Fundamental Rights
(c) Special treatment to Jammu & Kashmir
(d) Special treatment to Sikkim

Answer: (B) Primacy to Directive Principles over Fundamental Rights

Explanation: The 42nd Constitution Amendment gave Primacy to the Directive Principles over the Fundamental Rights, by stating that '*no law implementing any of the Directive Principles could be declared unconstitutional on the grounds that it violated any of the Fundamental Rights*'.

11. Consider the following statements regarding 'booth capturing' in an election: **(CSE - 1990)**

1. It has been defined in the Constitution of India after the 61st Amendment.
2. It includes the seizure of and taking possession of a polling booth to prevent the orderly conduct of elections.
3. It is also committed when any elector is threatened and prevented from going to the polling station to cast his vote.
4. It has been declared a cognizable offence punishable by imprisonment.

Of these statements

(a) 2, 3 and 4 are correct
(b) 1, 2 and 3 are correct
(c) 2 and 3 are correct
(d) 1, 2, 3 and 4 are correct

Answer: (A) 2, 3 and 4 are correct

Explanation: The Constitution (61st Amendment) Act, 1988, lowered the voting age of elections to the Lok Sabha and to the Legislative Assemblies of States from 21 years to 18 years. It does not define booth capturing. A detailed explanation of 'booth capturing' is provided under Section 135A of the Representation of the People Act, 1951.

12. Consider the following pairs: **(CSE - 1990)**

Constitutional Amendment	Subject
1. 52nd Amendment:	Anti Defection Law
2. 56th Amendment:	Statehood for Goa
3. 59th Amendment:	Emergency in Punjab
4. 62nd Amendment:	Reservation for Scheduled Castes and Tribes in services

Codes:

(a) 1, 2 and 3 are correctly matched
(b) 3 and 4 are correctly matched
(c) 1, 2, 3 and 4 are correctly matched
(d) 2, 3 and 4 are correctly matched

Answer: (A) 1, 2 and 3 are correctly matched

Explanation: 62nd Amendment extended reservation for SC/ST and nomination of Anglo-Indian members in Parliament and State Assemblies for another 10 years.

13. Which one of the following was not proposed by the 73rd Constitutional Amendment in the area of Panchayati Raj? **(CSE - 1997)**

(a) Thirty percent seats in all elected rural local bodies will be reserved for women candidates at all level

(b) The States will constitute their Finance Commissions to allocate resources to Panchayati Raj institutions

(c) The Panchayati Raj functionaries will be disqualified to hold their offices if they have more than two children

(d) The elections will be held in six months time if Panchayati Raj bodies are superseded or dissolved by the State government

Answer: (C) The Panchayati Raj functionaries will be disqualified to hold their offices if they have more than two children

Explanation: 73rd Constitutional Amendment did not provide for disqualification of Panchayati Raj functionaries from holding their offices if they have more than two children.

14. The 73rd Constitution Amendment Act, 1992 refers to the: **(CSE - 2000)**

(a) Generation of gainful employment for the unemployed and the under employed men and women in rural areas

(b) Generation of employment for the able-bodied adults who are in need and desirous of work during the lean agricultural season

(c) Laying the foundation for strong and vibrant Panchayati Raj institutions in the country

(d) Guarantee of right to life, liberty and security of person, equality before the law and equal protection without discrimination

Answer: (C) Laying the foundation for strong and vibrant Panchayati Raj institutions in the country

Explanation: The 73rd Constitution Amendment Act, 1992 laid the foundation for strong and vibrant Panchayati Raj institutions in the country.

15. Match List-I with List-II and select the correct answer using the codes given below the lists: **(CSE - 2000)**

List-I (Amendments to the Constitution)	List-II
A. The Constitution (69th Amendment) Act, 1991	**1.** Establishment of state-level Rent Tribunals

List-I (Amendments to the Constitution)	List-II
B. The Constitution (75th Amendment) Act, 1994	**2.** No reservations for Scheduled Castes in Panchayats in Arunachal Pradesh
C. The Constitution (80th Amendment) Act, 2000	**3.** Constitution of Panchayats in Villages or at other local level
D. The Constitution (83rd Amendment) Act, 2000	**4.** Accepting the recommendations of the Tenth Finance Commission
	5. According the status of National Capital Territory to Delhi

Codes:
(a) A-5, B-1, C-4, D-2
(b) A-1, B-5, C-3, D-4
(c) A-5, B-1, C-3, D-4
(d) A-1, B-5, C-4, D-2

Answer: (A)
Explanation: The Constitution (69th Amendment) Act, 1991 accorded the status of National Capital Territory to Delhi. The Constitution (75th Amendment) Act, 1994 provided for setting up Rent Control Tribunals.

The Constitution (83rd Amendment) Act, 2000 exempted Arunachal Pradesh from reservations for Scheduled Castes in Panchayats. The Constitution (80th Amendment) Act, 2000 accepted the recommendations of the Tenth Finance Commission.

16. The 93rd Constitution Amendment deals with the: **(CSE - 2002)**
(a) Continuation of reservation for backward classes in government employment
(b) Free and compulsory education for all children between the age of 6 and 14 years
(c) Reservation of 30 percent posts for women in government recruitments
(d) Allocation of more number of parliamentary seats for recently created States

Answer: (A) Continuation of reservation for backward classes in government employment
Explanation: The 93rd Constitution Amendment deals with the Continuation of reservation for backward classes in government employment.

17. The Ninth Schedule to the Indian Constitution was added by:

(CSE - 2003)

(a) 1st Amendment
(b) 8th Amendment
(c) 9th Amendment
(d) 42nd Amendment

Answer: (A) 1st Amendment

Explanation: The Ninth Schedule to the Indian Constitution was added by 1st Amendment to the Constitution in 1951, during the Prime Ministership of Shri Jawaharlal Nehru.

18. Consider the following statements: **(CSE - 2005)**

1. Part IX of the Constitution of India provisions for Panchayats and was inserted by the Constitution (Amendment) Act, 1992.
2. Part IX A of the Constitution of India contains provisions for Municipalities and the Article 243 Q envisages two types of Municipalities, a Municipal Council and a Municipal Corporation for every State.

Which of the statements given above is/are correct?

(a) 1 only
(b) 2 only
(c) Both 1 and 2
(d) Neither 1 nor 2

Answer: (A) 1 only

Explanation: Part IX and 11th Schedule were added by the 73rd Constitutional Amendment Act, 1992 which contain provisions for Panchayats.

Part IX A and 12th schedule were added by the 74th Constitutional Amendment Act, 1992 which contain provisions for Municipalities.

Article 243Q envisages three types of Municipalities: Nagar Panchayat, Municipal Council and Municipal Corporation.

19. Which one of the following statements is ***incorrect***? **(CSE - 2000)**

(a) Goa attained full statehood in 1987
(b) Diu is an island in the Gulf of Khambhat
(c) Daman and Diu were separated from Goa by the 56th Amendment of the Constitution of India
(d) Dadra and Nagar Haveli were under French colonial rule till 1954

Answer: (D) Dadra and Nagar Haveli were under French colonial rule till 1954

Explanation: 56th Amendment of the Constitution of India separated Daman and Diu from Goa. It granted full statehood to Goa and created separate Union territory of Daman and Diu.

Dadra and Nagar Haveli were under **Portuguese** colonial rule till 1954.

20. Consider the following statements: **(CSE - 2005)**

1. The Constitution of India has 40 parts.
2. There are 390 Articles in the Constitution of India in all.
3. Ninth, Tenth, Eleventh and Twelfth Schedules were added to the Constitution of India by the Constitution (Amendment) Acts.

Which of the statements given above is/are correct?

(a) 1 and 2
(b) 2 only
(c) 3 only
(d) 1, 2 and 3

Answer: (C) 3 only

Explanation: The Original Constitution of India had 22 parts and 395 Articles. Later parts related to fundamental duties, Tribunals, the municipalities and the cooperative society were added. Currently, the Constitution has more than 450 Articles.

The First Constitution (Amendment) Act added the Ninth schedule. The Tenth schedule was added in 1985. The Twelfth Schedule was added by the 74th Amendment Act of 1992.

21. What does the 104th Constitution Amendment Bill relate to? **(CSE - 2006)**

(a) Abolition of Legislative Councils in certain states.
(b) Introduction of dual citizenship for persons of Indian origin living outside India.
(c) Providing quota to socially and educationally backward classes in private educational institutions.
(d) Providing quota for religious minorities in the services under the central Government.

Answer: (C) Providing quota to socially and educationally backward classes in private educational institutions

Explanation: The 104th Constitution Amendment Bill (2005) dealt with providing quota to socially and educationally backward classes in private educational institutions.

22. Which of the following Constitution Amendment Acts seeks that the size of the Councils of Ministers at the Centre and in a State must not exceed 15% of the total number of members in the Lok Sabha and the total number of members of the Legislative Assembly of that State, respectively? **(CSE - 2007)**

(a) 91st Amendment
(b) 93rd Amendment
(c) 95th Amendment
(d) 97th Amendment

Answer: (A) 91st Amendment

Explanation: 91st Amendment Act restricted the size of the Council of Ministers to 15% of Legislative members.

23. Consider the following statements: **(CSE - 2005)**

1. Article 301 pertains to the Right to Property.
2. Right to Property is a legal right but not a Fundamental Right.
3. Article 300 A was inserted by the Constitutional Amendment.

Which of the statement given above is/are correct?

(a) 2 only
(b) 2 and 3
(c) 1 and 3
(d) 1, 2 and 3

Answer: (B) 2 and 3

Explanation: 44th Amendment of the Constitution removed the Right to property as a fundamental right and inserted a new article 300A making the Right to property a legal right.

24. Consider the following statements: **(CSE - 2006)**

1. Free and compulsory education to the children of 6-14 years age-group by the State was added by the 76th Amendment to the Constitution of India.
2. Sarva Shiksha Abhiyan seeks to provide computer education even in rural areas.
3. Education was included in the Concurrent List by the 42nd Amendment, 1976 to the Constitution of India.

Which of the statements given above are correct?

(a) 1, 2 and 3
(b) 1 and 2
(c) 2 and 3
(d) 1 and 3

Answer: (C) 2 and 3

Explanation: Free and compulsory education for the children of 6-14 years age group by the State was added by the **86th Amendment** to the Constitution of India.

Education was included in the Concurrent List by the 42nd Amendment, 1976 to the Constitution.

25. Under which one of the following Constitution Amendment Acts, four languages were added to the list of languages under the Eighth Schedule of the Constitution of India, thereby raising their number to 22?

(CSE - 2008)

(a) The Constitution (90th Amendment) Act
(b) The Constitution (91st Amendment) Act
(c) The Constitution (92nd Amendment) Act
(d) The Constitution (93rd Amendment) Act

Answer: (C) The Constitution (92nd Amendment) Act

Explanation: The Constitution (92nd Amendment) Act added Bodo, Dogri, Santali and Maithali to the list of languages under the **Eighth Schedule** of the Constitution of India, thereby raising their number to 22.

26. The Constitution (73rd Amendment) Act, 1992, which aims at promoting the Panchayati Raj Institutions in the country, provides for which of the following? **(CSE - 2008)**

1. Constitution of District Planning Committees.
2. State Election Commissions to conduct all panchayat elections.
3. Establishment of State Finance Commission.

Select the correct answer using the codes given below:

(a) 1 only
(b) 1 and 2 only
(c) 2 and 3 only
(d) 1, 2 and 3

Answer: (C) 2 and 3 only

Explanation: Article 243ZD of the Constitution (added by the 74th Amendment Act) provides for the Constitution of District Planning Committees.

27. Which principle among the following was added to the Directive Principles of State Policy by the 42nd Amendment to the Constitution?

(CSE - 2017)

(a) Equal pay for equal work for both men and women
(b) Participation of workers in the management of industries
(c) Right to work, education and public assistance
(d) Securing living wage and human conditions of work to workers

Answer: (B) Participation of workers in the management of industries

Explanation: 42nd Amendment inserted the following DPSP:

- The State shall take steps, by suitable legislation or in any other way, to secure the participation of workers in the management of undertakings, establishments or other organizations engaged in any industry.

- The State shall, in particular, direct its policy towards securing that children are given opportunities and facilities to develop in a healthy manner and in conditions of freedom and dignity and that childhood and youth are protected against exploitation and against moral and material abandonment.
- The State shall Endeavour to protect and improve the environment and to safeguard the forests and wildlife of the country.

28. Right to vote and to be elected in India is a **(CSE - 2017)**

(a) Fundamental Right
(b) Natural Right
(c) Constitutional Right
(d) Legal Right

Answer: (C) Constitutional Right

Explanation: Right to vote and to be elected in India is a Constitutional Right.

In ***Rajbala and Others v. State of Haryana and Others*** (2015), the Supreme Court held that the Right to Vote and Right to Contest are neither fundamental rights, nor merely statutory rights, but are **Constitutional Rights**. Further, the Right to Contest can be regulated and curtailed through laws passed by the appropriate legislature.

29. Consider the following statements: **(CSE - 2018)**

1. The Parliament of India can place a particular law in the Ninth Schedule of the Constitution of India.
2. The validity of a law passed in the Ninth Schedule cannot be examined by any court and no judgment can be made on it.

Which of the statements given above is/are correct?

(a) 1 only
(b) 2 only
(c) Both 1 and 2
(d) Neither 1 nor 2

Answer: (A) 1 only

Explanation: The Parliament of India can place a particular law in the Ninth Schedule of the Constitution of India. But the validity of a law passed in the Ninth Schedule **can be examined** by any court.

I R Coelho case in **2007** upheld the authority of the judiciary to review any law including those put in the 9th schedule.

30. Right to Privacy is protected as an intrinsic part of Right to Life and Personal Liberty. Which of the following in the Constitution of India correctly and appropriately imply the above statement? **(CSE - 2018)**

(a) Article 14 and the provisions under the 42nd Amendment to the Constitution
(b) Article 17 and the Directive Principles of State Policy in Part IV.
(c) Article 21 and freedom guaranteed in Part III
(d) Article 24 and provisions under the 44th Amendment to the Constitution.

Answer: (C) Article 21 and freedom guaranteed in Part III
Explanation: In ***Justice K. S. Puttaswamy (Retd) v. Union of India*** case, the Supreme Court held that the Right to Privacy is protected as an intrinsic part of the Right to Life and Personal Liberty under Article 21 and freedom guaranteed in Part III.

31. Consider the following statements: **(CSE - 2019)**

1. The 44th Amendment to the Constitution of India introduced an Article placing the election of the Prime Minister beyond judicial review.
2. The Supreme Court of India struck down the 99th Amendment to the Constitution of India as being violative of the independence of the judiciary.

Which of the statements given above is/are correct?
(a) 1 only
(b) 2 only
(c) Both 1 and 2
(d) Neither 1 nor 2

Answer: (B) 2 only
Explanation: The 39th Amendment (1975) placed the election of the President, the Vice President, the Prime Minister and the Speaker of the Lok Sabha beyond the scrutiny of the courts. In the ***Indira Nehru Gandhi v. Raj Narain case 1975***, the Supreme Court invalidated many provisions of the 39th CAA. The Parliament repealed the 39th Amendment of the Constitution by the Constitution (44th Amendment) Act, 1978.

99th Amendment provided for National Judicial Appointments Commission. The Supreme Court of India struck down the 99th Amendment to the Constitution of India as being violative of the independence of the judiciary and separation of powers.

32. Which Article of the Constitution of India safeguards one's right to marry the person of one's choice? **(CSE - 2019)**
(a) Article 19
(b) Article 21
(c) Article 25
(d) Article 29

Answer: (b) Article 21

Explanation: The right to marriage is considered as a fundamental right under Article 21 of the Indian Constitution. Even though it is not explicitly mentioned in Indian Constitution, there are various Supreme Court (SC) judgments connected with this. Further SC judgments are binding on all courts throughout India (Article 141)

In the ***Lata Singh v. State of UP case, 2006*** SC held that no law bars intercaste marriage and every individual has the right to choose a partner of his or her choice.

In the ***Salamat Ansari*** case in Allahabad high court (HC), the Court said, religious conversions, even when made solely for marriage, constitute a valid exercise of a person's liberties. By invoking the Supreme Court's judgment in the ***KS Puttaswamy*** case, the HC held that an individual's ability to control vital aspects of her life inheres to her right to privacy, which includes the right to marry the person of one's choice. It held that the judgment in Noor Jahan was incorrectly delivered. Marriage is a matter of choice, and every adult woman has a fundamental right to choose her partner. Even if such a decision encourages other concomitant decisions, including a choice of religion, the State has little to do with it.

33. The Ninth Schedule was introduced in the Constitution of India during the Prime ministership of **(CSE - 2019)**

(a) Jawaharlal Nehru
(b) Lal Bahadur Shastri
(c) Indira Gandhi
(d) Morarji Desai

Answer: (A) Jawaharlal Nehru

Explanation: The Ninth Schedule (Article 31-B) of the Constitution contains a list of central and state laws which cannot be challenged in courts. Currently, 284 such laws are shielded from judicial review.

The High Court of Patna in ***Kameshwar v. State of Bihar*** held a Bihar state legislation relating to land reforms was unconstitutional. The parties aggrieved had filed appeals before the Supreme Court. At the same time, certain Zamindars had also approached the Supreme Court under Article 32 of the Constitution.

It was, at this stage, that the Parliament amended the Constitution by adding Articles 31-A and 31-B to assist the process of legislation to bring about agrarian reforms and confer on such legislative measures immunity from a possible attack on the ground that they contravene the fundamental rights of the citizen. Article 31-B was inserted in the Constitution by the Constitution (1st Amendment) Act, 1951. The same Amendment also added a new schedule (Ninth Schedule) containing 13 items, all relating to land reform laws, immunizing these laws from challenge on the ground of contravention of Article 13 of the Constitution.

The Constitutional validity of the 1st Amendment was upheld in ***Sri Sankari Prasad Singh Deo v. Union of India and State of Bihar*** case. However, the Supreme Court declared in the ***I. R. Coelho case (2007)*** that laws appearing under the Ninth Schedule cannot enjoy blanket protection from judicial scrutiny. The judicial review is a 'basic structure' of the Constitution that cannot be taken away even if the Ninth Schedule is invoked.

34. Consider the following statements:

1. The Parliament (Prevention of Disqualification) Act, 1959 exempts several posts from disqualification on the grounds of 'Office of Profit'.
2. The above-mentioned Act was amended five times.
3. The term 'Office of Profit' is well-defined in the Constitution of India.

Which of the statements given above is/are correct? **(Prelims - 2019)**

(a) 1 and 2 only
(b) 3 only
(c) 2 and 3 only
(d) 1, 2 and 3

Answer: (A) 1 and 2 only

Explanation: Under Article 102 (1) and Article 191 (1) of the Constitution, an MP or an MLA (or an MLC) is barred from holding any office of profit under the central or state government.

The Parliament (Prevention of Disqualification) Act, 1959 exempts several posts from disqualification.

- Ministers of State and Deputy Ministers,
- Parliamentary Secretaries and Parliamentary Under-Secretaries,
- Deputy Chief Whips in Parliament,
- Vice-Chancellors of Universities,
- Officers in the National Cadet Corps and the Territorial Army
- The Chairman and members of Advisory Committees set up by the Government when they are not entitled to any fee or remuneration other than compensatory, etc.

The Act has been amended five times since its formulation in 1960, 1992, 1993, 2006 and 2013.

The term 'Office of Profit' has not been defined either in the law or in the Constitution but the definition has evolved over the years with judicial interpretations made in various judgments.

In ***Pradyut Bordoloi v. Swapan Roy (2001)*** case the Supreme Court outlined the four broad principles for determining whether an office attracts constitutional disqualification.

1. Whether the government exercises control over appointment, removal and performance of the functions of the office
2. Whether the office has any remuneration attached to it
3. Whether the body in which the office is held has government powers (releasing money, allotment of land, granting licenses, etc.).
4. Whether the office enables the holder to influence by way of patronage.

In the ***Jaya Bachchan*** case the Supreme Court, while upholding the disqualification of Jaya Bachchan from Rajya Sabha in 2006, had said that for deciding the question as to whether one is holding an office of profit or not, what is relevant is whether the office is capable of yielding a profit or pecuniary gain and not whether the person actually obtained a monetary gain.

35. With reference to the Constitution of India, prohibitions or limitations or provisions contained in ordinary laws cannot act as prohibitions or limitations on the constitutional powers under Article 142. It could mean which one of the following? **(CSE - 2019)**

(a) The decisions taken by the Election Commission of India while discharging its duties cannot be challenged in any court of law.

(b) The Supreme Court of India is not constrained in the exercise of its powers by the laws made by the Parliament.

(c) In the event of grave financial crisis in the country, the President of India can declare Financial Emergency without the counsel from the Cabinet.

(d) State Legislatures cannot make laws on certain matters without the concurrence of Union Legislature.

Answer: (B) The Supreme Court of India is not constrained in the exercise of its powers by the laws made by the Parliament.

Explanation: Article 142(1) reads: The Supreme Court in the exercise of its jurisdiction may pass such decree or make such order as is ***necessary for doing complete justice*** in any cause or matter pending before it, and any decree so passed or order so made shall be enforceable throughout the territory of India in such manner as may be prescribed by or under any law made by the Parliament and, until provision in that behalf is so made, in such manner as the President may by order prescribe.

Important instances when Article 142 was invoked

1. In the case of Perarivalan (***Rajeev Gandhi assassination*** case), the Supreme Court invoked Article 142(1) under which it was empowered to pass any order necessary to do complete justice in any matter pending before it.

2. In the ***Bhopal Gas tragedy*** case the Supreme Court awarded a compensation of $470 million to the victims and held that 'prohibitions or limitations or provisions contained in ordinary laws cannot, ipso facto, act as prohibitions or limitations on the constitutional powers under Article 142.'
3. In the ***Babri Masjid demolition*** case, the Supreme Court ordered the framing of a scheme by the Centre for the formation of a trust to construct Ram Mandir at the Masjid demolition site in Ayodhya.
4. In the ***Liquor sale ban*** case, the Supreme Court banned liquor shops within a distance of 500 metres from National as well as State highways to prevent drunken driving.

36. Which one of the following suggested that the Governor should be an eminent person from outside the State and should be a detached figure without intense political links or should not have taken part in politics in the recent past? **(CSE - 2019)**

(a) First Administrative Reforms Commission (1966)
(b) Rajamannar Committee (1969)
(c) Sarkaria Commission (1983)
(d) National Commission to Review the Working of the Constitution (2000)

Answer: (C) Sarkaria Commission (1983)

Explanation: The above suggestions in the question were made by the 'Sarkaria Commission', which was constituted in 1983 to examine the relationship between the Centre and the States.

The ***S. R. Bommai judgment*** passed by the nine-judge bench of the Supreme Court, extensively quoted from the Sarkaria Commission on Centre-State Relations constituted by the Central Government in 1983. The three-member commission headed by Justice R. S. Sarkaria remains to date the bedrock of any inquiry into the relations between the Centre and State. The Commission sought to reinfuse the spirit of cooperative federalism in Indian politics.

The Central Government appointed six members **Administrative Reforms Commission** in 1966 under the chairmanship of Morarji Desai to consider Centre-State relations.

A Centre-State Relations Inquiry Committee was set up by the then DMK Government of Tamil Nadu on 2nd September 1969 under the Chairmanship of **Dr P. V. Rajamannar** to consider the entire question regarding the relationship that should subsist between the Centre and the States in a federal set-up.

The **National Commission to Review the Working of the Constitution** was set up by a resolution of the Government of India in

2000. This 11-member Commission was headed by M.N. Venkatachaliah (former Chief Justice of India) and submitted its report in 2002.

37. With reference to the Constitution of India, consider the following statements:

1. No High Court shall have the jurisdiction to declare any central law to be constitutionally invalid.
2. An amendment to the Constitution of India cannot be called into question by the Supreme Court of India.

Which of the statements given above is/are correct? **(Prelims - 2019)**

(a) 1 only
(b) 2 only
(c) Both 1 and 2
(d) Neither 1 nor 2

Answer: (D) Neither 1 nor 2

Explanation: The 42nd Amendment Act of 1976 curtailed the judicial review power of High Courts and debarred the High Courts from considering the constitutional validity of any central law.

However, the 43rd Amendment Act of 1978 restored the original position of the High Courts and now the High Court shall have the jurisdiction to declare any central law to be constitutionally invalid.

Hence, both the Supreme Court and High Courts have the jurisdiction to declare any central law to be constitutionally invalid.

In the ***Kesavanada Bharati case, 1973***, Supreme Court declared that any constitutional amendment violating 'basic structure' would be declared unconstitutional by the courts.

38. Consider the following statements:

1. The Constitution of India defines its basic structure in terms of federalism, secularism, fundamental rights and democracy.
2. The Constitution of India provides for the 'judicial review' to safeguard the citizen's liberties and to preserve the ideals on which the Constitution is based.

Which of the above given statements is/are correct? **(CSE - 2020)**

(a) 1 only
(b) 2 only
(c) Both 1 and 2
(d) Neither 1 nor 2

Answer: (D) Neither 1 nor 2

Explanation: The Constitution of India does not define the basic structure.

It is the Supreme Court which has recognized the basic structure concept for the first time in the historic ***Kesavananda Bharati*** case in 1973. Ever since the Supreme Court has been the interpreter of the Constitution and the arbiter of all amendments made by the Parliament.

This doctrine of basic structure is not exactly defined but its contents have been provided by the judiciary from time to time.

However, the Supreme Court is yet to define the exact basic structure of the Constitution.

Some elements of the basic structure include:

- Supremacy of the Constitution
- Republican and democratic forms of government
- Secular character of the Constitution
- Separation of powers between the legislature, executive and the judiciary
- Federal character of the Constitution
- Sovereign democratic republic
- Welfare state, etc.

Judicial review refers to supervising the exercise of power by the judiciary of other bodies (legislative and executive) to ensure that they remain within the limits set by the Constitution on their powers.

- The judicial review doctrine is based on the principle of rule of law and separation of powers.
- Judicial review is the process of testing and balancing the separation of powers.
- Judicial review has been made a part of the basic structure in '***Indira Nehru Gandhi v. Raj Narain case 1975***'.

There is no explicit provision in the Indian Constitution for judicial review. However, it is an integral part of our Constitution as it is implicit in many provisions such as-Articles 13, 32 and 226, 131-137, 245, 246, 251 and 254.

39. The Preamble to the Constitution of India is

(a) A part of the Constitution but has no legal effect

(b) Not a part of the Constitution and has no legal effect either

(c) A part of the Constitution and has the same legal effect as any other part

(d) A part of the Constitution but has no legal effect independently of other parts. **(CSE - 2020)**

Answer: (D) A part of the Constitution but has no legal effect independently of other parts.

Explanation: In the ***Kesavananda Bharati case (1973)***, the Supreme Court rejected its earlier opinion expressed in the ***Berubari case (1960)*** and held that the Preamble is a part of the Constitution.

- It is observed that the Preamble is of extreme importance and the Constitution should be read and interpreted in the light of the grand and noble vision expressed in the Preamble.
- It plays an important role in the interpretation of statutes and provisions of the Constitution.

However,

- the Preamble is not the supreme power or source of any restriction or prohibition. Hence it has no legal effect independently of other parts.

In the ***Union Government v. LIC of India, 1995*** case, the Supreme Court has once again held that the Preamble is an integral part of the Constitution but is not directly enforceable in a court of justice in India.

40. 'Right to Privacy' is protected under which Article of the Constitution of India? **(CSE - 2021)**

(a) Article 15
(b) Article 19
(c) Article 21
(d) Article 29

Answer: (C) Article 21

Explanation: A nine-judge bench of the Supreme Court in the case of ***Puttuswamy v. Union of India*** has declared that the right to privacy is a fundamental right protected under Part III of the Constitution of India. It is a natural right that subsists as an integral part of the right to life and liberty under Article 21.

Note: It is however not an Absolute Right but subject to reasonable restrictions.

The Supreme Court held that the State can impose restrictions on the right to privacy to protect legitimate State interests but it can only do so by following the three-pronged test summarized below:

1. Existence of a law that justifies an encroachment on privacy;
2. A legitimate aim or need of the State that ensures that the nature or the content of this law falls within the zone of reasonableness and operates to guard against arbitrary State action; and
3. The means adopted by the State are proportional to the objects and needs sought to be fulfilled by the law.

41. With reference to Indian Judiciary, consider the following statements:

1. Any retired judge of the Supreme Court of India can be called back to sit and act as a Supreme Court judge by the Chief Justice of India with prior permission of the President of India.
2. A High Court in India has the power to review its own judgment as the Supreme Court does.

Which of the statements given above is/are correct? **(CSE - 2021)**

(a) 1 only
(b) 2 only
(c) Both 1 and 2
(d) Neither 1 nor 2

Ans: (A) 1 only

Explanation: The power of judicial review is vested in the Supreme Court and High Courts by Articles 32 and 226, respectively. However, the question deals with the review of its own judgments of the Supreme Court and High Court.

Under Article 137 of the Constitution of India and the rules made under Article 145, the Supreme Court of India has the power to review its judgment pronounced by it.

However, the power of the High Court to review its own judgment is not explicit as the Supreme Court.

Hence, only statement 1 is correct.

Nevertheless, as a court of record, a High Court in India also has the power to review its own judgment (***Pottakalathil Ramakrishnan v. Thahsildar, Tirur and Others*** case).

42. We adopted parliamentary democracy based on the British model, but how does our model differ from that model?

1. As regards legislation, the British Parliament is supreme or sovereign but in India, the power of the Parliament to legislate is limited.
2. In India, matters related to the constitutionality of the Amendment of an Act of the Parliament are referred to the Constitution Bench by the Supreme Court.

Select the correct answer using the code given below. **(CSE - 2021)**

A. 1 only
B. 2 only
C. Both 1 and 2
D. Neither 1 nor 2

Answer: (C) Both 1 and 2

Explanation: Britain follows 'Parliamentary Sovereignty', i.e., Parliament is supreme. But, India follows a constitutional government where the power of Parliament to legislate is limited by the Constitution.

The provision for a Constitution bench has been provided in the Constitution of India under Article 143 and Article 145(3). It is the Chief Justice of India who is constitutionally authorized to constitute a constitution bench and refer cases to it. A constitution bench consists of at least five or more judges of the court which is set up to decide substantial questions of law with regard to the interpretation of the Constitution in a case.

43. Consider the following statements:

1. Pursuant to the report of H.N. Sanyal Committee, the Contempt of Courts Act, 1971 was passed.
2. The Constitution of India empowers the Supreme Court and High Courts to punish for contempt of themselves.
3. The Constitution of India defines Civil Contempt and Criminal Contempt.
4. In India, the Parliament is vested with the powers to make laws on Contempt of Court.

Which of the statements given above is/are correct? **(CSE - 2022)**

(a) 1 and 2 only
(b) 1, 2 and 4
(c) 3 and 4 only
(d) 3 only

Answer: (B) 1, 2 and 4

Explanation: In 1961, a committee was established with the Late H. N. Sanyal serving as its head. He was the additional solicitor general at the time. The committee conducted a thorough analysis of the law and issues surrounding contempt of court in light of the stance established in our own nation and several other foreign countries. The H. N. Sanyal Committee's recommendations led to the passage of the 1971 Contempt of Courts Act.

The Supreme Court and the High Courts of India have been empowered with the power to penalize for Contempt of Court under Articles 129 and 215 of the Constitution of India.

The Constitution of India does not define Civil Contempt and/or Criminal Contempt.

Article 142 (2) of the Indian Constitution states that 'subject to the provisions of any law made on this behalf by the Parliament' the Supreme Court shall have all powers to make any order on the punishment of any contempt of itself. Thus, the Parliament is vested with powers to make laws on Contempt of Court.

44. With reference to the writs issued by the Courts in India, consider the following statements:

1. Mandamus will not lie against a private organization unless it is entrusted with a public duty.
2. Mandamus will not lie against a Company even though it may be a Government Company.
3. Any public-minded person can be a petitioner to move the Court to obtain the writ of Quo Warranto.

Which of the statements given above are correct? **(CSE - 2022)**

(a) 1 and 2 only
(b) 2 and 3 only
(c) 1 and 3 only
(d) 1, 2 and 3

Answer: (C) 1 and 3 only

Explanation: A court-issued mandate known as mandamus orders a public servant to carry out his mandated tasks after he has neglected or refused to do so. For the same reason, it may also be issued against any government, corporation, inferior court, or tribunal. In most cases, it cannot be used against a private organisation unless it has been given a public duty.

Mandamus can be used against a government company.

The court issues a quo warranto to investigate the legitimacy of a person's claim to a public position. As a result, it stops someone from illegitimately usurping public office. In contrast to the other writs, this can be requested by anybody interested, not just the party that has been aggrieved.

Appendix-8: Previous Years' UPSC CSE (Mains) Questions (Solved)

Based on the topic 'Important Judgments and Constitutional Evolution'

1. **What is the Basic Structure of the Indian Constitution? Briefly review the important amendments to the Constitution since its adoption by the Constituent Assembly. Specify any particular amendments which were later repealed and the reasons therefore. (CSE - 1979)**

The doctrine of 'Basic Structure' was evolved through the multiple judgments of the Supreme Court. It is not defined either in the Constitution or by the Supreme Court. However, the Supreme Court in ***Keshavananda Bharati*** case gave a non-exhaustive list of features which are essential and non-amendable under Article 368. It includes Supremacy of the Constitution; Separation of powers between the legislature, executive and the judiciary; Unity and integrity of the nation, etc. The Supreme Court decides from case to case whether a constitutional feature can be characterized as basic or not.

In simpler terms, the doctrine of 'Basic Structure' implies that certain basic or essential features of the Constitution cannot be taken away or damaged by the constitutional amendments by the Parliament.

Important amendments since the adoption of the Constitution:

The ***1st Amendment*** imposed reasonable restrictions on the rights conferred under Article 19(1)(a) in the interests of the security of the State, friendly relations with foreign States, public order, decency or morality, or in relation to contempt of court, defamation or incitement to an offence. It also inserted a new article 31A that provided for protection of laws providing for the acquisition of estates.

The ***24th Amendment Act*** expressly provided that the Parliament has the power to amend any provision of the Constitution. Thus, it brought the provisions of Part III within the scope of the amending power. It was mainly enacted to reverse the Supreme Court judgment in the well-known ***Golak Nath*** case (1967).

The ***25th Amendment Act*** introduced a new article 31C which provided that if any law is passed to give effect to the Directive Principles contained in Clauses (b) and (c) of Article 39, such law shall not be deemed to be void on the ground that it takes away or abridges any of the rights contained in Article 14, 19 or 31.

The ***29th Amendment Act*** placed certain land reforms laws in the Ninth Schedule to the Constitution so that they may have the protection under article 31B and any uncertainty or doubt that may arise in regard to the validity of those Acts is removed. This was done mainly to negate the Supreme Court Judgment in ***Keshavananda Bharati*** case (1973).

The ***42nd Amendment*** made the directive principles more comprehensive (added Articles 39A, 43A and 48A) and gave them precedence over fundamental rights. It provided for a requirement of the minimum number of Judges for determining the constitutionality of laws and for a special majority of not less than two-thirds for declaring any law to be constitutionally invalid. It took away the jurisdiction of High Courts with regard to the determination of Constitutional validity of Central laws and conferred exclusive jurisdiction in this regard on the Supreme Court. It spelt out expressly the ideals of socialism, secularism and the integrity of the nation in the Preamble to the Constitution. It made the advice of Council of Ministers, with the Prime Minister at the head, binding on the President.

The ***52nd Amendment*** outlawed political defections. The ***73rd Amendment*** and ***74th Amendment*** gave constitutional recognition to Panchayats and Urban Local bodies. The ***86th Amendment*** inserted a new article 21A, which made Right to Education a fundamental right. The ***99th Amendment*** inserted a new Article 124A that provided for the National Judicial Appointments Commission. The ***103rd Amendment*** provided reservation to Economically Weaker Sections of the society, who are not the beneficiaries of any other reservation provided under Article 15 and Article 16.

Of the above amendments, the ***42nd Amendment*** was the most controversial and unpopular. In 1977, there was a change in the government at the centre. The new government led by the Janata Party attempted to restore the Constitution to the condition it was in before the Emergency. It enacted the ***43rd Amendment*** and ***44th Amendment***, to restore the pre-1976 position of the Constitution. In ***Minerva Mill*** case, certain provisions of the ***42nd Amendment*** were held unconstitutional by the Supreme Court.

The Supreme Court of India struck down the ***99th Amendment*** to the Constitution of India as being violative of the independence of the judiciary.

Similar questions on 'Basic Structure':

1. What according to the Supreme Court, constituted 'the Basic Features' which is upheld in cases known as
   i. *Keshavananda Bharati v. State of Kerala*
   ii. *Minerva Mills v. Union of India* **(CSE - 1997)**

2. What constitutes the doctrine of 'Basic Structure' as introduced into the Constitution of India by the judiciary? **(CSE - 2000)**

2. The Office of the President of India was designed on the British Model. With this background, consider the modifications of the executive powers of the President by the 42nd Amendment, 1976 and thereafter by the 44th Amendment 1978 to the Constitution of India. Comment on the changes. (CSE - 1982)

The Indian constitution provides for a parliamentary form of government, and as a consequence, the President has been made only a nominal executive.

The Office of the President of India was designed on the British Model, with modifications to suit Indian democratic setup. Unlike the British Monarch which is hereditary, the President of India is elected indirectly. The President is the representative of the democracy embedded in the Indian Constitution. The President is the head of the State and acts as the symbol of unity, integrity and solidarity of the nation.

As a nominal executive, the President has to exercise his powers with the aid and advice of his ministers.

The ***42nd Constitutional Amendment*** **Act** (1976) made the President bound by the advice of the Council of Ministers headed by the Prime Minister. But, the ***44th Amendment Act*** (1978) authorised the President to require the Council of Ministers to reconsider such advice either generally or otherwise. The advice tendered by the Council of Ministers after such reconsideration is binding on the President.

In other words, after the ***44th Amendment***, the President can return the matter to the Council of Ministers only once for reconsideration. It is to be noted that, before 1976 there was no such restriction on the powers of the President. In fact, Rajendra Prasad, the first President of India, publicly questioned this ceremonial role of our President and argued that the Constitution had vested more power in the President of the Republic. The ***44th Amendment*** partly restored the power of the President to the pre-1976 position.

3. What was the amendment made, in 1976, in the Preamble of our Constitution? Discuss its significance. (CSE - 1983)

The Preamble to the Constitution outlines the main objectives of the Constitution. In 1976, through the ***42nd Amendment Act***, the Preamble was amended to add words 'Secular', 'Socialist' and 'Integrity'.

The words 'socialist' was added to pursue the goal of social and economic justice in a more pronounced way. It did not introduce a new ideology to the Constitution since the concept was already inherent with the Constitution. By the introduction of the word Socialist, the

Legislature sought to democratic socialism, which harmonizes the individual interests and public or social interests. The amendment made the idea of democratic socialism implicit in the Constitution.

Addition of 'Socialist' reassured the nation that the moneyed class would not dominate the economy. It strengthened the social protection the government offers to the poorest. Its significance can be noted from the fact that, even after the economic liberalisation in 1991, the successive governments followed socio-economic planning with a view to pursue a socialistic pattern of society.

The word 'secular' was meant to imply equality of all religions and religious tolerance. It was intended to emphasize the secular character of the Constitution. Secularism is built into the Constitution's provisions, including Article 25. Indian secularism does not recognize any religion as the official or state religion and treats all religions equally. It further strengthened the protection for minorities from discrimination. The judiciary has held secularism to be a part of the ***basic structure*** of the Constitution.

Addition of these words made explicit the commitments the nation had already made to itself.

4. Bring out the main change in the Panchayati Raj System in India through the 73rd Constitutional Amendment Act?

(CSE - 1993)

The ***73rd Constitutional Amendment Act*** (1992) provides for decentralized administration through local self-governing institutions (PRIs) at the district, intermediary and village levels. They are the prime instruments of decentralization at the grassroots level.

It provides for the participation of those groups of persons considered as weaker sections, namely, SCs, STs and women. Seats are reserved for SCs, STs in every Panchayat in proportion to their population in the area. One-third of the seats are reserved for women. Before the ***73rd Constitutional Amendment Act*** came into operation there was no effective participation for the weaker sections.

73rd Amendment also establishes the State Election Commission to conduct and regulate the elections to the local self-governments.

It establishes a finance commission to review the financial position of the Panchayats.

Significance:

- The amendment added a new Part-IX to the Indian Constitution to give constitutional status to the Panchayats. It made obligatory on the state governments to adopt the new Panchayati Raj System in accordance with the provisions of the 73rd Amendment Act.
- It gave shape to Article 40 of the Constitution which states that 'the State shall take steps to organize village Panchayats and

endow them with such powers and authority as may be necessary to enable them to function as units of self-government.'

- It is aimed at transforming India from 'representative democracy' to 'participatory democracy'.

The amendment empowers the Panchayats to prepare plans for economic development and social justice and also implement schemes. It associates people with the work of Government to the maximum possible extent with the aim to decide their own governance and development activities. However, the scope and range of functions to be discharged by these bodies are decided by the State Governments.

Similar question:

- Highlight the significance of the 73rd Constitutional Amendment to the Constitution of India? **(CSE - 1998)**

5. Describe the emergence of 'Basic Structure' concept in the Indian Constitution. (CSE - 1994)

The doctrine of 'Basic Structure' implies that certain basic or essential features of the Constitution cannot be taken away or damaged by the constitutional amendments by the Parliament. This doctrine was evolved through the multiple judgments of the Supreme Court.

After independence, the Government of India started implementing agrarian reforms scheme, which was violating the different Fundamental Rights, especially the Fundamental Right to Property. So, it was challenged in various High Courts and the Supreme Court. In ***Shankari Prasad*** case and in ***Sajjan Singh*** case, the Supreme Court upheld the power of the Parliament to amend the Fundamental Rights under Part III.

However, in ***Golak Nath*** case the Supreme Court held that the Parliament had no power to amend Part III of the Constitution. In order to nullify the Judgment of ***Golak Nath*** case, the Parliament enacted the ***24th Amendment Act, 1971***.

In 1972, the Parliament, through the ***29th Amendment Act,*** included the Kerala Land Reforms (Amendment) Act, 1969 and the Kerala Land Reforms (Amendment) Act, 1971 in the Ninth Schedule.

These Amendments were challenged in the Supreme Court in ***Keshavananda Bharati*** case. In this case, the Supreme Court held that the Parliament's constituent power under Article 368 was limited by the ***Basic Structure of the Constitution***, which is inviolable. The 'Basic Structure' of the Constitution cannot be destroyed or altered beyond recognition by a constitutional amendment.

The concept of 'Basic Structure' was again applied and further evolved by the Supreme Court in the ***Minerva Mills case***.

Through this doctrine, the Supreme Court denied the assertion of the supremacy of Parliament in a matter of amending the Constitution at solely on the basis of Parliamentary majority, quite unmindful of the basic or fundamental rights of citizens.

6. **Explain the significance of the April 1994 Supreme Court judgment on the proclamation of President's rule. (CSE - 1994)**

S. R. Bommai v. Union of India (1994) is a landmark case related to the proclamation of President's rule under Article 356 of the Constitution.

The Court ruled that '*Democracy and federalism are the essential features of our Constitution and are part of its basic structure. Any interpretation that is placed on Article 356 must, therefore, help to preserve and not subvert their fabric.*'

The Court held that the power under ***Article 356*** should be used very sparingly and only when the President is fully satisfied that a situation has arisen where the Government of the State cannot be carried on in accordance with the provisions of the Constitution.

The Court ruled that the Legislative Assembly of a State coming under President's Rule should not be dissolved until Presidential Proclamation is approved by the Parliament, till this approval, the President can only suspend the Assembly.

It further said the strength of the Government should be tested on the floor of the State Legislative Assembly and not anywhere else. The Court brought the validity of Proclamation issued by the President imposing President's Rule under judicial review. Thus it prevents the dismissal of democratically elected governments on flimsy grounds. It will be open to the court to restore the Legislative Assembly and the Ministry.

It also held that ***Secularism is a basic feature*** of the Indian Constitution and it cannot be violated. It further said politics and religion cannot be mixed. Any State Government which pursues policies or course of action that violates the concept of secularism may attract action under Article 356.

The judgment accorded '***secularism***' its rightful place, as a necessary condition for the survival of the Indian nation-state. It strengthened the principles of federal democracy in the country. It limited the constitutional power of the union government to dismiss State Governments and prevented the arbitrary use of the power of the Governors.

7. **Differentiate between the 'Due process of law' and the 'Procedure established by law' in the context of deprivation of personal liberty in India. (CSE - 1994)**

Deprivation of the right to life or personal liberty is an unusual course of action taken by the State against any person.

Article 21 states that 'No person shall be deprived of his life or personal liberty except according to the procedure established by law'. In other words, to deprive a person of life or personal liberty, there should be a legal procedure. However, this Article does not specifically prescribe any quality or standard for the procedure.

Due Process of Law is an American concept and has much wider significance. It not only checks if there is a law to deprive the life and personal liberty of a person but also sees if the law made is fair, just and not arbitrary. It empowers the Courts to invalidate the legislation enacted by the Parliament on the ground that procedures established were unjust, unfair and arbitrary.

In India, the ***Maneka Gandhi*** case introduced the 'due process' of American Constitution into Article 21 by articulating that 'procedure established by law' must be fair, just and reasonable. It is a landmark case in the field of protection of life and personal liberty. Post Maneka Gandhi's decision, Article 21 protects the right to life and personal liberty of persons not only from the executive action but also from the legislative action.

ClearIAS Article: https://www.clearias.com/procedure-established-by-law-vs-due-process-of-law/

8. What have been the observations of the Supreme Court in a recent judgment in respect of a Uniform Civil Code?

(CSE - 1995)

Article 44 of the constitution states that 'the State shall endeavour to secure for the citizens a Uniform Civil Code (UCC) throughout the territory of India.' Since it is a Directive Principle of State Policy under Part IV of the Constitution, it is non-justiciable.

The Supreme Court in ***Shah Bano*** case (1985) directed the Parliament to frame a UCC. It observed that a common civil code will help the cause of national integration by removing disparate loyalties to the law which have conflicting ideologies.

In ***Sarla Mudgal*** case, the Supreme Court again asked the Parliament to step in for framing a common civil code in the country. The common civil code will help the cause of national integration by removing the contradictions based on ideologies.

In ***John Vallamattom*** case (2003), the Court once again expressed its opinion on the subject of a UCC.

Thus, in several cases, the Supreme Court directed the Parliament to give effect to Article 44 under Part IV of the Constitution.

9. Bring out the issues involved in the appointments and transfer of judges of the Supreme Court and High Courts in India.

(CSE - 1998)

Article 124(2) of the Constitution states that every Judge of the Supreme Court shall be appointed by the President after 'consultation' with such of the Judges of the Supreme Court and of the High Courts in the States as the President may deem necessary for the purpose.

The Supreme Court interpreted the word 'consultation' differently, in different cases. In ***S. P. Gupta v. President of India and others*** (1981) case the Court held that consultation does not mean concurrence and it only implies an exchange of views. This ruling was overruled in the ***Advocate on Record Association v. Union of India*** (1993) case, which changed the meaning of the word 'consultation' to 'concurrence'. It made the advice tendered by the Chief Justice of India binding on the President in the matters of appointment of the judges of the Supreme Court.

In the ***Special Reference case of 1998***, the Court held that the consultation process to be adopted by the Chief Justice of India requires 'consultation of plurality judges'. Thus it established a collegium system.

Though the appointment by collegium insulated the judicial from executive interference and strengthened judicial independence, it clearly lacks transparency. It is inherently secretive, and provides for no oversight, due to which there are no checks or balances on the judiciary. Choosing judges based on undisclosed criteria in largely unknown circumstances has led to an increasing democratic deficit. Further, the executive can only once ask the collegium to reconsider its decision. If the collegium reiterates its decision, it is binding on the government.

Considerations for appointment to the higher judiciary often go beyond the minimum criteria prescribed in the Constitution. These must be pre-determined. Appointments cannot be done secretively by the collegium.

To bring in transparency in the appointment of judges, the government established the ***National Judicial Appointment Commission*** (NJAC), through the ***99th Amendment Act***. But, in ***Advocates on Record Association v. Union of India*** (2015) case, the apex court struck down the ***National Judicial Appointments Commission (NJAC) Act*** as unconstitutional and void for being violative of judicial independence.

Thus, through these judgments, the Supreme Court has considerably altered the process of appointment of judges of the Supreme Court and High Courts in India.

10. Highlight the significance of the 24th Amendment to the Constitution of India? (CSE - 1999)

In ***Golak Nath*** case (1967), the Supreme Court held that the Fundamental Rights cannot be amended for the implementation of the Directive Principles. The Constitution (24th Amendment) Act, 1971 was mainly enacted to reverse the Supreme Court judgment in the well-known ***Golak Nath*** case.

The ***24th Amendment*** expressly provided that the Parliament has the power to amend any provision of the Constitution. Thus, it brought the provisions of Part III within the scope of the amending power.

It made obligatory on the President to give his assent to the Constitution Amendment Bill passed by both Houses of the Parliament. Further, it placed any amendment of the Constitution under Article 368, outside the meaning of law under Article 13.

Supreme Court in ***Keshavananda Bharati*** case upheld the constitutional validity of the ***24th Amendment Act***. Thus, the amendment empowered the Parliament to amend any part of the Constitution, but without damaging the '***Basic Structure***'.

11. What is the constitutional position of the Directive Principle of State Policy? How has it been interpreted by the judiciary after the emergency in 1975-77? (CSE - 2001)

Part IV of the Indian Constitution contains the Directive Principle of State Policy. These are the ideals that the State should keep in mind while formulating policies and enacting laws. Dr. B. R. Ambedkar described these principles as 'novel features' of the Indian Constitution. The idea of DPSP was borrowed from the Irish Constitution.

Directive Principles are non-justiciable, but these principles are fundamental in the governance of the country. They impose a moral obligation on the state authorities for their application.

In the ***Champakam Dorairajan*** case (1951), the Supreme Court held that in the case of any conflict between the Fundamental Rights and the Directive Principles, the former would prevail.

In the ***Golaknath*** case, DPSP was made completely subservient to the Fundamental Rights. The Supreme Court held that the Fundamental Rights cannot be amended for the implementation of the Directive Principles.

The ***42nd Amendment Act*** accorded the position of legal primacy and supremacy to the Directive Principles over the Fundamental Rights conferred by Articles 14, 19 and 31.

After the emergency, in the ***Minerva Mills*** case (1980), the Supreme Court held that the Indian Constitution is founded on the bedrock of the balance between the Fundamental Rights and the Directive Principles. The harmony and balance between the two is an essential feature of the basic structure of the Constitution. The goals set out by the Directive Principles have to be achieved without the abrogation of the means provided by the Fundamental Rights.

Therefore, the present position is that the Fundamental Rights enjoy supremacy over the Directive Principles. But, the Parliament can amend the Fundamental Rights for the purpose of implementing the Directive Principles, without destroying the Basic Structure of the Constitution.

12. Comment on the nature of the Ordinance making the power of the President of India. What safeguards are there against the possible misuse? (CSE - 2001)

Article 123 of the Constitution empowers the President to promulgate ordinances when either House of the Parliament is not in session.

It is an important legislative power of the President. This power has been vested in the President to deal with unforeseen situations. However, the President can promulgate an ordinance only when both the Houses of Parliament are not in session or when either of the two Houses of Parliament is not in session. Further, an ordinance can be promulgated only when the President is satisfied that the circumstances exist that render it necessary for him to take immediate action.

However, the conditions for the promulgation of ordinances have been violated both in letter and spirit. Between 1952 and 2014, as many as 668 ordinances were promulgated by the President in the name of emergency. Many ordinances were re-promulgated several times. Some were promulgated just days before the sessions of the Parliament. For example, the bank nationalization ordinance was promulgated just two days before the convening of Parliament.

Such promulgation and re-promulgation of ordinance is an undemocratic route to lawmaking, which is the job of the legislature. Frequently passing ordinances violate the principle of separation of powers. The executive taking over a legislative business is nothing but a subversion of the democratic process.

In ***D. C. Wadhwa v. State of Bihar*** (1986) case the Supreme Court judgment declared that it was the 'constitutional duty' of the public to approach the court against re-promulgation of ordinances in a massive scale as a routine measure. Ordinances cannot be re-promulgated on a massive scale in a routine manner.

In ***Krishna Kumar Singh v. State of Bihar***, the Supreme Court held that re-promulgation of the ordinance is a fraud on the Constitution. The satisfaction of the President under Article 123 is not immune from judicial review.

Thus, several judgments of the Supreme Court have provided the safeguard against the misuse of the ordinance-making power.

13. What is the importance of the 84th Amendment of the Indian Constitution? (CSE - 2002)

The Constitution (84th Amendment) Act, 2001 extended the freeze on undertaking fresh delimitation up to the year 2026.

It provided for readjustment and rationalization of territorial constituencies in the States, without altering the number of seats allotted to each State in the House of the People and Legislative Assemblies of the States, including the Scheduled Castes and the Scheduled Tribes constituencies, on the basis of the population ascertained at the census for the year 1991.

It also provided for re-fixing the number of seats reserved for the Scheduled Castes and the Scheduled Tribes in the House of the People and the Legislative Assemblies of the States on the basis of the population ascertained at the census for the year 1991.

The amendment extended the freeze on undertaking fresh delimitation, keeping in view the progress of family planning programmes in different parts of the country. Many southern states achieved their targets under the family planning programme, whereas many northern states lagged behind. So, the freeze on delimitation up to 2026 is seen as a motivational measure to enable the State Government to pursue the agenda for population stabilization.

14. Highlight the significance of the 44th Amendment to the Constitution of India. (CSE - 2003)

The main objective of the ***44th Amendment*** was to restore the pre-1976 position of the Constitution. It provided adequate safeguards against the recurrence of a contingency like the one happened between 1975 and 1977 in the future and to ensure to the people themselves an effective voice in determining the form of government under which they are to live.

As per the ***44th Amendment***, proclamation of Emergency can be issued only when the security of India or any part of its territory is threatened by war or external aggression or by armed rebellion. Internal disturbance not amounting to armed rebellion would not be a ground for the issue of a Proclamation. It further provided that an Emergency can be proclaimed only on the basis of written advice tendered to the President by the Cabinet and must be approved by the Parliament within a period of one month.

It provided that the power to suspend the right to move the court for the enforcement of a fundamental right cannot be exercised in respect of the fundamental right to life and liberty.

The right to property ceased to be a fundamental right and became only a legal right. The amendment provided that no person shall be deprived of his property except in accordance with the law.

It restored the term of Loksabha to five years, which was increased to six years through the ***42nd Amendment Act***.

Thus, the ***44th Amendment***, along with the ***43rd Amendment***, partly succeeded in restoring the pre-1976 position of the Constitution.

15. Discuss the Section 66A of IT Act, with reference to the alleged violation of Article 19 of the Constitution. (CSE - 2013)

The Information Technology (IT) Act, 2000 provided legal recognition for transactions through electronic communication. The Act was amended in 2009 to insert a new section 66A. This section was aimed at addressing the cases of cybercrime. It criminalized sending of false, misleading and offensive messages through a computer or other communication devices.

Under the section, many arrests were made for social media posts directed at notable personalities. There were allegations that the law was misused.

The terms used under the Section 66A, like *causing of annoyance, inconvenience, danger, obstruction, insult, injury, criminal intimidation, enmity, hatred or ill-will* are very subjective and these terms were not defined in the Act. They are all outside the purview of Article 19(2). Further, the Act does not refer to what the content of 'information' can be.

Interpretation and application of Section 66A and the terms under it depend on law enforcement officers.

Thus, Section 66A authorized the imposition of restrictions on the fundamental right contained in Article 19(1)(a) in language wide enough to cover restrictions both within and without the limits of constitutionally permissible legislative action.

In the ***Shreya Singhal*** case (2015), the Supreme Court held that mere discussion or even advocacy of a particular cause, howsoever unpopular, is at the heart of Article 19(1)(a). Only when the discussion or advocacy reaches the level of incitement, restrictions under Article 19(2) can be invoked. Only at this stage, a law may be made to curtail the speech or expression.

16. Does the right to clean environment entail legal regulation on burning crackers during Diwali? Discuss in the light of the Indian Constitution and Judgments of the apex court in this regard. (CSE - 2015)

Studies by CPCB had categorically found that burning of crackers during Diwali was contributing to air as well as noise pollution in an alarming manner. This has a direct consequence on the health of a person.

By expanding the ambit of ***Article 21*** of the Constitution of India, the Supreme Court has held that the right to live in a clean and healthy environment is a fundamental right under the right to life.

Subhash Kumar v. State of Bihar case as well as in ***M. C. Mehta*** case, the Court observed that 'right to life guaranteed by Article 21 includes the right of enjoyment of pollution-free water and air.'

Further, it is the duty of the State to ensure a healthy environment in terms of ***Article 48A***, as well as the duty of the citizens to ensure the same under ***Article 51A(g)*** of the Constitution.

So, the right to health coupled with the right to breathe clean air is important, but, any legal regulation on burning crackers should take into account the rights of the cracker manufacturers to carry on trade under ***Article 19***.

It should also be noted that burning of the cracker is not the only cause for air pollution. Citizens have the right to celebrate a festival under the Right to freedom of expression.

But, in ***Vellore Citizens Welfare Forum v. Union of India*** case, the Supreme Court held that '*industry has no right to destroy the ecology, degrade the environment and pose a health hazard*'.

Thus, there is a need to strike a balance between the right to health of citizens and the right to carry on trade by fireworks manufacturers. This entails the legal regulation on burning crackers during Diwali.

17. Discuss the essentials of the 69th Constitutional Amendment Act and anomalies, if any, that have led to recent reported conflicts between the elected representatives and the institution of the Lieutenant Governor in the administration of Delhi. Do you think that this will give rise to a new trend in the functioning of the Indian federal politics? (CSE - 2016)

The ***69th Amendment*** (1991) changed the federal status of Delhi from a UT to a National Capital Territory. Still, the National Capital Territory of Delhi (NCT) is not a full-fledged State. The first schedule of the Constitution lists it as a Union Territory (UT).

The amendment inserted ***Article 239AA*** to provide for an elected government and co-extensive executive powers. It also provides for a legislature with power to legislate on all subjects contained in the State List of Schedule VII except some fields.

But Delhi is a lesser state in comparison to other states. Three key jurisdictions of the **state list** - public order, police and land - are not within the purview of the Delhi government.

Despite empowering the Delhi legislature from making laws on state list subjects, it does not curtail the power of Parliament to make a law on any subject.

Delhi is a Union territory and the Lieutenant Governor is the President's representative. Lt. Governor is appointed by the President on the advice of the Union government. However, Delhi also has an elected Assembly, a Chief Minister and a Council of Ministers.

Article 239-AA(4) states that the Lieutenant Governor shall act on the aid and advice of the Council of Ministers of the NCTD. But, the Union government often tries to control the Delhi government through the office of the Lt. Governor. This has led to a situation where there is a constant tussle between the elected representatives and the institution of the Lieutenant Governor in the administration of Delhi.

18. What was held in the Coelho case? In this context, can you say that judicial review is of key importance amongst the basic features of the Constitution? (CSE - 2016)

In ***I. R. Coelho v. State of Tamil Nadu*** (2007) case, the Supreme Court upheld the authority of the judiciary to review any law including those laws placed under the Ninth Schedule of the Constitution, after 14th April 1973. This case is popularly known as The Ninth Schedule Case.

The Ninth Schedule to the Constitution was added by the ***First Amendment Act*** in 1951. ***Article 31B***, inserted by the ***First Amendment*** to the Constitution in 1951, says that none of the Acts and Regulations specified in the Ninth Schedule shall be void on the grounds of inconsistency with the fundamental rights guaranteed under the Constitution.

The main objective of this was to place certain laws, especially those related to the land reforms, beyond the judicial review. Such laws often were in conflict with the Fundamental Rights under Articles 14, 19, 21, etc. They were perceived as discriminatory. But those laws were important from the point of view of social justice.

After the ***Keshavananda Bharati*** case, which gave the ***doctrine of 'basic structure'***, a large number of Acts and Regulations were placed under the Ninth Schedule.

I. R. Coelho case opened all laws inserted under the Ninth Schedule after April 24, 1973, to judicial review. Now a law placed under the Ninth Schedule can be challenged by anyone for a perceived violation of fundamental rights that might affect the basic structure of the Constitution.

The judgment attempted to put a check on misuse of the provision of the Ninth Schedule in the Constitution. However, the judgment completely neglected the content of the laws placed under the Ninth Schedule. It was mainly concerned with the number of laws placed under the Ninth Schedule.

The judgment was mainly criticized on the fact that the nine-Judge Bench showed no interest in analyzing these laws. The Supreme Court overlooked a key Directive Principle of State Policy as enshrined in ***Article 38(2)***, which directs the state to strive to minimize the inequalities in income and endeavour to eliminate inequalities in status, facilities and opportunities.

Though the judicial review is a key 'Basic Feature', puts a check on the power of the Parliament and necessary to uphold the rights of citizens, it cannot be unmindful to the other parts of the Constitution like Directive Principle of State Policy.

19. Critically examine the Supreme Court's judgment on 'National Judicial Appointments Commission Act, 2014' with reference to the appointment of judges of higher judiciary in India.

(CSE - 2017)

The ***99th Amendment*** paved the way for an appointment and transfer in the higher judiciary by creating the National Judicial Appointment Commission. It inserted three new Articles – 124A, 124B and 124C. The composition, power and functions of the Commission were provided under the National Judicial Appointments Commission Act, 2014 and not by the Constitution.

Since the power and functions of the NJAC are determined by the statutory Act, it is vulnerable to the amendment by the Parliament by a simple majority.

Article 124C enabled the Parliament to empower the Commission to make regulations for selecting judges and for 'other matters'. Thus, constitutional provisions and safeguards can easily be negated by regulations framed by the Commission.

Section 6(4) of the NJAC provided for consultation with senior-most judges and eminent advocates in the High Courts. But their opinion is not binding on the NJAC.

Further, the views of the Governor of the state are not binding in the case of appointment of judges to the concerned High Courts. This means, the central government, through NJAC, will select the High Court Judges. This goes against the federal trait of the Constitution.

Thus, both the ***99th Amendment*** and the NJAC Act were struck down by the Supreme Court in ***Advocates on Record Association v. Union of India*** (2015) case for being violative of judicial independence.

However, the NJAC judgment raised important questions, since the Supreme Court struck down a law passed by the Parliament and ratified by more than 20 states. The most important structure of the Constitution is parliamentary democracy and the Parliament represents the will of the sovereign.

The ability of the two 'eminent persons' to veto any appointment flowed not from the 99th Constitutional Amendment but the NJAC Act. Therefore, it defied logic to render the entire amendment invalid solely because of this provision.

There is no doubt that judicial independence, based on the principle of separation of powers, is part of the basic structure of the Constitution. However, it is wrong to equate judicial independence to judicial primacy.

20. Examine the scope of Fundamental Rights in the light of the latest judgment of the Supreme Court on Right to Privacy. (CSE - 2017)

The Supreme Court in ***Justice (retd) K. S. Puttaswamy*** case, overruling its earlier judgments in ***M. P. Sharma*** case and ***Kharak Singh*** case held that Right to Privacy is a fundamental right under Article 21 of the Constitution.

Three elements are considered as the core to the right to privacy: physical privacy, informational privacy and decisional autonomy. These aspects are reflected throughout Part III of the Constitution of India, which guarantees fundamental rights.

As per the judgment, the laws interfering with privacy will have to be just, fair and reasonable. They have to be based on the grounds enunciated in Part III. This expands the scope of judicial review of such laws and raises the burden on governments to ensure the constitutionality of laws. Thus the Right to Privacy has considerably strengthened and expanded the scope of fundamental rights under Part III.

Further, Right to privacy has wider implication as it includes sexual orientation, the right to choose one's food habits and many more. The principles laid down in the judgment of the Supreme Court on Right to Privacy will go a long way in striking down some of the laws, which are considered as regressive.

In the rapidly changing technological world, the Right to Privacy protects the right of individuals to make a choice of how and where they want to live, work and pursue their individual dreams.

21. Whether the Supreme Court Judgment (July 2018) can settle the political tussle between the Lt. Governor and elected government of Delhi? Examine. (CSE - 2018)

Article 239-AA(4) states that the Lieutenant Governor shall act on the aid and advice of the Council of Ministers of Delhi. However, the Union government often tried to control the Delhi government through the office of the Lt. Governor. For example, in a May 2015 notification, it gave the Lieutenant Governor new powers such as control over the bureaucracy.

In ***Government of NCT of Delhi v. Union of India*** (2018) case, the Supreme Court held that the Lieutenant Governor of Delhi is bound by the 'aid and advice' of the Council of Ministers of the Delhi government in all matters under its jurisdiction. The real authority to make decisions lies with the elected government.

The Lieutenant Governor can only refer differences of opinion under Article 239AA (4) to the President only in exceptional matters. The decision of the President in such matter is binding.

The court also observed that Lieutenant Governor is the administrative head but he cannot act as an obstructionist. He has to act in the spirit of constitutional trust and morality.

Even though Delhi does not have the status of a state, the Supreme Court held that the Central government cannot usurp powers on areas within the dominion of states.

The judgment of the Supreme Court has fairly settled the powers and functions of both the elected government and the Lieutenant Governor. It has also put a check on unnecessary interference by the Central government in the administration of Delhi. Thus, the judgment is expected to settle the political tussle between the Lt. Governor and elected government of Delhi.

22. How far do you agree with the view that tribunals curtail the jurisdiction of ordinary courts? In view of the above, discuss the constitutional validity and competency of the tribunals in India. (CSE - 2018)

Based on the recommendations of the Swaran Singh Committee, Part XIV-A was added by the ***42nd Constitution Amendment Act***, titled as 'Tribunals' which provided for the establishment of 'Administrative Tribunals' under ***Article 323-A*** and 'Tribunals for other matters' under ***Article 323-B***.

Administrative Tribunals Act, 1985, brought a large number of cases relating to service matters pending before various Courts were brought within the jurisdiction of the Tribunals. Tribunals have replaced High Courts for disputes under the Companies Act, Competition Act, SEBI Act, Electricity Act, Consumer Protection Act, etc. Thus, the tribunals have curtailed the jurisdiction of ordinary courts.

Tribunals are the administrative bodies established for the purpose of discharging quasi-judicial duties. Increase in the State activities of techno-legal nature, reducing the arrears in High Courts and the need for speedy disposal of cases has led to the establishment of Tribunals. The Tribunals are not bound by the procedure to be followed in the regular courts. They work on the principles of natural justice. As they also include technical experts along with judicial experts, they are more competent than a regular court of law, especially in the cases that are more technical in nature than legal.

In ***L. Chandra Kumar v. Union of India*** (1997) case, the Supreme Court has upheld the constitutional validity of the tribunals. However, it brought tribunals under the jurisdiction of the respective High Courts. The Court held that the power vested in the High Courts to exercise judicial superintendence over the decisions of all Courts and Tribunals within their respective jurisdictions is part of the ***basic structure*** of the Constitution. The tribunals are competent to hear the matters where the statutory provisions are questioned, but they cannot act as substitutes for the High Courts and the Supreme Court.

23. Do you think the Constitution of India does not accept the principle of strict separation of powers rather it is based on the principle of checks and balances? Explain. (CSE - 2019)

The principle of strict separation of power refers to the complete division of executive, legislative and judicial powers among different branches of government while the principle of checks and balances limits the misuse of power.

Provisions for separation of power in the Constitution of India

Article 50: the state shall take steps for separation of power between judiciary and executive.

Articles 121 and 211: Parliament cannot discuss the judicial conduct of the Supreme Court and High Court judges.

Articles 122 and 212: validity of legislative proceedings cannot be called into question in any court.

But, in the ***Raj Narain case***, the Supreme Court held that a rigid Constitution with strict separation of powers as under American and Australian Constitutions does not apply in the context of India. The Court also mentioned the principle of checks and balances provided in the Indian Constitution.

Principle of checks and balances in the Constitution of India

1. Articles 75: Executive is collectively responsible to the Lok Sabha.
2. Judicial review: It is implicit in Articles 13, 32, 226, 246, etc. It is used to strike down any law violating the Constitution.
3. Appointment of Judges: Judges of High Courts and supreme court shall be appointed by the President of India (Articles 124 and 217)
4. Removal of Judges: Parliament has the power to remove judges of the Supreme Court and the High Courts.
5. Parliamentary Instruments: Instruments like censure motion-confidence hence motion, etc, to control the executive.

In the ***Ram Jawaya case (1955)***, the Supreme Court held that functions of different branches of the government have been sufficiently differentiated. Yet, the Indian Constitution has not recognised the strict separation of powers.

24. From the resolution of contentious issues regarding the distribution of legislative powers by the courts, the principle of Federal Supremacy and Harmonious Construction has emerged. Explain (CSE - 2019)

Judicial interpretations in contentious issues, especially about the distribution of legislative powers such as one surrounding recent acts, have given rise to certain principles such as the 'principle of federal supremacy'; and 'principle of harmonious construction'.

Article 131 empowers the Supreme Court to interpret the lists under the 7th schedule regarding the distribution of legislative powers.

Principle of federal supremacy

It states even though both the Union and States derive legislative powers from the same Constitution, States have no legal rights against overriding powers of the Union. In the ***West Bengal case of 1963,*** the court held that structure of the Indian Union is centralised with the Union government occupying the central position.

Principle of harmonious construction

It holds that when two provisions of legal text seem to conflict, they should be interpreted in such a way that each has a separate effect and neither is made redundant or nullified. In the ***CIT v. Hindustan bulk carriers case of 2003,*** the Court laid down certain principles to be used in situations where the Court is unable to reconcile differences.

For cooperative and competitive federalism, the judiciary shall interpret laws to highlight the essence of the enactments based on the established principles. This will not only help in resolving contentious issues but also in minimizing federal disputes.

25. Parliament's power to amend the Constitution is limited and it cannot be enlarged into absolute power. In light of this statement, explain whether parliament under Article 368 of the constitution can destroy the basic structure of the Constitution by expanding its amending power. (CSE - 2019)

Article 368 empowers the Parliament of India to amend the Indian Constitution. However, the Supreme Court of India has put forward the doctrine of basic structure which restraints the Parliament from using absolute power. Now, it is well established that the Parliament of India cannot amend the basic foundational features of the Indian Consitution even by using a constitutional amendment.

Why the Power of Parliament under Article 368 is limited in nature?

1. Amendment shall follow the procedure: Constitution Amendment Bill must be passed with a special majority in both the houses and it shall be assented by the President.
2. Amendment is subject to Judicial review: If the Judiciary finds the amendment unlawful or against the provisions of the Constitution, it can declare it ultra vires or unconstitutional.
3. Amendment needs ratification by States: At least half of the states shall ratify such amendments which affect federal principles.

Can the Parliament destroy the basic structure of the Indian Constitution?

Even before the concept of basic structure was introduced by the Supreme Court, the Court had given some judgments regarding amending the powers of the Parliament.

1. In the ***Shankari Prasad case, 1951*** and ***Sajjan Singh case, 1965*** the Supreme Court held that Parliament under Article 368 can amend any part of the Constitution including Part 3.
2. In the ***Golaknath case, 1967*** the Supreme Court reversed this stand and held that the Parliament cannot amend the fundamental rights.
3. In the ***Keshavanand Bharati case of 1973***: Supreme Court further ruled that the Parliament can amend the Constitution but such power is limited. The Court introduced the concept of the ***doctrine of basic structure*** as a fundamental feature which the Parliament cannot destroy.
4. ***Minerva Mills case 1980***: The judgment struck down many provisions of the 42nd Constitutional Amendment Act. The Court held that the Constitution and not the Parliament is supreme.
5. ***IR Coelho case 2007***: The Supreme Court held that judiciary can review any law which may destroy basic structure even if such laws are put in the Ninth Schedule.

The Indian Constitution is a living document. It responds to the changing times by amending the power of the Parliament. However, such a power cannot uproot or destroy the basic features of the Constitution.

26. Judicial legislation is antithetical to the doctrine of separation of powers as envisaged in the Indian Constitution. In this context, justify the filing of a large number of public interest petitions praying for issuing guidelines to executive authorities. (CSE - 2020)

Judicial legislation is the law pronounced by the judiciary by filling the gaps in the laws made by the legislature, usually by issuing guidelines to the executive. This extension of legislative function to the courts to some extent violates the doctrine of separation of powers which pitches for the exclusivity of functions of each body of the state.

However, a large number of Public Interest Litigations (PIL) are pending before the Supreme Court with prayers for issuing guidelines to executive authorities. When the legislature and executive fail their duties, the judiciary should come as the final rescue to the common man.

Need for the Supreme Court to issue guidelines to executive authorities in PIL

1. To fill the lacunae in the functions of the executive or legislature: In India, there are instances when the legislative and executive bodies neglect their respective roles. In this context, the judiciary should fill the gap when the petitions seek grievance redressals through the courts.
2. As part of the constitutional obligation to guarantee fundamental rights:
   The Supreme Court is the custodian of the Constitution. As a redressal body, the judiciary must protect the fundamental rights of citizens.
3. As part of judicial assurances:
   In the ***Asiad Workers judgment*** case, Justice P. N. Bhagwati held that anyone getting less than the minimum wage can approach the Supreme Court directly without going through the Labour Commissioner or lower courts.
4. To enforce accountability:
   Public interest petitions work as a significant tool in the hands of marginalized and deprived people to hold the executive and legislative accountable to the judiciary.
   For example, in the ***Hussainara Khatoon*** case, the petition has highlighted the inhumane conditions prevailing in the prisons concerning the undertrials.
5. To counter the decline in the parliament's efficiency:
   There is around a 50% decrease in parliamentary sittings between 1960 and the present.
6. To counter the reduced parliamentary scrutiny:
   Bills subjected to scrutiny by parliamentary committees are decreasing.

These conditions point to the need for delegated legislation. However, despite the decisive roles played by public interest petitions, the judiciary needs to be cautious about the violation of the doctrine of separation of power. The Apex Court should avoid judicial overreach while using judicial legislation.

27. The judicial systems in India and the UK seem to be converging as well as diverging in recent times. Highlight the key points of convergence and divergence between the two nations in terms of their judicial practices. (CSE - 2020)

The Indian judicial system is mainly based on the Government of India Act,1935. Further, the judiciary as an organ of the state is incorporated into the Constitution of India. However, the judicial system of the UK is the result of gradual evolution.

The judicial systems of India and the UK have influenced each other which resulted in many points of convergence and divergence.

Converging elements:

1. In theory, both the systems follow 'procedure established by law'. It means the judiciary in both nations is empowered to review executive actions and procedures.
2. Judiciary is the highest interpreter of laws, bye-laws, etc. in both India and the UK.
3. Both India and UK have a system of integrated judiciary.
4. Both enjoy writ jurisdiction. The mechanism of writ jurisdiction in the Indian constitution has been borrowed from the UK.

Diverging elements:

1. The Indian Judiciary is now leaning more toward the concept of ***due process of law*** than the ***procedure established by law*** after the ***Maneka Gandhi*** case.
2. The judicial innovation of the 'doctrine of the basic structure' (***Kesavananda Bharati*** *case*) made the legislature more accountable to the Judiciary. This concept is absent in the UK.
3. Unlike the UK, the jury system does not exist in India.
4. Judicial appointment in the UK is more transparent as it is carried out through the 'judicial appointment commission' while in India it is based on the 'collegium system'.
5. Some overarching powers enjoyed by the Indian judiciary such as one enjoyed under Article 142 (the power of the Supreme Court to pass any order for doing complete justice) and under 136 (Special Leave Petition) are not present in the UK.

Judicial systems of the world inspire and influence one another. For a more evolved system of judicial practice, both India and UK need to adopt the best practices of the world to eliminate common issues such as the large pendency of cases. At the same time, more vigorous works need to be done to induct the mechanisms of Alternative Dispute Resolutions (ADR).

28. Constitutional morality is rooted in the Constitution itself and is founded on its essential facets. Explain the doctrine of constitutional morality with the help of judicial decisions.

(CSE - 2021)

Constitutional morality refers to the adherence to bottom-line principles of constitutional values. It may not always align with public persceptions or mass opinions. Constitional morality is rooted in the values upheld by the Constitution such as:

1. Values mentioned in the Preamble: core democratic values such as **justice** (social, economic and political), **liberty** (of thought, expression, belief, faith and worship), **equality** and **fraternity**.
2. Values mentioned in the Fundamental Rights (Part 3): fundamental rights such as Article 14, Article 19 and Article 21 (rule of law, freedom of speech and expression, and right to life)
3. Values mentioned in the Directive Principles (Part 4): directives for the state to fulfil the vision of makers of the Constitution such as welfare state, reduction of inequalities, upliftment of weaker sections, grass-root level democracy, gender equality, etc.

Judicial decisions expounding constitutional morality

1. **Kesavananda Bharati case 1973**: The Supreme Court limited the Parliament's ability to violate basic features of the Constitution.
2. **Sabarimala case**: The Supreme court gave primacy to constitutional morality over the doctrine of essentiality.
3. **Naz Foundation case**: The Supreme Court ruled that only constitutional morality and not public morality shall prevail.
4. **Navtej Johar case:** The Supreme Court established a framework to reaffirm the dignity, life, and liberty of the LGBTQ community.

The term 'constitutional morality' is an outcome of judicial interpretation and is not explicitly mentioned in the Constitution. However, it is rooted in the Constitution itself. The concept of constitutional morality should be the guiding principle of all citizens in the country and not just of the courts.

Conclusion

Even though it may not sound so, the law and the common man are highly connected.

We resist whenever somebody tries to interfere in our lives; we claim our rights.

But how do we come to enjoy those democratic liberties we take for granted every day?

Of course, it is granted to us - 'WE, THE PEOPLE' - by the Indian Constitution. However, without a powerful judiciary, all good things can easily come to an end.

To come out of the fist of the archaic colonial laws, to settle disputes which hinder India's growth, and to prevent the might to become right, we need a strong and independent judiciary.

As the custodian of Indian Constitution, the Supreme Court of India has not only been assertive of the fundamental rights of Indian Citizens but also prevented the State from encroaching on it.

The evolution of the Supreme Court of India from its apparent weakness during the emergency period to a powerful and independent Constitutional Court has been phenomenal. It has transformed India. The path is now clear - a progressive and liberal society, with a Constitutional and Limited Government.

The common man's faith in the Supreme Court of India has been restored by several important judgments. The landmark judgments articulate not only the wisdom of the judges or the founding fathers of the Indian Constitution but also the conscience of the nation altogether.

The stories of landmark cases when compiled together is the story of the **evolution of the Indian Constitution**. It is also the story of the **transformation of India.**